Dr. B.R. Ambedkar

Dalit Movement in India

DR. B.R. AMBEDKAR

Dalit Movement in India

Geetanjali

CENTRUM PRESS
NEW DELHI-110002 (INDIA)

CENTRUM PRESS
H.O.: 4360/4, Ansari Road, Daryaganj,
New Delhi-110002 (India)
Tel: 23278000, 23261597, 23255577, 23286875
B.O.: No. 1015, Ist Main Road, BSK IIIrd Stage,
IIIrd Phase, IIIrd Block, Bangalore-560085 (INDIA)
Tel: 080-41723429
Email: centrumpress@gmail.com
Visit us at: www.centrumpress.com

Dr. B.R. Ambedkar: Dalit Movement in India

First Edition, 2011

ISBN 978-93-80921-77-8

PRINTED IN INDIA

Printed at Tarun Offset Printers, Delhi-110053

Preface

Bhimrao Ramji Ambedkar which is also known as Babasaheb, was an Indian Jurist, Political Leader, Buddhist Activist, Philosopher, Thinker, Anthropologist, Historian, Orator, Prolific Writer, Economist, Scholar, Editor, Revolutionary and a Revivalist for Buddhism in India. He was also the chief architect of the Indian Constitution. Born into a poor Mahar family, Ambedkar spent his whole life fighting against social discrimination, the system of Chaturvarna - the categorization of Hindu society into four varnas - and the Hindu caste system. He is also credited with providing a spark for the conversion of hundreds of thousands of untouchables to Theravada Buddhism.

Dr. Ambedkar was posthumously awarded the Bharat Ratna, India's highest civilian award, in 1990. There are at present 100,000,000 Untouchables in India, the vast majority of who are underprivileged in every sense of the term. Each year between four and five hundred of them are murdered by their Caste Hindu compatriots, while thousands more are beaten, raped, and tortured and their homes looted and burned. An incalculable number of them are not only subject to social, economic, and religious discrimination but daily suffer personal harassment and humiliation. In the course of the last thousand or so years saints and reformers have sought to ameliorate the lot of the Untouchables-none of them with any great success. The latest and most heroic of these attempts were made by Dr. Bhimrao Ramji Ambedkar.

Author

Contents

1

Quotations of Dr. B. R. Ambedkar

- Men are mortal. So are ideas. An idea needs propagation as much as a plant needs watering. Otherwise both will wither and die.
- The conception of secular state is derived from the liberal democratic tradition of west. No institution which is maintained wholly out of state funds shall be used for the purpose of religious instruction irrespective of the question whether the religious instruction is given by the state or any other body.
- If you ask me, my ideal would be the society based on liberty, equality and fraternity. An ideal society should be mobile and full of channels of conveying a change taking place in one part to other parts.
- To idealise the real which more often than not is full of inequities is a very selfish thing to do. It is only when a person finds a personal advantage in things, as they are that he tries to idealise the real. To proceed to make such an ideal real is nothing short of criminal. It means perpetuating inequity on the ground that whatever is settled is settled for all times. Such a view is opposed to all morality. No society with ideal conscience has ever accepted it. On the contrary whatever progress in improving the terms of associated life between individuals and classes has been made in the course of history is due entirely to the recognition of the ethical doctrine that whatever is wrongly settled is never settled and must be resettled.

- A historian ought to be exact, sincere and impartial; free from passion, unbiased by interest, fear, resentment or affection; and faithful to the truth, which is the mother of history the preserver of great actions, the enemy of oblivion, the witness of the past, the director of the future.
- In every country the intellectual class is the most influential class. This is the class which can foresee, advice and lead. In no country does the mass of the people live the life for intelligent thought and action. It is largely imitative and follows the intellectual class. There is no exaggeration in saying that the entire destination of the country depends upon its intellectual class. If the intellectual class is honest and independent, it can be trusted to take the initiative and give a proper lead when a crisis arises. It is true that the intellect by itself is no virtue. It is only a means and the use of a means depends upon the ends which an intellectual person pursues. An intellectual man can be a good man but he may easily be a rogue. Similarly an intellectual class may be a band of high-souled persons, ready to help, ready to emancipate erring humanity or it may easily be a gang of crooks or a body of advocates of narrow clique from which it draws its support.
- My final words of advice to you are educate, agitate and organize; have faith in yourself. With justice on our side I do not see how we can loose our battle. The battle to me is a matter of joy. The battle is in the fullest sense spiritual. There is nothing material or social in it. For ours is a battle not for wealth or for power. It is battle for freedom. It is the battle of reclamation of human personality.
- You must abolish your slavery yourselves. Do not depend for its abolition upon god or a superman. Remember that it is not enough that a people are numerically in the majority. They must be always watchful, strong and self-respecting to attain and

maintain success. We must shape our course ourselves and by ourselves.

- Untouchability shuts all doors of opportunities for betterment in life for Untouchables. It does not offer an Untouchable any opportunity to move freely in society; it compels him to live in dungeons and seclusion; it prevents him from educating himself and following a profession of his choice.
- Untouchability has ruined the Untouchables, the Hindus and ultimately the nation as well. If the depressed classes gained their self-respect and freedom, they would contribute not only to their own progress and prosperity but by their industry intellect and courage would contribute also to the strength and prosperity of the nation. If the tremendous energy Untouchables are at present required to fritter away in combating the stigma of Untouchability had been saved them, it would have been applied by them to the promotion of education and development of resources of their nation as a whole.
- There have been many Mahatmas in India whose sole object was to remove Untouchability and to elevate and absorb the depressed classes, but everyone has failed in their mission. Mahatmas have come, Mahatmas have gone but the Untouchables have remained as Untouchables.
- From the point of view of annihilation of caste, the struggle of the saints did not have any effects on society. The value of a man is axiomatic and self-evident; it does not come to him from the gilding of Bhakti. The saints did not struggle to establish this point. On the contrary their struggle had very unhealthy effect on the depressed classes. It provided the Brahmins with an excuse to silence them by telling them that they would be respected if they attained the status of Chokhamela.
- It is mischievously propagated by Hindu scriptures

that by serving the upper classes the Shudras achieve salvation. Untouchability is another appellation of slavery. No race can be raised by destroying its self-respect. So if you really want to uplift the Untouchables, you must treat them in the social order as free citizens, free to carve out their destiny.

- What you have lost others have gained. Your humiliations are a matter of pride with others. You are made to suffer wants, privations and humiliations not because it was pre-ordained by the sins committed in your previous birth, but because of the overpowering tyranny and treachery of those who are above you. You have no lands because others have usurped them; you have no posts because others have monopolised them. Do not believe in fate; believe in your strength.
- Learn to live in this world with self-respect. You should always cherish some ambition of doing something in this world. But remember that the age of selflessness has ended. A new epoch is set in. All things are now possible because of your being able to participate in the politics and legislature of your country.
- Some people think that religion is not essential to the society. I do not hold this view. I consider the foundations of religion are essential to the society. At the roots of Hindu social system lies a Dharma as prescribed in the Manusmriti. Such being the case I do not think it is possible to abolish the inequality in the Hindu society unless foundations of the Smriti-religion is removed and a better one laid in its place. I however, despair of Hindu society, being able to reconstruct itself on such a better foundation.
- My religious conversion is not inspired by any material motive. This is hardly anything I cannot achieve even while remaining an Untouchable. There is no other feeling than that of a spiritual feeling underlying my religious conversion. Hinduism does

not appeal to my conscience. My self-respect cannot assimilate Hinduism. In your case change of religion is imperative for worldly as well as spiritual ends. Do not care for the opinion of those who foolishly ridicule the idea of conversion for material ends. Why should you live under the fold of that religion which has deprived you of honour, money, food and shelter?

- I tell you, religion is for man and not man for religion. If you want to organise, consolidate and be successful in this world, change this religion. The religion that does not recognise you as a human being, or give you water to drink, or allow you to enter in temples is not worthy to be called a religion. The religion that forbids you to receive education and comes in the way of your material advancement is not worthy of the appellation 'religion'. The religion that does not teach its followers to show humanity in dealing with its co-religionists is nothing but a display of a force. The religion that teaches its followers to suffer the touch of animals but not the touch of human beings is not a religion but a mockery. The religion that compels the ignorant to be ignorant and the poor to be poor is not a religion but a visitation!
- The basic idea underlying religion is to create an atmosphere for the spiritual development of the individual. This being the situation, it is clear that you cannot develop your personality at all in Hinduism.
- In Hinduism, conscience, reason and independent thinking have no scope for development.
- It is your claim to equality which hurts them. They want to maintain the status quo. If you continue to accept your lowly status ungrudgingly, continue to remain dirty, filthy, backward, ignorant, poor and disunited, they will allow you to live in peace. The moment you start to raise your level, the conflict

starts. Untouchability is not transitory or temporary feature; it is eternal, it is lasting. Frankly it can be said that the struggle between the Hindus and the Untouchables is a never-ending conflict. It is eternal because the religion which assigns you the lowest status in society is itself divine and eternal just as to the belief of the so-called high caste Hindus. No change warranted by change of time and circumstances is possible.

- We have never claimed to be a universal leader of suffering humanity. The problem of the untouchables is quite enough for my slender strength. I do not say that other causes are not equally noble. But knowing that life is short, one can only serve one cause and we have never aspired to do more than serve the Untouchables.
- Every man must have a philosophy of life, for everyone must have a standard by which to measure his conduct. And philosophy is nothing but a standard by which to measure.
- Negatively I reject the Hindu social philosophy propounded in Bhagvad Gita, based as it is on the Triguna of Sankhya Philosophy which in my judgement is a cruel perversion of the philosophy of Kapila, and which had made the caste system of graded inequality the law of Hindu social life.
- Positively, my social philosophy may be said to be enshrined in three words: liberty, equality and fraternity. Let no one however say that we have borrowed my philosophy from the French Revolution. We have not. My philosophy has its roots in religion and not in political science. We have derived them from the teachings of my master, the Buddha.
- Indians today are governed by two different ideologies. Their political ideal set in the preamble of the Constitution affirms a life of liberty, equality and fraternity. Their social ideal embodied in their religion denies them.

- Unlike a drop of water which loses its identity when it joins the ocean, man does not lose his being in the society in which he lives. Man's life is independent. He is born not for the development of the society alone, but for the development of his self.
- Freedom of mind is the real freedom. A person whose mind is not free though he may not be in chains, is a slave, not a free man. One whose mind is not free, though he may not be in prison, is a prisoner and not a free man. One whose mind is not free though alive, is no better than dead. Freedom of mind is the proof of one's existence.
- What is the proof to judge that the flame of mental freedom is not extinguished in the mind of person? To whom can we say that his mind is free. I call him free who with his conscience awake realises his rights, responsibilities and duties. He who is not a slave of circumstances and is always ready and striving to change them in his flavour, I call him free. One who is not a slave of usage, customs, of meaningless rituals and ceremonies, of superstitions and traditions; whose flame of reason has not been extinguished, I call him a free man. He who has not surrendered his free will and abdicated his intelligence and independent thinking, who does not blindly act on the teachings of others, who does not blindly accept anything without critically analysing and examining its veracity and usefulness, who is always prepared to protect his rights, who is not afraid of ridicule and unjust public criticism, who has a sound conscience and self-respect so as not become a tool in the hands of others, I call him a free man. He who does not lead his life under the direction of others, who sets his own goal of life just as to his own reasoning and decides for himself as to how and in what way life should be lead, is a free man. In short, who is a master of his own free will, him alone I call a free man.

- Caste cannot be abolished by inter caste dinners or stray instances of inter caste marriages. Caste is a state of mind. It is a disease of mind. The teachings of the Hindu religion are the root cause of this disease. We practice casteism and we observe Untouchability because we are enjoined to do so by the Hindu religion. A bitter thing cannot be made sweet. The taste of anything can be changed. But poison cannot be changed into nectar.
- What struck me most was that my community still continues to accept a position of humiliation only because caste Hindus persist in dominating over them. You must rely on your own strength, shake off the notion that you are in any way inferior to any community.
- Constitutional morality is not a natural sentiment. It has to be cultivated. We must realise that our people have yet to learn it. Democracy in India is only a top dressing on an Indian soil which is essentially undemocratic.
- Majorities are of two sorts:
  1. Communal majority and
  2. Political majority.

  A political majority is changeable in its class composition. A political majority grows. A communal majority is born. The admission to a political majority is open. The door to a communal majority is closed. The politics of political majority are free to all to make and unmake. The politics of communal majority are made by its own members born in it.
- The minorities in India have loyally accepted the rule of the majority which is basically a communal majority and not a political majority. It is for the majority to realise its duty not to discriminate against minorities. Whether the minorities will continue or will vanish must depend upon this habit of majority. The moment the majority looses the habit of

discriminating against the minority, the minorities can have no ground to exist. They will vanish.

- We want our own people, people who will fight tooth and nail for our interest and secure privilege for the underprivileged; people who will undo the wrongs done to our people; people who will voice our grievances fearlessly; people who can think, lead and act; people with principles and character. Such people should be sent to the legislatures. We must send such people to Legislatures who will be slaves to none but remain free to their conscience and get our grievances redressed.
- Why does a human body become deceased? The reason is that as long as the human body is not free from suffering, mind cannot be happy. If a man lacks enthusiasm, either his body or mind is in a deceased condition.... Now what saps the enthusiasm in man? If there is no enthusiasm, life becomes drudgery - a mere burden to be dragged. Nothing can be achieved if there is no enthusiasm. The main reason for this lack of enthusiasm on the part of a man is that an individual looses the hope of getting an opportunity to elevate
- himself. Hopelessness leads to lack of enthusiasm. The mind in such cases becomes deceased.... When is enthusiasm created? When one breaths an atmosphere where one is sure of getting the legitimate reward for one's labour, only then one feels enriched by enthusiasm and inspiration.
- The fundamental principle of Buddhism is equality... Buddhism was called the religion of Shudras. There was only one man who raised his voice against separatism and Untouchability and that was Lord Buddha.
- The teachings of Buddha are eternal, but even then Buddha did not proclaim them to be infallible. The religion of Buddha has the capacity to change just as to times, a quality which no other religion can

claim to have...Now what is the basis of Buddhism? If you study carefully, you will see that Buddhism is based on reason. There is an element of flexibility inherent in it, which is not found in any other religion.

- I am myself a believer in Animas (non-violence). But I make a distinction between Animas and meekness. Meekness is weakness and weakness is voluntarily imposed upon oneself is not a virtue. I am believer in Animas but in the sense defined by the saint Takuma. Takuma has quite rightly said that Animas consisted of two things:
  1. Love and kindness towards all creatures and
  2. Destruction of evil doers.

  The second part of this definition is often lost sight of that the doctrine of Animas becomes so ridiculous.
- Religion must mainly be a matter of principles only. It cannot be a matter of rules. The moment it degenerates into rules, it ceases to be a religion, as it kills responsibility which is an essence of the true religious act.
- We must begin by acknowledging that there is a complete absence of two things in Indian Society. One of these is equality. On the social plane we have an India based on the principles of graded inequality, which means elevation for some and degradation for others. On the economic plane we have a society in which there are some who have immense wealth as against many who live in abject poverty.
- The second thing we are wanting in is the recognition of the principle of fraternity. What does fraternity mean? Fraternity means a sense of common brotherhood of all Indians, all Indians being one people. It is a principle that gives solidarity to social life. It is difficult thing to achieve. It seems to me that there lies a heavy duty to see that democracy does not vanish from the earth as a governing principle of human relationship. If we believe in it, we must both be true and loyal to it. We must not

only be staunch in our faith in democracy but we must resolve to see that whatever we do, we do not help the enemies of democracy to uproot the principles of liberty, equality and fraternity. It follows that we must strive along with other democratic countries to maintain the basis of democratic civilization. If democracy lives we are sure to reap the benefit of it. If democracy dies it will be our doom. On that there can be no doubt.

- The basis of my politics lies in the proposition that the Untouchables are not a sub-division or sub-section of Hindus, and that they are a separate and distinct element in the national life of India.
- The true function of law consists in repairing the faults in society. Unfortunately ancient societies never dared to assume the function of repairing their own defects; consequently they decayed. This country has seen the conflict between ecclesiastical law and secular law long before Europeans sought to challenge the authority of the Pope. Kautilya's Arthshastra lays down the foundation of secular law. In India unfortunately ecclesiastical law triumphed over secular law. In my opinion this was the one of the greatest disasters in the country. The unprogressive nature of the Hindu society was due to the notion that the law cannot be changed.
- Civilization has never been a continuous process. There were states and societies which at one time had been civilised. In the course of time something happened which made these societies stagnant and decayed. This could be showed by India's history itself. There could be no doubt that one of the countries which could boast of ancient civilization is India. When the inhabitants of Europe were living under the barbaric conditions, this country had reached the highest peak of civilization, it had parliamentary institutions when the people of Europe were mere nomads.

- I measure the progress of a community by the degree of progress which women have achieved.
- Justice has always evoked ideas of equality, of proportion of compensation. Equity signifies equality. Rules and regulations, right and righteousness are concerned with equality in value. If all men are equal, then all men are of the same essence, and the common essence entitles them of the same fundamental rights and equal liberty... In short justice is another name of liberty, equality and fraternity.
- Anyone who studies working of the system of social economy based on private enterprise and pursuit of personal gain will realise how it undermines, if it does not actually violate the individual rights on which democracy rests. How many have to relinquish their rights in order to gain their living? How many have to subject themselves to be governed by private employers?
- I hate injustice, tyranny, pompousness and humbug, and my hatred embraces all those who are guilty of them. I want to tell my critics that I regard my feelings of hatred as a real force. They are only the reflexes of love I bear for the causes I believe in and I am in no wise ashamed of it.
- Indifferentism is the worst kind of disease that can affect people.
- Political tyranny is nothing compared to the social tyranny and a reformer who defies society is a more courageous man than a politician who defies Government.
- Every man who repeats the dogma of Mill that one country is no fit to rule another country must admit that one class is not fit to rule another class.
- One cannot have any respect or regard for men who take the position of the reformer and then refuse to see the logical consequences of that position, let alone following them out in action.
- History shows that where ethics and economics come

in conflict, victory is always with economics. Vested interests have never been known to have willingly divested themselves unless there was sufficient force to compel them.

- Slavery does not merely mean a legalised form of subjection. It means a state of society in which some men are forced to accept from others the purposes which control their conduct.
- This condition obtains even where there is no slavery in the legal sense. It is found where as in caste system, some persons are forced to carry on the prescribed calling which are not their choice.
- India is a peculiar country and her nationalists and patriots are a peculiar people. A patriot and a nationalist in India is one who sees with open eyes his fellow men treated as being less than man. But his humanity does not rise in protest. He knows that men and women for no cause are denied their rights. But it does not prick his civil sense of helpful action. He finds a whole class of people shut out from public employment. But it does not rouse his sense of justice and fair play. Hundreds of evil practices that injure man and society are perceived by him. But they do not sicken him with disgust. The patriot's one cry is power for him and his class. I am glad I do not belong to that class of patriots. I belong to that class which takes its stand on democracy and which seeks to destroy monopoly in every form. Our aim is to realise in practice our ideal of one man one value in all walks of life - political, economical and social.
- There is no nation of Indians in the real sense of the world, it is yet to be created. In believing we are a nation, we are cherishing a great delusion. How can people divided into thousand of castes be a nation? The sooner we realise that we are not yet a nation, in a social and psychological sense of the world, the better for us.

- It is not enough to be electors only. It is necessary to be law-makers; otherwise those who can be law-makers ill be the masters of those who can only be electors.
- Walter Bagehot defined democracy as ' Government by discussion'. Abraham Lincoln defined democracy as ' A Government of the people, by the people and for the people'.
- My definition of democracy is - A form and a method of Government whereby revolutionary changes in the social life are brought about without bloodshed. That is the real test. It is perhaps the severest test. But when you are judging the quality of the material you must put it to the severest test.
- Democracy is not merely a form of Government. It is primarily a mode of associated living, of conjoint communicated experience. It is essentially an attitude of respect and reverence towards our fellow men.
- A democratic form of Government presupposes a democratic form of a society, The formal framework of democracy is of no value and would indeed be a misfit if there was no social democracy. It may not be necessary for a democratic society to be marked by unity, by community of purpose, by loyalty to public ends and by mutuality of sympathy. But it does unmistakably involve two things. The first is an attitude of mind, and attitude of respect and equality towards their fellows. The second is a social organisation free from rigid social barriers. Democracy is incompatible and inconsistent with isolation and exclusiveness resulting in the distinction between the privileged and the unprivileged.
- Democracy is not a Form of Government, but a form of social organisation.
- What we must do is not to content ourselves with mere political democracy. We must make our political democracy a social democracy as well. Political democracy cannot last unless there is at the base of

it, a social democracy. What does social democracy mean? It means a way of life which recognises liberty, equality and fraternity as the principles of life. These principles of liberty, equality and fraternity are not to be treated as separate items. They form a union in the sense that, to divorce one from the other is to defeat the very purpose of democracy. Liberty cannot be divorced from equality, nor can liberty and equality be divorced from fraternity.

- Without social union, political unity is difficult to be achieved. If achieved, it would be as precarious as a summer sapling, liable to be uprooted by the gust of wind. With mere political unity, India may be a state. But to be a state is not to be a nation and a state which is not a nation has small prospects of survival in the struggle of existence. This is especially true where nationalism - the most dynamic force of modern times, is seeking everywhere to free itself by the destruction and disruption of all mixed states. The danger to a mixed and composite state, therefore lies not so much in external aggression as in the internal resurgence of nationalities which are fragmented, entrapped, suppressed and held against their will.
- The idea of fundamental rights has become a familiar one since their enactment in the American Constitution and in the Constitution framed by the Revolutionary France. The idea of making a gift of fundamental rights to every individual is no doubt very laudable. The question is how to make them effective? The prevalent view is that once the rights are enacted in law then they are safeguarded. This again is an unwarranted assumption. As experience proves, rights are protected not by law but by social and moral conscience of the society. If social conscience is such that it is prepared to recognise the rights which law proposes to enact, rights will be safe

and secure. But if the fundamental rights are opposed by the community, no Law, no Parliament, no Judiciary can guarantee them in the real sense of the world. What is the use of Fundamental rights to the Untouchables in India? As Burke said, there is no method found for punishing the multitude. Law can punish a single solitary recalcitrant criminal. It can never operate against the whole body of people who choose to defy it. Social conscience is the only safeguard of all rights, fundamental or non-fundamental.

- Rights are real only if they are accompanied by remedies. It is no use giving rights if the aggrieved person has no legal remedy to which he can resort when his rights are invaded.
- Lost rights are never regained by appeals to the conscience of the usurpers, but by relentless struggle.... Goats are used for sacrificial offerings and not lions.
- Life should be great rather than long.
- For a successful revolution it is not enough that there is discontent. What is required is a profound and thorough conviction of the justice, necessity and importance of political and social rights.
- I feel that the constitution is workable, it is flexible and it is strong enough to hold the country together both in peacetime and in wartime. Indeed, if I may say so, if things go wrong under the new Constitution, the reason will not be that we had a bad Constitution. What as suggested, have to say is that Man was vile.
- Equality may be a fiction but nonetheless one must accept it as a governing principle.
- What are we having this liberty for? We are having this liberty in order to reform our social system, which is full of inequality, discrimination and other things, which conflict with our fundamental rights.
- Our object in framing the Constitution is rally two-

fold: (1) To lay down the form of political democracy, and (2) To lay down that our ideal is economic democracy and also to prescribe that every Government whatever is in power shall strive to bring about economic democracy. The directive principles have a great value, for they lay down that our ideal is economic democracy.

- If I find the constitution being misused, I shall be the first to burn it.
- On the 26th January 1950, we are going to enter into a life of contradictions. In politics as suggested, have equality and in social and economic life as suggested, have inequality. In politics as suggested, be recognising the principle of one man one vote and one vote one value. In our social and economic life, we shall by reason of our social and economic structure, continue to deny the principle of one man one value. How long shall we continue to live this life of contradictions? How long shall we continue to deny equality in our social and economic life? If we continue to deny it for long, as suggested, do so only by putting our political democracy in peril. We must remove this contradiction at the earliest possible moment else those who suffer from inequality will blow up the structure of democracy which this Constituent Assembly has so laboriously built up.
- There can be no gain saying that political power in this country has too long been the monopoly of the few, and the many are not beasts of burden but also beasts of prey.
- The monopoly has not merely deprived them of their chance of betterment, it has sapped them of what may be called the significance of life. Those downtrodden classes are tired of being governed. They are impatient to govern themselves. This urge of self-realisation in the downtrodden must not be allowed to devolve into class struggle or class war.

It would lead to the division of the House. That would indeed be a day of disaster. For, as has been well-said by Abraham Lincoln: "A house divided against cannot stand very long". Therefore the sooner room is made for realisation of their aspiration, the better for the few, the better for the country, the better for the independence and the better for the continuance of its democratic structure. This can only be done by the establishment of equality and fraternity in all walks of life.

- It is disgraceful to live at the cost of one's self-respect. Self-respect is the most vital factor in life. Without it, man is a cipher. To live worthily with self-respect, one has to overcome difficulties. It is out of hard and ceaseless struggle alone that one derives strength, confidence and recognition.
- Cultivation of mind should be the ultimate aim of human existence.
- Sincerity is the sum of all moral qualities.
- Man is mortal. Everyone has to die some day or the other. But one must resolve to lay down one's life in enriching the noble ideals of self-respect and in bettering one's human life. We are not slaves. Nothing is more disgraceful for a brave man than to live life devoid of self-respect.
- My social philosophy may be said to be enshrined in three words: liberty, equality and fraternity. My philosophy has roots in religion and not in political science. We have derived them from the teachings of my master, the Buddha.
- Emerson has said that consistency is a virtue of an ass. No thinking human being can be tied down to a view once expressed in the name of consistency. More important than consistency is responsibility. A responsible person must learn to unlearn what he has learned. A responsible person must have the courage to rethink and change his thoughts. Of course there must be good and sufficient reason for

unlearning what he has learned and for recasting his thoughts. There can be no finality in rethinking.

- John Dewey said: "Every society gets encumbered with what is trivial, with what is dead wood from the past and what is positively perverse. As a society becomes more enlightened, it realises that it is responsible not to conserve and transmit the whole of its achievement, but only such as makes a better future society"
- There is nothing fixed, nothing eternal, nothing sanatan; everything is changing, change is the law of life for individuals as well as for society. In a changing society there must be constant revolution of old values.
- No civilised society of today presents more survivals of primitive times than does the Indian society. Its religion is essentially primitive and its tribal code, in spite of the advance of time and civilization, operates in all its pristine vigour even today. Indian society still savors of the clan system, even though there are no clans.
- An ideal society should be mobile, should be full of channels for conveying a change taking place in one part to other parts. In an ideal society there should be many interests consciously communicated and shared.
- The strength of a society depends upon the presence of points of contacts, possibilities of interaction between different groups that exist in it. These are what Carlyle calls "Organic filaments", *i.e.* the elastic threads which helps to bring the disintegrating elements together and to reunite them.
- Heroes and hero-worship is a hard fact in India's political life. I agree that hero-worship is demoralising for the devotee and dangerous to the country. I welcome the criticism so far as it conveys the caution that you must know your man is really great before you start worshipping him. This

unfortunately is not an easy task. For in these days with the Press in hand it is easy to manufacture Great Men. Carlyle used a happy phrase when he described the Great Men of history as so many bank notes. Like bank notes they represent gold. What we have to see that they are not forged notes. I admit that we ought to be more cautious in our worship of Great Men. For in this country we have arrived at such a stage when alongside the notice boards saying "Beware of pickpockets", we need to have notice boards saying "Beware of Great Men". Even Carlyle who defended the worship of Great Men warned his readers how: "Multitudes of Great Men have figured in history who were false and selfish ".

- Hero-worship in the sense of expressing our unbound admiration is one thing. To obey the hero is a totally different kind of worship. There is nothing wrong in the former while the latter is no doubt a most pernicious thing. The former is man's respect for which is noble and of which the great men are only an embodiment. The latter is the serf's fealty to his lord. The former is consistent with respect, but the latter is a sign of debasement. The former does not take away one's intelligence to think and independence to act. The latter makes one perfect fool. The former involves no disaster to the state. The latter is a source of positive danger to it.
- In India, 'Bhakti' or what may be called the path of devotion or hero-worship plays a part in politics unequalled in magnitude by the part it plays in the politics of any other of the world. 'Bhakti' in religion may be a road to salvation of the soul. But in politics, 'Bhakti' or hero-worship is a sure road to degradation and to eventual dictatorship.
- The questions which President Roosevelt propounded for the American public to consider will arise here, if they have not already arisen: Who shall rule - wealth or man? Which shall lead - money or intellect?

Who shall fill the public stations - educated and patriotic free men or the feudal serf's of the corporate capital? For the president, Indian politics, at any rate the Hindu part of it, instead of being spiritualised has become grossly commercialised, so much so that it has become a byword for corruption. Many men of culture are refusing to concern themselves in this cesspool. Politics has become a kind of sewage system intolerably unsavory and insanitary. To become a politician is like going to work in the drain.

- History bears out the proposition that political revolutions have always been preceded by social and religious revolutions. Social reform in India has few friends and many critics.
- Law and order are the medicine of the body politic and when the body politic gets sick, medicine must be administered.
- The world owes much to rebels who would dare to argue in the face of the pontiff (high priest) and insist that he is not infallible.
- A people and their religion must be judged by social standards based on social ethics. No other standard would have any meaning if religion is held to be necessary good for the well-being of the people.
- Ethnologists are of the opinion that men of pure race exist nowhere and that there has been admixture of all races in all parts of the world - especially is this the case with the people if India. Mr. D.R. Bhandarkar has stated: "There is hardly a class or caste in India which has not a foreign strain in it. There is as an admixture of alien blood not only among the warrior classes - the Rajputs and Marathas - but among the Brahmins who are under the happy delusion that they are free from all foreign elements.
- The question is not whether a community lives or dies, the question is on what plane does it live. There are different modes of survival. But all are not equally

honourable. For an individual as well as a society, there is a gulf between merely living and living worthily. To fight in a battle and live in a glory is one mode. To beat a retreat to surrender and to live the life of a captive is also a mode of survival.

- The sovereignty of scriptures of all religions must come to an end if we want to have a united integrated modern India.
- Law and religion are two forces which govern the conduct of men. At times they act as handmaids to each other. At other times they act as check and counter-check. Of the two forces, Law is personal while religion is impersonal. Law being personal it is capable of being unjust and iniquitous. But religion being impersonal, it can be impartial, it is capable of defeating the inequity committed by law. Religion is believed to ennoble man and not degrade him. Hinduism is an exception.
- I like the religion that teaches liberty, equality and fraternity.
- The relationship between husband and wife should be one of closest friends.
- To open or not to open the temples is a question for you to consider and not for me to agitate. If u think it is bad manners not to believe in the sanctity of human beings, then throw open the doors and be a gentleman, but if u wish to remain a orthodox Hindu then shut the doors and damn yourself, for I don't care to come.
- We are Indians, firstly and lastly
- Given the time and circumstances, nothing under the sun shall stop this country from becoming a super power.
- Being grateful has limitations, no man can be grateful at the cost of his dignity, no woman at the cost of her chastity and no country at the cost of its freedom.
- I hope that Mr. Gandhi will not drive me to the

necessity of making a choice between his life and rights of my people, for I shall never consent to deliver my people bound hand and foot to the orthodox for generations to come.

- A great man is different from an eminent one in that he is ready to be the servant of the society.
- So long as you do not achieve social liberty, whatever freedom is provided by the law is of no avail to you.
- On 26th Jan. 1950, India will be an independent country. What would happen to her independence? Will she maintain or will she lose it again? This is the first thought that comes to my mind. It is not that India was never an independent country. The point is that she once lost the independence she had. Will she lose it a second time? It is this thought which makes me most anxious for the future. What perturbs me greatly is the fact that not only India has once before lost her independence, but she lost it by treachery of some of her own people... Will history repeat itself ?It is this thought which fills me with anxiety. This anxiety is deepened by the realization of the fact that in addition to our old enemies in the form of castes and creeds, we are going to have many political parties with diverse and opposing political creeds. Will Indians place the country above their creed or creed above their country? I do not know, But this much is certain that if the parties place creed above country, our independence will be put in jeopardy a second time and probably be lost forever. This eventuality we all must resolutely guard against. We must be determined to defend our independence with the last drop of our blood!

2

Dr. Ambedkar: A Brief Biography

Bhimrao Ramji Ambedkar (14 April 1891 — 6 December 1956), also known as Babasaheb, was an Indian jurist, political leader, Buddhist activist, philosopher, thinker, anthropologist, historian, orator, prolific writer, economist, scholar, editor, revolutionary and a revivalist for Buddhism in India. He was also the chief architect of the Indian Constitution.

Born into a poor Mahar family, Ambedkar spent his whole life fighting against social discrimination, the system of Chaturvarna — the categorization of Hindu society into four varnas — and the Hindu caste system. He is also credited with providing a spark for the conversion of hundreds of thousands of untouchables to Theravada Buddhism. Dr. Ambedkar was posthumously awarded the Bharat Ratna, India's highest civilian award, in 1990. Overcoming numerous social and financial obstacles, Ambedkar became one of the first so called "Outcasts" to obtain a college education in India. Eventually earning law degrees and multiple doctorates for his study and research in law, economics and political science from Columbia University and the London School of Economics, Ambedkar gained a reputation as a scholar and practiced law for a few years, later campaigning by publishing journals advocating political rights and social freedom for India's so-called untouchables. He is regarded as a Bodhisattva by Indian Buddhists, though he never claimed himself to be a Bodhisattva.

EARLY LIFE AND EDUCATION

Bhimrao Ramji Ambedkar was born in the British-founded town and military cantonment of Mhow in the

Central Provinces (now in Madhya Pradesh). He was the 14th and last child of Ramji Maloji Sakpal and Bhimabai. His family was of Marathi background from the town of Ambavade in the Ratnagiri district of modern-day Maharashtra. They belonged to the Hindu, Mahar caste, who were treated as untouchables and subjected to intense socio-economic discrimination.

Ambedkar's ancestors had for long been in the employment of the army of the British East India Company, and his father Ramji Sakpal served in the Indian Army at the Mhow cantonment. He had received a degree of formal education in Marathi and English, and encouraged his children to learn and work hard at school. Belonging to the Kabir Panth, Ramji Sakpal encouraged his children to read the Hindu classics. He used his position in the army to lobby for his children to study at the government school, as they faced resistance owing to their caste.

Although able to attend school, Ambedkar and other untouchable children were segregated and given no attention or assistance by the teachers. They were not allowed to sit inside the class. Even if they needed to drink water somebody from a higher caste would have to pour that water from a height as they were not allowed to touch either the water or the vessel that contained it. This task was usually performed for the young Ambedkar by the school peon, and if the peon was not available then he had to go without water, Ambedkar states this situation as "No peon, No Water". Ramji Sakpal retired in 1894 and the family moved to Satara two years later. Shortly after their move, Ambedkar's mother died. The children were cared for by their paternal aunt, and lived in difficult circumstances. Only three sons — Balaram, Anandrao and Bhimrao — and two daughters — Manjula and Tulasa — of the Ambedkars would go on to survive them. Of his brothers and sisters, only Ambedkar succeeded in passing his examinations and graduating to a higher school. Bhimrao Sakpal Ambavadekar the surname comes from his native village 'Ambavade' in Ratnagiri District. His Bhramin teacher Mahadev Ambedkar who was so much fond of him, has changed his surname from 'Ambavadekar' to his own surname 'Ambedkar' in school records.

HIGHER EDUCATION

Ramji Sakpal remarried in 1898, and the family moved to Mumbai (then Bombay), where Ambedkar became the first untouchable student at the Government High School near Elphinstone Road. Although excelling in his studies, Ambedkar was increasingly disturbed by the segregation and discrimination that he faced. In 1907, he passed his matriculation examination and entered the University of Bombay, becoming one of the first persons of untouchable origin to enter a college in India.

This success provoked celebrations in his community, and after a public ceremony he was presented with a biography of the Buddha by his teacher Krishnaji Arjun Keluskar also known as Dada Keluskar, a Maratha caste scholar. Ambedkar's marriage had been arranged the previous year as per Hindu custom, to Ramabai, a nine-year old girl from Dapoli. In 1908, he entered Elphinstone College and obtained a scholarship of twenty five rupees a month from the Gayakwad ruler of Baroda, Sahyaji Rao III. By 1912, he obtained his degree in economics and political science from Bombay University, and prepared to take up employment with the Baroda state government.

His wife gave birth to his first son, Yashwant, in the same year. Ambedkar had just moved his young family and started work, when he dashed back to Mumbai to see his ailing father, who died on February 2, 1913. In 1913 he received Baroda State Scholarship of 11.50 British pounds a month for three years to join the Political Department of the Columbia University as a Post Graduate Student. In New York he stayed at Livingston Hall with his friend Naval Bhathena, a Parsi; the two remained friends for life. He used to sit for hours studying in Low Library. He passed his M.A. exam in June 1913, majoring in Economics, with Sociology, History, Philosophy, and Anthropology as other subjects of study; he presented a Thesis," Ancient Indian Commerce". In 1916 he offered another M.A. thesis, "National Dividend of India-A Historic and Analytical Study". On May 9, he read his document Castes in India: Their Mechanism, Genesis and Development" before a seminar conducted by the anthropologist. Alexander Goldenweiser. In October 1916 he was admitted to Gray's Inn for Law, and to the London School of Economics and Political Science for Economics where he started work on a Doctoral thesis. In 1917 June he was obliged to go back to India as the term of his scholarship from Baroda ended, however he was given permission to return and submit his thesis within four years. He sent his precious and much-loved collection of books back on a steamer, but it was torpedoed and sunk by a German submarine.

FIGHT AGAINST UNTOUCHABILITY

As he was educated by the Baroda State, he was bound to serve the State. He was appointed as Military Secretary to the Gaikwar of Baroda, which he had to quit within short time, this fiasco was described by Ambedkar in his autobiography "Waiting for a Visa" he states that "This scene of a dozen Parsis armed with sticks line before me in a menacing mood, and myself standing before them with a terrified look imploring for mercy, is a scene which so long a period as eighteen years had not succeeded in fading away. I can even vividly recall it— and I never recall it without tears in my eyes. It was then for the first time that I learnt that a person who is an untouchable to a Hindu is also an untouchable to a Parsi". Then after he tried to find ways to make a living for his growing family.

He worked as private tutor, as an accountant, investment consulting business, but it failed when his clients learned that he was an untouchable. In 1918 he became Professor of Political Economy in the Sydenham College of Commerce and Economics in Bombay. Even though he was successful with the students, but other professors objected to his sharing the same drinking-water jug that they all used. As a leading Indian scholar, Ambedkar had been invited to testify before the South borough Committee, which was preparing the Government of India Act 1919. At this hearing, Ambedkar argued for creating separate electorates and reservations for untouchables and other religious communities. In 1920, he began the publication of the weekly Mooknayak (Leader of the Silent) in Mumbai with the help of Shahu I (1884–1922), Maharaja of Kolhapur. Ambedkar used this journal to criticize orthodox Hindu politicians and a perceived reluctance of the Indian political community to fight caste discrimination. His speech at a Depressed Classes Conference in Kolhapur impressed the local state ruler Shahu IV, who described Ambedkar as the future national leader and shocked orthodox society by dining with Ambekdar. Having resigned from his teaching position, in July he returned to London, relying on his own savings, supplemented by loans from the Maharaja of Kolhapur and his friend Naval Bhathena.

He returned to the London School of Economics, and to Gray's Inn to read for the Bar. He lived in poverty, and studied constantly in the British Museum. In 1922 through unremitting hard work, Ambedkar once again over fulfilled all expectations: he completed a thesis for a M.Sc. (Econonics) degree at London School of Economics, and was called to the bar, and submitted a Ph.D. thesis in economics to the University of London. Ambedkar established a successful legal practice. Early on his legal career, Ambedkar was engaged in a very important lawsuite file by some Brahmins against three non-Bhramin leaders K.B.Bagde, Keshavrao Jedhe and Dinkarrao Javalkar. They were being prosecuted for writing a pamphlet that Bhramins had ruined India. On the prosecution side was L. B. Bhopatkar, a great lawyer from Poona, Ambedkar argued his case very ably, put up a very eloquent defence and won the case in October 1926. The victory was resounding, both socially and individually for the clients.

MISSIONS

While practicing law in the Bombay High Court he ran head long in to uplift the untouchable to educate them. To achieve these goals his first organizational attempt was the Bahishkrit Hitakarini Sabha. An organisation to promote education, socio-economic uplifting and for welfare of "outcastes" or the depressed classes. By 1927 Dr. Ambedkar decided to launch active movements against untouchability. He began with public movements and marches to open up and share public drinking water resources, also he began a struggle for the right to enter Hindu temples.

He led a satyagraha in Mahad to fight for the right of the untouchable community to draw water from the main water tank of the town. He was appointed to the Bombay Presidency Committee to work with the all-European Simon Commission in 1925. This commission had sparked great protests across India, and while its report was ignored by most Indians, Ambedkar himself wrote a separate set of recommendations for future constitutional

POONA PACT

By now Ambedkar had become one of the most prominent political figures of the time. He had grown increasingly critical of mainstream Indian political parties for their perceived lack of emphasis for the elimination of the caste system. Ambedkar criticized the Indian National Congress and its leader Mohandas Gandhi, whom he accused of reducing the untouchable community to a figure of pathos. Ambedkar was also dissatisfied with the failures of British rule, and advocated a political identity for untouchables separate from both the Congress and the British.

At a Depressed Classes Conference on August 8, 1930 Ambedkar outlined his political vision, insisting that the safety of the Depressed Classes hinged on their being independent of the Government and the Congress. Ambedkar's political work, such as this demand for a Separate Electorate System, had made him unpopular amongst Hindus, as well as with many Congress politicians who had earlier condemned untouchability while stopping short of advocating full equality for untouchables.

Due to Ambedkar's prominence and popular support amongst the untouchable community, he was invited to attend the Second Round Table Conference in London in 1932.

Gandhi fiercely opposed separate electorate for untouchables, though he accepted separate electorate for all other minority groups such as Muslims and Sikhs, saying he feared that separate electorates for untouchables would divide Hindu society for future generations. When the British agreed with Ambedkar and announced the awarding of separate electorates, Gandhi began a fast-unto-death while imprisoned in the Yerwada Central Jail of Pune in 1932 against the separate electorate for untouchables only. Gandhi asked for the political unity of Hindus.

Gandhi's fast provoked great public support across India, and orthodox Hindu leaders, Congress politicians and activists such as Madan Mohan Malaviya and Palwankar Baloo organized joint meetings with Ambedkar and his supporters at Yeravada. Fearing a communal reprisal and killings of untouchables in the event of Gandhi's death, Ambedkar agreed under massive coercion from the supporters of Gandhi. This agreement, which saw Gandhi end his fast, while dropping the demand for separate electorates that was promised through the British Communal Award prior to Ambedkar's meeting with Gandhi. Ambedkar was to later criticise this fast of Gandhi as a gimmick to deny political rights to the untouchables and increase the coercion he had faced to give up the demand for separate electorates.

POLITICAL CAREER

In 1935, Ambedkar was appointed principal of the Government Law College, Mumbai, a position he held for two years. Settling in Mumbai, Ambedkar oversaw the construction of a house, and stocked his personal library with more than 50,000 books. His wife Ramabai died after a long illness in the same year. It had been her long-standing wish to go on a pilgrimage to Pandharpur, but Ambedkar had refused to let her go, telling her that he would create a new Pandharpur for her instead of Hinduism's Pandharpur which treated them as untouchables. Speaking at the Yeola Conversion Conference on October 13 near Nasik, Ambedkar announced his intention to convert to a different religion and exhorted his followers to leave Hinduism. He would repeat his message at numerous public meetings across India In 1936, Ambedkar founded the Independent Labour Party, which won 15 seats in the 1937 elections to the Central Legislative Assembly. He published, The Annihilation of Caste in the same year, based on the thesis he had written in New York. Attaining immense popular success, Ambedkar's work strongly criticized Hindu orthodox religious leaders and the caste system in general. Ambedkar served on the Defence Advisory Committee and the Viceroy's Executive Council as minister for labour.

With What Congress and Gandhi Have Done to the Untouchables, Ambedkar intensified his attacks on Gandhi and the Congress, hypocrisy. In his work Who Were the Shudras?, Ambedkar attempted to explain the formation of the Shudras *i.e.* the lowest caste in hierarchy of Hindu caste system. He also emphasised how Shudras are separate from Untouchables. Ambedkar oversaw the transformation of his political party into the All India Scheduled Castes Federation, although it performed poorly in the elections held in 1946 for the Constituent Assembly of India. In writing a sequel to Who Were the Shudras? in 1948, Ambedkar lambasted Hinduism in The Untouchables: A Thesis on the Origins of Untouchability:

- The Hindu Civilization.... is a diabolical contrivance to suppress and enslave humanity. Its proper name would be infamy. What else can be said of a civilization which has produced a mass of people.... who are treated as an entity beyond human intercourse and whose mere touch is enough to cause pollution?

PAKISTAN OR THE PARTITION OF INDIA

Between 1941 and 1945, he published a number of books and pamphlets, including Thoughts on Pakistan, in which he criticized the Muslim League's demand for a separate Muslim state of Pakistan but considered its concession if Muslims demanded so as expedient. Ambedkar wrote a subchapter titled If Muslims truly and deeply desire Pakistan, their choice ought to be accepted. He wrote that if the Muslims are bent on Pakistan, then it must be conceded to them. He asked whether Muslims in the army could be trusted to defend India. In the event of Muslims invading India or in the case of a Muslim rebellion, with whom would the Indian Muslims in the army side? He concluded that, in the interests of the safety of India, Pakistan should be acceded to, should the Muslims demand it.

Ambedkar, the Hindu assumption that though Hindus and Muslims were two nations, they could live together under one state, was but an empty sermon, a mad project, to which no sane man would agree. Ambedkar was also critical of Islam and its practices in South Asia. While justifying the Partition of India, he condemned the practice of child marriage in Muslim society, as well as the mistreatment of women. He said,

- No words can adequately express the great and many evils of polygamy and concubinage, and especially as a source of misery to a Muslim woman. Take the caste system. Everybody infers that Islam must be free from slavery and caste. [While slavery existed], much of its support was derived from Islam and Islamic countries. While the prescriptions by the Prophet regarding the just and humane treatment of slaves contained in the Koran are praiseworthy, there is nothing whatever in Islam that lends support to the abolition of this curse. But if slavery has gone, caste among Musalmans [Muslims] has remained.

He wrote that Muslim society is "even more full of social evils than Hindu Society is" and criticized Muslims for sugarcoating their sectarian caste system with euphemisms like "brotherhood". He also criticized the discrimination against the Arzal classes among Muslims who were regarded as "degraded", as well as the oppression of women in Muslim society through the oppressive purdah system. He alleged that while Purdah was also practiced by Hindus, only among Muslims was it sanctioned by religion. He criticized their fanaticism regarding Islam on the grounds that their literalist interpretations of Islamic doctrine made their society very rigid and impermeable to change. He further wrote that Indian Muslims have failed to reform their society unlike Muslims in other countries like Turkey.

- In a "communal malaise", both groups [Hindus and Muslims] ignore the urgent claims of social justice.

FATHER OF INDIA'S CONSTITUTION

Upon India's independence on August 15, 1947, the new Congress-led government invited Ambedkar to serve as the nation's first law minister, which he accepted. On August 29, Ambedkar was appointed Chairman of the Constitution Drafting Committee, charged by the Assembly to write free India's new Constitution. Ambedkar won great praise from his colleagues and contemporary observers for his drafting work. In this task Ambedkar's study of sangha practice among early Buddhists and his extensive reading in Buddhist scriptures were to come to his aid.

Sangha practice incorporated voting by ballot, rules of debate and precedence and the use of agendas, committees and proposals to conduct business. Sangha practice itself was modelled on the oligarchic system of governance followed by tribal republics of ancient India such as the Shakyas and the Lichchavis. Thus, although Ambedkar used Western models to give his Constitution shape, its spirit was Indian and, indeed, tribal. Granville Austin has described the Indian Constitution drafted by Dr Ambedkar as 'first and foremost a social document.'... 'The majority of India's constitutional provisions are either directly arrived at furthering the aim of social revolution or attempt to foster this revolution by establishing conditions necessary for its achievement.'

The text prepared by Ambedkar provided constitutional guarantees and protections for a wide range of civil liberties for individual citizens, including freedom of religion, the abolition of untouchability and the outlawing of all forms of discrimination Ambedkar argued for extensive economic and social rights for women, and also won the Assembly's support for introducing a system of reservations of jobs in the civil services, schools and colleges for members of scheduled castes and scheduled tribes, a system akin to affirmative action. India's lawmakers hoped to eradicate the socio-economic inequalities and lack of opportunities for India's depressed classes through this measure, which had been originally envisioned as temporary on a need basis.

The Constitution was adopted on November 26, 1949 by the Constituent Assembly. Ambedkar resigned from the cabinet in 1951 following the stalling in parliament of his draft of the Hindu Code Bill, which sought to expound gender equality in the laws of inheritance, marriage and the economy. Although supported by Prime Minister Nehru, the cabinet and many other Congress leaders, it received criticism from a large number of members of parliament. Ambedkar independently contested an election in 1952 to the lower house of parliament, the Lok Sabha, but was defeated. He was appointed to the upper house, of parliament, the Rajya Sabha in March 1952 and would remain a member until his death.

CONVERSION BACK TO BUDDHISM

As a profound life long student of anthropology Dr. Babasaheb Ambedkar made a remarkable discovery that the Mahar people are originally ancient Buddhist people of India. They have been forced outside a village to live like an outcast as they refused to leave Buddhist practices and eventually they were made into untouchables. He wrote a scholarly book on this topic- Who were Sudras? How they became Untouchables. Dr. Babasaheb Ambedkar studied Buddhism all his life, and around 1950s, Ambedkar turned his attention fully to Buddhism and travelled to Sri Lanka (then Ceylon) to attend a convention of Buddhist scholars and monks. While dedicating a new Buddhist vihara near Pune, Ambedkar announced that he was writing a book on Buddhism, and that as soon as it was finished, he planned to make a formal conversion back to Buddhism. Ambedkar twice visited Burma in 1954; the second time in order to attend the third conference of the World Fellowship of Buddhists in Rangoon.

In 1955, he founded the Bharatiya Bauddha Mahasabha, or the Buddhist Society of India. He completed his final work, The Buddha and His Dhamma, in 1956. It was published posthumously. After meetings with the Sri Lankan Buddhist monk Hammalawa Saddhatissa, Ambedkar organised a formal public ceremony for himself and his supporters in Nagpur on October 14, 1956. Accepting the Three Refuges and Five Precepts from a Buddhist monk in the traditional manner, Ambedkar completed his own conversion. He then proceeded to convert an large number (some 500,000) of his supporters who were gathered around him. He prescribed the 22 Vows for these converts, after the Three Jewels and Five Precepts. He then traveled to Kathmandu in Nepal to attend the Fourth World Buddhist Conference. His work on The Buddha or Karl Marx and "Revolution and counter-revolution in ancient India" remained incomplete.

DEATH

Since 1948, Ambedkar had been suffering from diabetes. He was bed-ridden from June to October in 1954 owing to clinical depression and failing eyesight. He had been increasingly embittered by political issues, which took a toll on his health. His health worsened as he furiously worked through 1955. Just three days after completing his final manuscript The Buddha and His Dhamma, it is said that Ambedkar died in his sleep on December 6, 1956 at his home in Delhi.

A Buddhist-style cremation was organised for him at Dadar Chowpatty beach on December 7, attended by hundreds of thousands of supporters, activists and admirers. A conversion programme was supposed to be organised on 16 December 1956. So, those who had attended cremation function also got converted to Buddhism at same place. Ambedkar was survived by his second wife Savita Ambedkar and converted to Buddhism with him. His wife's name before marriage was Sharda Kabir. Savita Ambedkar died as a Buddhist in 2002. His Son Yashwant [Known as Bhaiyasaheb Ambedkar] and daughter-in-low Meetatai Ambedkar is working as National prisident of Bhartiya Baudh Mahasabha and Ambedkar's grandson, Prakash Yaswant Ambedkar leads the Bharipa Bahujan Mahasangha and has served in both houses of the Indian Parliament. A number of unfinished typescripts and handwritten drafts were found among Ambedkar's notes and documents and gradually made available. Among these were Waiting for a Visa, which probably dates from 1935–36 and is an autobiographical work, and the Untouchables, or the Children of India's Ghetto, which refers to the census of 1951. A memorial for Ambedkar was established in his Delhi house at 26 Alipur Road. His birthdays is celebrated as a public holiday known as Ambedkar Jayanti or Bhim Jayanti. He was posthumously awarded India's highest civilian honour, the Bharat Ratna in 1990. Many public institutions are named in his honour, such as the Dr Babasaheb Ambedkar Marathwada university—Aurangabad [Maharashrta]

Dr. Babasaheb Ambedkar Open University in Hyderabad; Dr BR Ambedkar University in Srikakulam, Andhra Pradesh; B. R. Ambedkar Bihar University, Muzaffarpur and Dr. B.R. Ambedkar National Institute of Technology, Jalandhar. The other being Dr. Babasaheb Ambedkar International Airport in Nagpur, which was otherwise known as Sonegaon Airport. A large official portrait of Ambedkar is on display in the Indian Parliament building. On the anniversary of his birth (14 April) and death (6 December) and on Dhamma Chakra Pravartan Din, 14th Oct at Nagpur, at least half a million people gather to pay homage to him at his memorial in Mumbai.

DR. BABASAHEB AMBEDKAR, WRITINGS AND SPEECHES

The Education Department, Government of Maharastra (Bombay) Published the Collection of Dr. B. R. Ambedkar's writings and speeches in different volumes.

Volume No.	Description
Vol. 1.	Castes in India: Their Mechanism, Genesis and Development and 11 other essays
Vol. 2.	Dr Ambedkar in the Bombay Legislature, with the

	Simon Commission and at the Round Table Conferences, 1927–1939
Vol. 3.	Philosophy of Hinduism ; India and the pre-requisites of communism ; Revolution and counter revolution ;Buddha or Karl Marx
Vol. 4.	Riddles in Hinduism
Vol. 5.	Essays on untouchables and untouchability
Vol. 6.	The evolution of provincial finance in British India
Vol. 7.	Who were the shudras? ; The untouchables
Vol. 8.	Pakistan or the partition of India
Vol. 9.	What Congress and Gandhi have done to the untouchables ; Mr. Gandhi and the emancipation of the untouchables
Vol. 10.	Dr. Ambedkar as member of the Governor General's Executive Council, 1942–46
Vol. 11.	The Buddha and his Dhamma
Vol. 12.	Unpublished writings ; Ancient Indian commerce ; Notes on laws; Waiting for a Visa; Miscellaneous notes, etc.
Vol. 13.	Dr. Ambedkar as the principal architect of the Constitution of India
Vol. 14.	(2 parts) Dr. Ambedkar and The Hindu Code Bill
Vol. 15.	Dr. Ambedkar as free India's first Law Minister and member of opposition in Indian Parliament (1947– 1956)
Vol. 16.	Dr. Ambedkar's The Pali grammar
Vol. 17	(Part I) Dr. B.R. Ambedkar and his Egalitarian Revolution – Struggle for Human Rights. Events starting from March 1927 to 17 November 1956 in the chronological order (Part II) Dr. B. R. Ambedkar and his Egalitarian Revolution–Socio-political and religious activities. Events starting from November 1929 to 8 May 1956 in the chronological order (Part III) Dr. B. R. Ambedkar and his Egalitarian Revolution – Speeches. Events starting from 1 January to 20 November 1956 in the chronological order

Vol. 18	(3 parts) Dr. B. R. Ambedkar's Speeches and writing in Marathi
Vol. 19	Dr. B. R. Ambedkar's Speeches and writing in Marathi
Vol. 20	Dr. B. R. Ambedkar's Speeches and writing in Marathi
Vol. 21	Dr. B. R. Ambedkar's Photo Album and correspondence.

CRITICISM AND LEGACY

Ambedkar's legacy as a socio-political reformer, had a deep effect on modern India. In post-Independence India his socio-political thought has acquired respect across the political spectrum. His initiatives have influenced various spheres of life and transformed the way India today looks at socio-economic policies, education and affirmative action through socio-economic and legal incentives. His reputation as a scholar led to his appointment as free India's first law minister, and chairman of the committee responsible to draft a constitution.

He passionately believed in the freedom of the individual and criticised equally both orthodox casteist Hindu society. His condemnation of Hinduism and its foundation of caste system, made him controversial, although his conversion to Buddhism sparked a revival in interest in Buddhist philosophy in India and abroad. Ambedkar condemned Gandhi's support for the caste system and perpetuating untouchability. Dr. Ambedkar warned people, "Don't call Gandhi a saint. He is a seasoned politician.

When everything else fails, Gandhi will resort to intrigue." "Don't fall under Gandhi's spell, he's not God... Mahatmas have come and Mahatmas have gone but untouchables have remained untouchables." Ambedkar's political philosophy has given rise to a large number of Dalit political parties, publications and workers' unions that remain active across India, especially in Maharashtra. His promotion of the Dalit Buddhist movement has rejuvenated interest in Buddhist philosophy in many parts of India. Mass conversion ceremonies have been organized by Dalit activists in modern times, emulating Ambedkar's Nagpur ceremony of 1956. Some scholars, including some from the affected castes, took the view that the British were more even-handed between castes, and that continuance of British rule would have helped to eradicate many evil practices. This political opinion was shared by quite a number of social activists including Jyotirao Phule. Some, in modern India, question the continued institution of reservations initiated by Ambedkar as outdated and anti-meritocratic.

However, such arguments have always been dismissed by the Dalit masses. They express that the opposition of Caste-based reservations in India, primarily comes from the antagonism rooted in the Hindu society towards the Dalits. And, that the Caste-based reservations in India, in fact, have become the uplifting of Dalits in the post-colonial period. Outside India, at the end of the 1990s, some Hungarian Romani people drew parallels between their own situation and the situation of the Dalits in India. Inspired by Ambedkar's approach, they started to convert to Buddhism.

3

Indian Historiography and Ambedkar

INTRODUCTION

Ambedkar came to forefront in Indian academics from the decade of nineties with the intensified struggles of Dalits. The struggles of the ordinary people forced the centres of power and knowledge to consider the importance of Ambedkar and his ideas in social reconstruction of the nation. With Ambedkar as the source of inspiration, Dalits are struggling to write their own history by interrogating the dominant Brahminical traditions. The project of De- Brahiminisation of Indian history has appeal among the Dalit scholars in writing Indian history, culture and philosophy.

The relevance of Ambedkar has to be read with the fifty years developments of post Ambedkar of post independent India. His approach to Indian society and its history are crucial in understanding contemporary India and the struggles of the oppressed. The document will focus on the importance of historical method of Ambedkar in relation to the theories of contemporary historiography of India. Ambedkar's notion of history is identified with 'moral community' imbibed with the principles of equality, liberty and fraternity. His historical method borrows tools from Marxism in understanding the ancient history. Rather than mechanically applying Marxism, he had creatively used it in keeping the specific context of Indian society. He approached Indian society from the point of religion and finds the religion as source for the different ideological position. For instance, Buddhism is considered as revolutionary and Hinduism as counter revolutionary. 'Rationality' is the guiding principle in evaluating the principles and practices of religion. For the claims of religion he applied rationalistic principle.

He brings the religion as a focal point in reference to caste system. To construct the Indian history in proper, he avail all the convincing ideas of his times, from liberal to Marxist. This may go in tune of pragmatism. The pragmatism of Ambedkar differs from the context of western societies. The pragmatic method of Ambedkar came out of his social responsibility and in presenting the history from the victim's point of view. In essence he made a serious attempt in constructing the Indian history in which one finds dignified place for 'sudras' and 'untouchable communities'. Ambedkar is a source of inspiration for contemporary dalit movement and so for constructing history from dalit point of view. Dalit historiography establishes its own method by challenging the colonial, nationalist, marxists and subaltern approaches of Indian historiography.

PHILOSOPHY OF HISTORY

Historians have always tried to provide rationally justified knowledge about past, cause and effects of events. Philosophy of history can function as a conceptual enhancement for working historians and also it can function as a source of rational criticism of specific methods or approaches within contemporary historiography. Historically, there are various attempts to read history from diverse ideological and methodological positions. Many thinkers contributed to the philosophy of historical ideas.

Many who have concerned themselves with questions about the nature of historical knowledge and interpretation of the past have spent a good deal of time studying the history of various historical concepts and ideas; and in doing so some have concluded that there are no absolute ideals of historical method or truth which can be isolated from their own peculiar historical and social contexts. Broadly there are two streams identified in approaching the historical knowledge- idealistic and materialistic. In the realm of epistemological understanding of truth value of historical knowledge-rationalistic and empiricist methods were followed. The empiricist views past as an ordinary object of empirical investigation. The rationalist views past as an object of rational reconstruction and understanding. There raised a basic questions what is history about? Kant, Hegel and Marx have common strand and answered this question differently. For Hegel, history is unfolding of human freedom. Hegel's conception of history presupposes an abstract or absolute spirit.

History of humanity becomes history of abstract spirit of humanity, a spirit above and beyond the real man. The clue to history, in Hegel's view, is to be found in the idea of freedom. 'World history', in his words, 'exhibits the development of the consciousness of freedom on the part of spirit, and of the consequent realization of that freedom.' Marx answered in another way – that the underlying driver in historical change is the tension between the forces and relations of production or class struggle. For Marx, the first premise of all human history is, of course the existence of living human beings. All historiography must begin with these natural bases and their modification in the course of history by men's activity.

Unlike the idealist view of history, it does not have to look for category in each period, but remains constantly on the real ground of history, it does not explain the practice from the idea but explains the formation of ideas from material practice. The whole previous conception of history has either completely neglected this real basis of history. Consequently, history has always to be written in accordance with external standard, the real production of life appears to be a historical. During the Nineteenth century the central concern is changed from metaphysical issues about 'direction of history' to epistemological issues about 'historical truth'. In twentieth century these concerns about truths in history focus on dispute between two views on question into what is history.

A good part of the twentieth century was devoted to a debate sparked by the philosopher of science Carl Hempels claiming that historical explanations — to be legitimately scientific ones have to be developed from the physical sciences. In contrast with Hempel's thesis, some, such as R. G. Collingwood and William Dray' have insisted that the historian is more concerned with understanding the motives of historical agents than with predicting events.

Collingwood, author of 'The Idea of History' argues that all history is the history of thought. He replaced the 'positivistic' notion of history with one which treats thought as the fundamental concept of historical inquiry. Philosophy of history-as-discipline has also addressed concerns about the justification and limitations of historical objectivity, the truth of historical claims, and the nature of historical explanations. Are there any proper methods in understanding history? Is it possible to find the historical method without any ideological and political positions?

The discussion further continued that historians' ideological and political positions play a role either approaching the knowledge of past or constructing the ideas of past. The historians are selective in interpreting the knowledge of past. In other words, the contemporary demands force them to probe into the past. As the historian Croce said 'all history is contemporary'. As Carl Becker declares, 'the facts of history do not exist for any historian till he creates them.' As E H Carr explains, 'history is a continuous process of interaction between the historian and his facts and unending dialogue between the past and the present.' 'All history depends ultimately upon its social purpose.'

HISTORIOGRAPHIES IN WRITING INDIAN HISTORY

This document gives emphasis on the historical method of Ambedkar in countering the dominant social groups' construction of the Indian history. Both in construction of history of India and in having its historical method- Colonial, Orientalist, Nationalist, Marxists, Cambridge historians and

Subaltern historians who played a vital role. History writing in India as a conscious exercise began with scholars of Colonial and Orientalist persuasion and followed by nationalist elite and others. At present four dominant streams in Indian historiography are important - Colonial, Nationalist, Marxist and Subaltern schools.

Each school has its historical social context in emphasizing its method in writing Indian history. Each school argued its case in relation to other. The decade of eighties is turning point in Indian history in bringing new epistemological positions corresponding to the struggles of Dalits, Women, Adivasis. In writing history, categories wise, caste, gender, region became reference points. On the other hand, struggles rallying religious nationalism are trying to invoke the 'glorious past'. With the many contesting positions, to reach out historical objectivity is not an easy task.

When researches into India's past began in the late 18th century and early 19th centuries, Orientalist ideas structured historical representations. Inspired by the romanticism and classicism of the time, Orientalists like William Jones and H.T. Colebrooke returned to the ancient past, discovered its greatness and defined a specific notion of a glorious classical age. It was in this age, so the Orientalists told us, that the essence of Indian civilization – embodied in its language, laws, institutions and religious texts – came into being. Subsequent to this golden age there was a continuous or cyclical decline to a degenerate present before the British rule.

If India had to develop, its lost past had to be rediscovered, its essence had to be properly understood, its juridical and religious texts had to be translated and canonized, its poetry had to be recaptured. The Orientalists saw themselves as the mediators who would define this relationship between the past and the present. As codifiers and translators they would be the ones to discover the ancient texts and ascribe to them their true meanings. By the early 19th century, with liberalism gaining ground, Orientalist histories were questioned from within the fold of imperial thought. If Orientalists had glorified

India's past, the liberals condemned it. From a veneration of classicality we moved to a phase of arrogant deification of modernity. Liberal histories idealized the modern West and the assumed principles of its order – individualism, freedom and democracy. Other societies – of the past and present – were understood and characterized only in terms of the presence and non-presence of liberal values.

While Orientalists had discovered in India's past a succession of golden ages, liberals like James Mill and Thomas Macaulay could see only shades of darkness. In the West liberal histories traced a series of great transitions – from darkness to light, irrationality to rationality, magic to science, superstition to reason. Modernity had emerged from the age of darkness, through the Renaissance and Enlightenment into the modern age. In India and other 'dark continents', as the liberals saw it, this transition never took place. India had remained unchanged, constrained by the social institutions that defined it – caste, village community and Oriental despotism. The colonial historians were tried to construct the Indian history that suits their political interests.

The colonial historians tried to show that Indian nationalism was nothing more than an unprincipled, selfish, amoral bid for power by a few Indian elites. They had used the traditional bonds of caste and communal ties to mobilize masses for their own ends. The colonial assumptions of historical thought was enshrined by Hegel and expounded by Macaulay, Mill, Seeley, and many others. In the historical literature, colonial powers escaped serious interrogation outside of the specific contestations of the nationalist struggle until new critical inquiries were initiated by figures as various as Bernard Cohn, Edward Said, and Ranjit Guha.

Nicholas Dirks argues that British colonialism played a critical role in both the identification and production of Indian 'tradition'. Essentially colonial history of India is Eurocentric and imperialistic. The tendency to read Indian history in terms of a lack, an absence, or incompleteness that translates into 'inadequacy' is obvious in these excerpts. The British conquered and represented the diversity of 'Indian' pasts through a homogenizing narrative of transition from a 'medieval' period to 'modernity'. The terms have changed with time. The 'medieval' was once called 'despotic' and the 'modern', the 'rule of law'. 'Feudal/capitalist' has been a later variant. While the nationalists mounted a critique of colonial ideas, they continued to accept many of the key categories through which imperial representations of Indian society were fashioned.

But in their critiques, nationalists still borrowed from the Orientalists, transforming the founding Orientalist notions of India's past – the idea of classical golden ages and the corollary myth of a subsequent civilizational decline – into accepted orthodoxies of Indian history. But most nationalist histories continued to periodize pre-colonial history through religious categories. They referred to ancient India as Hindu and medieval India as Muslim – as if a unitary religious essence permeated the entire age and the whole society. By the 1980s history writing in India saw a new phase of dramatic change. Influenced by the new social history in England and the cultural turn in social sciences, Subaltern Studies challenged the elitism of earlier histories that attributed historical agency to the elites and looked at the world from above.

Subaltern histories emphasized the need to understand the experiences and lives of the dominated – peasants and workers, tribals and lower castes, women and dalits – people who leave few written records, whose voices are difficult to hear, whose actions appear inconsequential. The cultural turn in history writing all over the world shifted the focus away from economist and reductive reading of historical processes. Power and domination, economy and society, experience of work and leisure, identities and interests, were all seen as culturally constituted.

The real break came with the rise of a much more sophisticated historiography from the 1950s and '60s pioneered by scholars, to name few of the most important, like D.D. Kosambi, R.S. Sharma and Irfan Habib. There was a veritable paradigm shift, particularly in ancient and medieval Indian history. The historiography of the Hindu Right necessarily sticks to periodization by religion: in effect, the religion of rulers, for that is the only way through which the premise of medieval 'Muslim domination' or 'tyranny' can be made credible. The only real evil for it is religious, cultural or political domination coming from sources it considers external and alien, because non-Hindu.

The failure to go beyond the single evaluative standard set by the colonial/anti-colonial binary produces similar problems for histories of subordinate caste and Dalit protest. Arun Shourie's onslaught on Ambedkar typifies this tendency at its worst, but an indication of the difficulties is revealed by the interesting recent attempt by G. Aloysius to write an alternative history of modern India from a 'Dalit-Bahujan' perspective. Its many virtues include a valid stress on the complicities between colonialism and continued or refurbished high caste domination (a theme which Jyotiba Phule had opened up), as well as on the numerous overlaps between 'mainstream' nationalism and Hindutva.

Even Nehru's Discovery of India is revealed as being not entirely immune from such contamination. In the decade of eighties, a group of scholars identifying with subaltern historiography got prominence by differing with earlier nationalist and Marxist historiography. This rise coincided with that of the Dalit movement which was taking aspiration from the philosophy of Ambedkar. Dalit movement, on the one hand, questions Brahminism and its basic assumptions and on the other hand finds 'faults' with Marxism in practice as an alternative to dominant classes.

The scholars influenced by the Dalit movement are even critical about the subaltern studies especially their treatment of the issue of caste. Subaltern studies came into prominence from the decade of eighties in projecting a new method of historiography by countering the earlier ones. This approach came along the line of 'history from below' approach of European history writing in 1970 and 1980s. It came in opposition to both colonialist and nationalist historiography. It is skeptical about the established orthodoxies of both liberal nationalist and Marxist historiographies. Writing history from subaltern point of view was to show that neither nationalist nor left progressive historiography had a place for autonomous historical actions of the subaltern classes. 'The historiography of Indian nationalism has for a long time been dominated by elitism- colonialist elitism and bourgeois-nationalist elitism.' The thrust of the argument is subaltern consciousness is distinct and autonomous.

The histories of class divided societies have been written and preserved in accordance with interests of dominant classes. Only rarely does subaltern consciousness appear in its autonomous form in these accounts. Subaltern consciousness evolved out of the experience of subordination, out of struggle, despite the daily routine of servitude, exploitation and deprivation. The subaltern consciousness can not be found in archival material conventionally used by historians, since it is prepared and preserved by dominant groups.

For the most part, those materials only show the subaltern as subservient. It is only the moment of rebellion that subaltern appears as the bearer of independent personality. The subaltern studies are criticized by scholars on different grounds. The criticism is on the agency involved in this project and on the method. Many complained that subaltern history was becoming bhadralok history, the history of elites. Sumit Sarkar, 'The decline of the subaltern in subaltern studies' argued that in the name of theory, a tendency emerged towards essentializing the categories of 'subaltern' and 'autonomy', in the sense of assigning to them more or less absolute, fixed, de-contextualized meanings and qualities.

They were not advanced further by pointing out the economic reductionism of Marxism. What is conveniently forgotten is that the problems do not disappear through a simple substitution of 'class' by 'subaltern' or 'community'. Reifying tendencies can be actually strengthened by the associated detachment from socio-economic contexts and determinants out of a mortal fear of economic reductionism. The handling of the new concepts, further, may remain equally naive. The subaltern studies, symptomatically has ignored histories of the left and of organized anti-caste movements throughout, and the line between past and present-day neglect can be fairly porous. He further argues that subaltern studies don't have ideological strength to counter the communal violence. There is another criticism by branding the subaltern school as idealistic. 'Guha masks his idealism by formulating a critique of official, liberal and left historiography. Guha's idealism can be seen most clearly in his attempt to criticize the analysis of the social and economic conditions which generate rebellion. By accepting the basic premises of idealism, peasant consciousness is rendered supra-historical as it is not determined by any objective historical forces. It is at a par with the Hegelian 'geist' which is not determined by history, while the development of history is march towards the self realization of this spirit. Guha's idealism consists not in emphasizing the importance of consciousness, but in placing consciousness beyond the pale of historical determination or mediation.

Definitely there is a breakthrough in methodology in constructing the history with much authenticity. Subaltern Studies becomes a blanket term for all subaltern communities like dalits, women, peasants, adivasis etc. in countering the hegemony of the dominance. Within the subaltern studies, if each community had its own logic and approach to history, then the project of subaltern studies is in trouble. For instance, the issue of caste is important in writing the history so as the historians/scholars from the dalit communities had altogether different approach in constructing/imagining Indian history. Immediately, it even dismisses the so called subaltern by dismissing them as elite/ or non dalits.

Dalit historiography throws a challenge to colonial, nationalist, Marxist and right wing and even to the so called historians of subaltern studies. In this context, Ambedkar's method of constructing the history from dalit perspective is path breaking, and provides insights for contemporary historians of all shades. Infact, very few historians worked out in the field of ancient history with sound ideological commitment and with a purpose of liberating the oppressed masses from dominant social and philosophical systems.

AMBEDKAR: IN PURSUIT OF HISTORICAL TRUTH

One may derive Ambedkar's 'historical method' in all his major writings on Indian history, culture and philosophy. The writings on this kind of issues not only provoked the scholars, political leaders of nationalist movement and orthodox Hindus of his times but helped deconstruct the dominant construction of ideas of Indian society.

He made a systematic attempt to construct the histories and genealogies of the submerged social groups of Indian society by questioning the elite and dominant established Brahminical positions. He seems confident of his position by declaring it as 'fresh insights and new visions' in looking at Indian history and philosophy. In the year 1946, Ambedkar identified five streams of thoughts among the Hindus of Indian society in his writing on 'who are Shudras'- Orthodox, Aryasamajists, respecters of law (Hindu social system is all wrong, but who holds that there is no necessity to attack it.

Since law does not recognize it, it is dying, if not dead system) Political minded (Swaraj is important than social reform) and Rationalists (regard social reform as primary and even more important than Swaraj). Among these five classes of Hindus, Ambedkar would like to identify his position with rationalist Hindus who were arguing for social reform as immediate agenda rather than any other.

In the words of Ambedkar; "I claim that in my research I have been guided by the best tradition of the historian who treats all literature as vulgar- I am using the word in its original sense of belonging to the people –to be examined and tested by accepted rules of evidence without recognizing any distinction between the sacred and profane and with the sole object of finding the truth." As has been well said, an historian ought to be exact, sincere, and impartial; free from passion, unbiased by interest, fear, resentment or affection; and faithful to the truth, which is the mother of history, the preserver of great actions, the enemy of oblivion, the witness of the past, the director of the future. In short he must have an open mind, though it may not be an empty mind, and readiness to examine all evidence even though it be spurious.

The non-brahmin scholar may find it difficult to remain true to this spirit of historian. He is likely to import the spirit of non-brahmin politics in the examination of the truth or falsity of ancient literature which is not justifiable. I feel certain that in my research I have kept myself free from such prejudice. In writing about sudras I have had present in my mind no other consideration except that of pure history. Respect and reverence for the sacred literature cannot be made to order. They are results of social factors which make such sentiments natural in one case and quite unnatural in another. Respect and reverence for sacred literature of the hindus is natural to a Brahmin scholar. But it is quite unnatural in a non-Brahmin scholar.

In the historical method of Ambedkar; man is the maker of history: Ambedkar evaluates the three different views on the causes of historical changes, Augustine, Buckle and Marx. Augustinian, history is only an unfolding of divine plan in which mankind is to continue through war and suffering until that divine plan is completed at the day of judgment. Ambedkar pointed out that this is not acceptable to many except theologians. For Buckle, history was made by geography and physics. As per Marx, history was the result of economic forces.

Ambedkar finds the limitations of these three arguments by holding the opinion that none of these would admit that history is the biography of great men. Indeed they deny man any place in making of history. He considers there is a truth in Buckle and Marx, but their views do not represent the whole truth. They are quite wrong in holding that impersonal forces are everything and that man is no factor in the making of history. That these impersonal forces are a determining factor can not be denied, however, the effect of impersonal forces depends on man must also be admitted.' The methods employed by Ambedkar in reconstructing the history are unique and convincing. In developing an historical method he followed Goethe, as he said 'the historian's duty is to separate the truth from false, the certain from the uncertain...' Ambedkar agrees with Goethe in bringing out the relevant and necessary facts to forefront. Ambedkar proceeds further and points out into what the duty of historian in reconstructing the authentic history in situations, where he confronts with many missing links, *i.e.* when no direct evidence of connected relations between important events is available. He himself faced this kind of situation in explaining the origin of sudras and untouchables as in both cases no documentary evidences were available or its antiquity. "In case of reconstructing history where there are no texts, and if there are, they have no direct bearing on the question. In such circumstances what one has to do is to strive to divine what the texts conceal or suggest without being even quite certain of having found the truth.

The task is one of gathering survivals of the past, placing hem together and making them tell the story of their birth. The task is analogous to that of the archaeologist who constructs a city from broken stones or of the paleontologist who conceives an extinct animal from scattered bones and teeth or of a painter who reads the lines of the horizon and the smallest vestiges on the slopes of the hill to make up a scene." Ambedkar appears very much aware of the role of historian's social affinity in dealing the material in relation to the problems of social history.

In an introduction to 'who are the Shudras', he made this point more clear. He finds the difference between the non-Brahmin scholar and Brahmin scholar in treating the same source material of sacred literature of Hindus. The Brahmin scholar's attitude is identified as uncritical commendation, and where as the Non-Brahmins attitude in dealing this is unsparing condemnation. Ambedkar finds both the attitudes are harmful to historical research. It is often argued by many Brahmins that sacred literature has to be treated with reverence and respect. Ambedkar staunchly believes that in pursuit of historical truth, there is nothing wrong in exposure of these very sacred texts which are responsible for the decline and fall of nation and society. It is the duty of a scholar to treat the literature without having any distinction of sacred or profane in pursuing truth. It is quite natural for Brahmin scholar to treat it as sacred with lot of respect and reverence. More over its object is to sustain the superiority and privileges of Brahmins as against the non-brahmins. Since he finds the comfort and privilege, it is not possible for the Brahmin scholar to be critical about sacred literature. In fact, it is his whole production and finds livelihood on it.

'Knowing that what is called the sacred literature contains an abominable social philosophy which is responsible for their social degradation, the non-brahmin reacts to it in a manner quite opposite to that of the brahmin.....I am a non-brahmin, not even a non-brahmin, but an untouchable.' Ambedkar had more focus on philosophy of religion in understanding the socio-historical phenomenon and the moral basis of Indian society, than exclusively depending on either religion or philosophy.

He developed it as a method. It seems in evolving this method, he got influenced by John Dewey. Dewey is one of those pragmatic philosophers who wrote extensively on philosophy of religion from this perspective. In the west, religion is identified with faith, and philosophy is with reason/ science/rationality, in the age of enlightenment. It is also understood as tradition and modernity dichotomy. Religion and science started considering adverse to each other. In this backdrop pragmatism of Dewey got importance by considering religion on practical utility.

Religion is an institution or an influence and like all social influences and institutions, it may help or harm a society which is in its grip. Religion not only crossed everywhere the wrap of Indian history it forms the wrap and woof of Hindu mind. The life of the Hindu is regulated by religion at every moment of his life. Besides religion acts as a social force, and it stands for a scheme of divine governance. The scheme becomes an ideal for society to follow. 'The power of religious ideal depends upon its power to confer material benefit'. Ambedkar favours for religion that stand for reason rather negating religion. He felt that Hindu religion need to undergo a reform. Caste is a natural outcome of certain religious beliefs which have the sanction of shastras. To abolish the sanctity and sacredness of caste, one has to destroy the authority of the shastras and Vedas. One has to destroy the religion of sruti and smriti. Ambedkar not only proposed the religion that should stand for reason, but also tries to link it up with the governing principle of politics. In simple terms, he thought reason and critical analysis as a method used for the study of religion.

CASTE AS KEY PRINCIPLE IN UNDERSTANDING INDIAN HISTORY

Ambedkar identified caste as an important institution, in understanding the Indian society. In evolving his political theory, one could not ignore the role of caste system in India. No political theory is possible without some understanding of the caste. Ambedkar is the first thinker who systematized the conception of caste in analytical way. Earlier discussions on caste are ethnographic and descriptive in nature. His approach is more political rather etnographical.

He made an attempt to understand the origin and functioning of caste in order to understand the lives of the victims of the caste system. He understood that whole Indian social system was founded on the caste and the beliefs, customs, knowledge all are centred around caste system. All the human activities are determined by the caste. Caste has social, political and economical implications. In simple caste is the primary institution of Indian society and other institutions like family, state, nation, school are directly or indirectly related/ influenced by it.

Most of his writing occupied the discussions on caste. It is generally understood that Indo-Aryan society of ancient India was based upon varna system, where the society was divided into Brahmins, kshtriyas, vaishyas and sudras based on the principle of labour and heredity. Some of the scholars would like to argue that chaturvarna system based on economic theory of division of labour and that the varna system is scientific. In later days where the people deprived of this varna system contesting it is argued that the individuals are defined as their innate qualities (guna) but not by birth. However, Ambedkar refutes the chaturvarna system and argued that it is not only divided the society but also divided the labourers. Further, this chaturvarna is opposed to natural law and spirit of human development. Ambedkar argued that initially there were only three varnas in indo Aryan society. The shudras were not a separate varna but were part of kshatriya varna. There was a constant fued between sudra kings and Brahmins. Brahmins were insulted and tortured by these kshtriya kings. Ambedkar believes that Brahmins began to take revenge upon kshtriyas through 'divinity' and 'infinity' ideas which later on came to be attached to religious laws continued in course of time as sacred laws. Brahmins hatred towards sudras culminated into a situation where Brahmins refused to invest the sudras with sacred thread. The sacred thread in ancient India presupposed a higher social and economic status. Owing to the loss of sacred thread, the sudras were socially degraded and demoted to the rank of the fourth varna. Amedkar shows this point through the examples from Hindu mythology.

REINTERPRETATION OF MARXISM IN INDIAN CONTEXT

Ambedkar made an attempt to interpret Indian society by using Marxian methodology for his own convenience. Contrary to the opinion that ancient India doesn't have any history, Ambedkar tried to dig out its history with the help of Buddhist literature. The rise of Budhism considered by him as a revolutionary against Aryan Brahminism in the history of India. More than religious revolution, it is social and political. The Brahmins were the custodians of religion by monopolizing the priestly profession and guided the people in all its moral and spiritual matters. They set the standards to be followed by all others. The Aryan community at the time of Budha was steeped in the worst kind of debauchery: social, religious and spiritual. The Aryan religion never concerned itself with what is called a righteous life. In the Aryan society the shudra or low caste man could never become Brahmin. But Budha not only preached against caste but admitted them at the rank of bhikku.

The phenomena of the decline of Budhism, followed by the triumph of Brahminism - was considered by him as counter revolution and attempted to situate the sudras, women in relation to this counter revolution. In understanding this phenomenon, Ambedkar made an attempt to understand the Brahminic literature and mythology from historical point of view. He finds the riddles of Hinduism in its sacred literature. He questioned the very authority of Vedic literature and its privilege of apaurusheya. 'Present day hindus are probably the strongest opponents of Marxism. They are horrified at its doctrine of class- struggle. But they forget that India has been not merely the land of class struggle but she has been the land of class wars'.

The bitterest class war took place between Brahmins and kshatriyas. The classical literature of hindus abounds in reference to class wars between these two varnas. Conceptual structures will grow only when they are used in everyday life and in the context of thought and when contemporary thinkers in India begin to articulate their experiences about man, society, and polity in terms of classical thought, a new direction will be given to concepts. In a sense, Indian thinkers from the time of Ramamohan Roy have been trying to do this, but the focus has mostly been on matters primarily non intellectual and non conceptual in nature. Indian philosophy like Indian culture approached with either too much enthusiasm or total negation of it.

To assess Indian Polity properly, one has to keep aside both positive and negative emotions. There are certain myths about IP and claimed as facts. The claim of spirituality was never put to the test. In fact it seems so self evident as to require any argument or evidence on its behalf. No body feels it to question the worthiness of this claim. Amedkar's contributions are not only significant in writing Indian history but in evolving a method which is more relevant even for contemporary historians of different schools. On the one hand, he tried to prove that historian's social affiliation plays a role in interpreting the past. This he shows by citing the Brahminical scholarship. On the other, he argues for objectivity in case of non-brahminical scholars rather carried by the romanticism of non-brahmin struggles. He identifies the historical change with socio- economical, political and cultural struggles of the people. He observed that this historical phenomenon reflected as a whole in evolution of religion. He considers the religion on moral basis that stand for the reason. For Ambedkar, religion had become important category in constructing/interpreting Indian history.

Further he proceeds by understanding religion in historical dialectical way. He borrowed the tools of Marxism in understanding Indian history in this fashion. Buddhism had been considered as revolutionary strand against Brahminism and against the triumph of Brahminism. Moreover, he made a systematic attempt to bring in view the history of victims of Indian society, where one finds no trace of any historical evidence in official records or narratives of dominant Brahminical class.

DALIT HISTORIOGRAPHY

There is a significant scholarship coming up from Dalits in writing their own history. Their intervention is crucial in many ways. The history writing came along with the dalit struggles. In search of their identity, they dig the past in all possible ways. In writing of dalit history or interrogating dominant history from Dalit point of view, Dalit scholars/ activists/ writers may not be systematic, argumentative but are striking in their attack and provide an alternative forcefully. One may find many missing links in the construction of the dalit history or questioning the dominance from Dalit point of view.

They are in vernacular languages. These writings are often reproduction of oral narratives. Some of them are in the form of autobiographies. In this connection this document presents historical claims of dalits of Telugu society as a case study. The word 'Dalit' in telugu society become familiar with Dalit Mahasabha, which came into existence with Karamchedu massacre of 1985. Dalit movement had taken roots at popular level and oppressed Dalit masses started questioning the dominance and hegemony of the upper caste people. The newly emerged dalit middle class, however small, played a role in production of knowledge systems in the fields of literature, culture, politics, philosophy and history. Dalit movement provided the spectacle through which they could uphold the culture, history and politics of the lower caste. Dalit intelligentsia is making serious attempt to construct their cultured past and history as against the upper caste Brahminical hegemony. The literature coming in the name of Dalit, shattered the existing canons of Telugu society.

As a Telugu Dalit writer G. Kalyana Rao (2000) felt, 'We have to dig a lot and simultaneously bury a lot.' The Dalit intelligentsia is active in this mission to strengthen the on going Dalit struggles. Of course, within Dalit movement, there exists a variety of political positions. However, caste becomes a reference point in understanding history, philosophy, culture and politics, with active Dalit struggles. From the trained historians, though negligible, there exists significant number of historical writings. Kancha Ilaih's Why I'm Not a Hindu (Nenu Hindunetlaitha in telugu) is a prominent intervention from Dalit-Bahujan perspective against Brahmanism.

It is a critique on hindutva, culture, politics and economics from a sudra perspective. He reflected on these issues from his social experience. He argues that dalit-bahujans have different food habits, culture, customs, and religious practices, which are unique, democratic and different from brahminical Hinduism. Dalit bahujans culture emerged from their involvement in labour. They are productive classes and so their culture is real, natural and authentic. The Dalitbahujan Understanding of Telugu culturtal and Literary History, he argues that construction of history taking place from two opposite and conflicting views: the Brahminical and dalit bahujan. He questions us to whether the brahminical writings (based on Sanskrit language, Sanskrit texts, and Sanskrit lipi, etc.) should really be called history at all? 'For brahminical people, history is a march of god on earth; where as for dalit bahujans, history is the march of people (that is, the dalit bahujan majority) on the earth.' Further, the dalit bahujans history mostly lies in folklore/oral tradition. The language of this folklore is far richer, humanitarian and democratic-perhaps that is the reason why it has been relegated to the margins by the brahminical historians. On the other hand, productive castes had their own Telugu language, but it never figured in the brahminical writings. Though it is in autobiographical form, the arguments directly go against the dominant forms of knowledge systems. A. Sayanarayana, Professor in History made an attempt to write history from dalit bahujan perspective in his book Dalits and Upper Caste, Essays in Social History.

He tried to construct dalit history by using the alternative literary discourses of dalits which are marginalized in the mainstream literary discourses. Y. Chinna Rao's doctoral dissertation Dalit Movement in Andhra, 1900-1950 captures the dalit struggles of colonial times. This tried to establish that alternative struggles of dalits in colonial times rarely found mention in both colonialism and nationalism. To focus on the specific nature of resistance and struggles of dalits against the dominance, he uses the framework of James Scott's 'Weapons of the Weak.' The major argument is that contemporary dalit struggles are in continuation of these struggles. In other words, charging the mainstream historians for not documenting the dalit struggles.

'Dalit movements have not become a part of Indian historiography yet, even though their study is of immense importance in view of their inherent radical democratic identity and their interrelation with contemporary movements. The available studies on dalit movement in India suffer from lack of historical and written documentation, leaving scope for ambiguity.' Moreover, there are attempts from the conscious Dalit activists also. From late nineties, there are considerable numbers of books on history. Katti Padma Rao, Sanskrit teacher and activist in rationalist movement turned to a leader of Dalit Mahasabha. In the process of his active involvement in dalit struggles reflected on many issues in relation to the liberation of dalit community. His Dalitula Charitaconstructs the history of the dalits based on the sources of Sanskrit texts. His Caste and Alternative Culture makes an attempt to construct history and struggles of the untouchable and sudra castes against Aryan –Brahmin-Hindu culture. He explores this theme from ancient times to contemporary times. He is even critical of the communist movement of contemporary times led by the upper castes like Reddy and Kamma communities and their silence on the issue of annihilation of caste. He explains the philosophical background of dalit movement. The matriarchal culture, Carvakas materialism, Budhist sangha philosophy and humanism are the foundation of dalit movement. He argues that in the Indian sub- continent, the makers of history are the dalit people.

Ancient Indian culture was matriarchal in character, founded on the principle of equality. The Aryans after arriving in India established Hindu kingdom and tried the culture of the ancient indigenous Indians. They introduced casteism, patriarchal culture and politico-economic dictatorship. Suppressing all the indigenous castes, they propagated their own Hindu culture in Indian society, and forcefully implemented Hindu way of life. Dr. Vijaya Bharathicame out with three books on Puranalu-Kulavyavastha. She has critically evaluates the puranas and their role in protection of caste system.

Though the puranas are not considered as history, but are intend to cultivate ideal society to control the different social groups. On analysing the story of Satya Harischandra, though this story seems to uphold the truth, but its purpose is essentially to consolidate the varna system and controlling the women in the name of pativratyam. She made her analysis based on Markandeya puranam, skandha puranam and Harischandropakyanam. 'If we observe the stories and the constructed ideology around the avataramurthi's of different yugas, the whole effort is to implement and introduce the sanctions of the varna systems in the lives of ordinary people. Dharmasamsthapanam means varna dharma samsthapanam. The stories of the shatchakravarties (Pururudu, Purukutsudu, Harischandrudu, Sagarudu, Naludu, Karyaveeryarjunudu) are made popular because they stand as the symbols in protection of varnadharma. In a similar fashion the mythological god Rama represents the dominant brahminical system. Bonigala Rama Rao made an attempt to trace out history of untouchables. In his Antarani Jathula Charitra, he tried to establish that untouchable communities are not only the sons of the soil but also earlier ruling communities. Though weakened economically, they are protecting their culture and social ideology.

He proposes an arugument that the names of the untouchable communities are nothing but the relics of the vanished kingdoms. To construct the history of untouchable communities he relied mostly on historical texts, books of linguistics and inscription rather puranas and epics. He further wrote Mala Kannamaneedu and Adiguruvu Acharya Chandala. The writings of Kathi padma rao and Bonigala Ramarao have influenced the later writings on the history of dalits – this includes Dr. K. Lakshmi Narayana who tried to explore history of dalits in the Aadibharatteyula Charitra (from 2500 BC to 2500 AD) and Pilli Rambabu's Adi Baratheeyulu.

Apart from these, Dalit literature as a creative intervention of dalit intelligentsia played a significant role in constructing dalit history. The historical consciousness is very much internalized in the structure of their literary narratives. The importance of dalit writings lies in authentic representation of the community by questioning the existing brahminical and progressive writings. The protest against the caste and class dominance is central to the dalit writings. Mostly, Dalit literary writings are autobiographical reflections of the community.

Dalit writings are conscious effort of bridging the oral and written cultures. Dalit writings often invoke social memory as the source of their knowledge system. This also helps in maintaining the historical continuity. Dalit literature enriched with content and description of dalit struggles for human dignity. There has been constant effort from dalit writers in translating the condemned life styles and practices of marginalized people into symbols of protest and pride. In the process of writing their own history, they thoroughly interrogated the existing histories of dominant caste/class groups in their literary writings. As Dalit writer, Sivasagar marking the assertion of dalits in writing their own history against the brahminical history centred around advaita of Sankara. With a smile on his face/Shambhuka is slaying rama/ with his axe/Ekalavya is cutting drona's thumb away/with his small feet/ Bali is sending Vamana down to pathala/ With needles in his eyes/ and lead in is ears/Manu, having cut his tongue is seen rolling on the graveyard/standing on the merciless sword of time/and roaring with rage/The chandala is seen hissing four hounds on Sankaracharya/ Oh..!/ The history that is occurring today/Is the most Chandala history

CONCLUSION

The historical writings and method employed by Ambedkar had serious implication for writings of colonial, nationalist, Marxist and even subaltern historiographies on Indian history. As against the colonial writings, he showed that Indians had a tradition of rich democratic struggles throughout its history and overcomes the dichotomy of tradition and modernity created by the colonial scholarship. He countered the nationalist historiographies. In order to counter colonial rule, the nationalist projects Indian spiritual tradition of their glorious past.

Ultimately, the elite Brahminical ideology valorized through the writings of nationalists in the name of nation. Ambedkar was critical against this kind of brahminical scholarship by showing the other worldview of oppressed groups. He totally dismisses the glorious past of vedic and upanishadic times. He is critical about the brahminical past and at the same time he valorizes the democratic past of the oppressed parts of India. Altogether he gave different meaning for nationalism of oppressed. Although Ambedkar was lenient towards Marxism, he is against mere economic reductionistic approach of it. He forcefully argues that other factors like culture and religion too influencing the world view of people.

This may come as a parallel to Frankfort school of late sixties and cultural studies of contemporary times. He argues Marxism had to creatively interpret by considering specificity of Indian context rather than mechanically interpreting it. He throws a challenge to Marxists on understanding the issue of caste. The subaltern studies are much concentrated on modern Indian history. It masks the socio-economic realities in the name of consciousness.

In the context of communalization of history with the rise of hindutva forces, theoretically it does not have strength to counter it. As subaltern studies argue in favour of indigenous culture, this may be appropriated by right wing politics. But Ambedkar's method had potential to counter religious nationalism of hindutva kind and in place of it proposes democratic nationalism of the oppressed. Ambedkar's idea of history came out of the struggles of the oppressed communities and had the imagination of better future by owning the reasoned/democratic past.

4

Transnational Advocacy and the Dalit Rights Movements

INTRODUCTION

October 2, 2006: The tension and excitement were palpable. Thousands of blue bandana-wearing youth shouted and waved their fists towards the sky from atop buses, rooftops, and the numerous teetering light-posts that dotted the divided thoroughfare. Crowds of revelers lined the street leading to the main entrance of the giant stupa -like structure that marked the spot in Nagpur City where in October of 1956 Dr. B.R. Ambedkar led one of human history's largest mass religious conversion ceremonies. Like much in India, this celebratory atmosphere, in which people seemed to fill every crevice of available space, attacked all the senses.

It was clear that many of the revelers were happy to be there—not simply to revere Ambedkar or his embrace of Buddhism, but to show that they existed; that they had a distinctly new identity; and that they could not be simply disregarded and de-legitimized. Yet, it was also clear that this was a religious pilgrimage for many—a show of support for the deified bodhisattva Ambedkar and his important embrace of a socially engaged Buddhism aimed at the betterment of Dalits. From an outsider's perspective the excitement and revelry of the crowd was only eclipsed by a veneer of social conflict. Across from the Dikshabhumi was a different kind of reveler, because October 2, 2006 was also the confluence of the start of a major Hindu festival, Divali and a national holiday, Gandhi Jayanti. While the tension between Ambedkar supporters and either those celebrating the beginning of Divali, or those celebrating the birth anniversary of M.K. Gandhi, could have easily risen to a level of violence, it did not on this auspicious day in Nagpur.

The sacredness of the religious experience of a pilgrimage to Dikshabhumi seemed to trump secular disagreements that Ambedkar Dalits in the crowd would surely share with their Hindu counterparts and/or supporters of Gandhi. This distinctly religious framing of an Ambedkar Buddhist identity, and interconnection of it with the social problematic of the caste system fits the Indian socio-political context well – a context where such distinctions are rarely made. But the absence of secular political voices in this crowd was stark, with religion holding all answers. Even to those shouting, blue bandana-wearing, youth, Buddhist flags and religious ritual seemed to hold sway over secular speeches or public signs of Dalit organization and mobilization.

June 7, 2007: Cut to a hotel room in Sterling, Virginia, not far from Dulles International Airport. Seven Dalit professionals conduct a meeting of a newly formed organization called DANRIA, converting a vacant fifth-floor hotel suite into a makeshift meeting space. DANRIA, The Dr. Ambedkar Non-Resident Indian Association, is a confederation of Dalit Diaspora professionals that has just recently registered as a local NGO in Maryland.

They are seeking to collaborate with others to bring development to Dalit communities in India. On this day they are meeting with a representative of the International Association for the Advancement of Dalits to plan for a proposed upcoming symposium on Dalits to be held in Washington, D.C.

This organization of Diaspora Dalits is comprised of a neurosurgeon, a NASA scientist, The CEO and Founder of a Chain of Car Repair shops, an IT professional, and a number of academics from various theoretical disciplines. These are first-generation Indian Americans from all over India, yet they share the common identity as Dalit. Such an identity shares similar narratives of caste discrimination, but not necessarily similar religious foundations or ideologies, which gives the group its fiercely secular character. While the idea of the "promotion of shared values" does come up during the meeting, these shared values are framed as strictly secular, underlining simply that each human has rights to pursue, whether vaguely articulated or not, a shared sense values.

One member even takes the opportunity to remind the inter-religious membership that DANRIA is a "strictly secular" organization and that he will leave if this reality changes. While there is an implicit knowledge of the Dalit Sikh, Muslim, Buddhist, and Christian conversion movements in modern India among these DANRIA members, each of these movements' sacred import is clearly perceived as a secondary to the goal of Dalit liberation or Dalit human rights, which is broadly defined and seen as at hand. In other words, the need for a secular frame of human rights takes precedence, and provides a perceived legitimacy to these professionals' framing of Dalit oppression. This strictly secular identity is seen as evolved from communal-based religious ideologies and, in turn, as a more effective vehicle for social change.

They represent the tendency among Ambedkar followers to make prescient either a religious or a secular narrative structure for achieving social justice, and then to highlight those aspects of Ambedkar's career and thinking which support this narrative structure. Neither is less legitimate than the other, but both problematize social justice in different ways, and thus articulate its desired advent differently. The religious narrative structure stresses the pious individual as a model for building a new community, while the secular emphasizes the individual's rights as the basis for modernizing Dalit community. These different narrative structures can be seen best in the distinction between two meaningful words that have gained widespread usage among former 'untouchables' – 'Dalit' versus 'bahujan'. While divergent narrative structures—which tend towards either more religious or more secular expressions—lead to different ideal conceptions of the socially just society, they also complicate movements' attempts to mobilize for activism. Scholars have been inattentive to these varying conceptions of social justice because frequently a community of speakers does not have a clearly-defined notion, and/or lacks the consensus or ability to express their projective vision of such an ideal concept as justice.

However, what is most startling is that social actors are disempowered by such narrative confusion or hesitancy, not that they simply cannot articulate their confusion. Social mobilization scholars often ignore the importance between either secular or religious narrative frames. To see justice from a multifaceted perspective— both one based on ensuring the realization of equity or balance and the other based on the creative possibilities which underpin any state of justice— requires a broad projective outlook.

While many social movement theorists argue this difference focuses on movement's ideals and not what is 'real' or seen to be objectively understandable, the fact is to some social movements, such as those created by Ambedkar Buddhists, the religious narrative is all that they see as really real. Of course, in the practice of movement dynamics, like other social science phenomenon, the real and the ideal often become blurred. The result is that Ambedkar's followers proceed unawares of the fine implications of the divergent narrative structures they deploy. Another important scholarly critique of such a secular-religious distinction comes from post-colonial theorists.

Despite the fact that "the ultimate aim of postcolonial theories is to feed into some form of social activism for a more egalitarian society," such theories tend to deconstruct case study and theory-building about post-colonial social movements as 'always-already' lodged in Western hegemonic leaning and constructs. Thus, the post-colonial critique of drawing conclusions based on the pictures argues that such dialectic constructs as secular and religious are Western and therefore value-laden with imperialist and/or individualistic homogenization of experience. Though such critique is valuable in questioning bias and presumptions, from a pragmatic perspective it hinders a movement's self-reflective and emancipatory potential. Ambedkarite social justice movements for the eradication of caste discrimination must overcome this post-colonial tendency in order to develop a pragmatic conception of social justice.

Despite a few attempts to point out the lack of a clearly defined notion of justice in social movements, few scholars have chosen to address the sticky business of understanding movements' efforts at conceptualizing social justice, or more broadly their own conceptions in relation to human rights. The scholarly dearth of research into social movements' social justice conceptions underscores both the complexity of defining justice, and, until recently, a sense that global interrelations were unimportant or unquantifiable.

In the case of Dalit rights, as activists have attempted to actualize their social justice conceptions which were previously blocked by their government, what Keck and Sikkink call a "boomerang pattern" gets created in which activists attempt to circumvent traditional channels by developing transnational ties and strategies. The global resources afforded by modernity have allowed new means to achieve social justice. But, do these new means portend new ends? My own study of Ambedkar Buddhists has shown that religiously-based social actors have been slow to realise these new ends Rinker.

As Ganguly has argued, what is needed to understand the caste system's encounter with modernity is an ability to "scrutinize hegemonic knowledge formations that frame our outlook on the world and tell most of us in South Asia that the caste system smacks of times past and is ingloriously retrogressive." To understand the recent proliferation of transnational Dalit rights discourse, understanding movement narrative structures is a mandatory precursor.

While religious-based movements for Dalit rights, like their secular big brother before them, have begun to develop transnational linkages in recent years, social actors projecting religious-based narrative structures have had to work harder than their secular counterparts to tailor frame their message for specific audiences and supporters, both secular and religious. This becomes especially evident within an increasingly global environment in which justice concerns are no longer local. The modernist disdain for religion that is seen as traditionalist and identity-forming continues to be challenged in the marketplace of ideas, and in a spiritually inclined society, like India, the modernist thinking is loosing. In such context, religion is understood for its instrumental and communal nature, which makes an outwardly religious narrative of individual attainment helpful in forging local community, but also makes it more difficult to the success of a national or international movement.

In India, the challenge to modernist ideas has been both successful and unwieldy—witness respectively the rise of the Hindutva politics of the 1990s; and the point counterpoint and social contention over various anti-conversion laws. In the U.S. and the West, however, this challenge to modernism receives less traction, as for rational individualist Westerners, religious frames of social justice seem more problematic. Such secular-religious dialectic cries for further analysis as global attempts to empower the voiceless gain strength and inclusive versus exclusive narratives of justice compete for both consumers and beneficiaries. Despite the confusion it is apparent that both religious-based and strictly secular movements have something to learn from each other and the narratives they deploy.

Using narrative analysis methods to analyse the secular and religious narrative structures that Dalit leaders employ, this research draws out the implications of the worldview frames of Dalit activists from a multi-disciplinary conflict theory perspective. While this document extrapolates a narrative theory from exemplary cases of only three social movements narratives it does point to the centrality of narrative structures to social justice conceptions and foregrounds possible strategies and tactics of contention. The prevalent narrative apparent in the narrative structure of religiously-based movements focuses on overcoming victimization through the reclamation of one's identity upon conversion. This assumes a responsibility for action, which resides intrinsically within each individual. The opposite and secular narrative, by focusing on the re-humanization of past victims, assumes there is a need to push the collective mentality to a tipping-point in which a rights regime can be adequately enforced. Highlighting the lack of analysis of this dialectic between religious and secular narratives of social justice within the Ambedkar movement, this research aims to develop a sense of shared values between those inclined towards particularly strict versions of these two opposing worldviews.

Based on preliminary fieldwork such shared values do not yet exists, or at best only exist in small pockets of Dalit activism and coordination. By privileging such shared values both a better understanding of Dalit contention and a fulfillment of Dalit rights movements' potential with best be achieved.

HISTORY OF DALIT ACTIVISM IN INDIA

The word Dalit means broken or downtrodden in Sanskrit and was "used as far back as 1931 in journalistic writing". Popularized by Dr. B.R. Ambedkar in the 1920s and 30s, and later by the Dalit Panthers movement in the 1970s, the term became a new secular identity for millions of those formerly known as 'untouchables' in India. Today, modern Dalit identity is in a discursive competition with various religious identities for control of between one-fourth and one-fifth of India's billion-person population, which is classified as scheduled caste.

The life and thought of Dr. B.R. Ambedkar, the father of Dalit rights and assertion, as well as the modern Indian constitution, was foundational to this discursive competition, which can be clearly seen in the following quote from Gangadar Pantawane, the founding editor of Asmitadarsh, a journal devoted to Dalit literature:

- To me Dalit is not a caste. He is a man exploited by the social and economic traditions of this country. He does not believe in God, Rebirth, Soul, Holy Books teaching separatism, Fate and Heaven because

> they have made him a slave. He does believe in humanism. Dalit is a symbol of change and revolution.

Compared to the rhetorical calls by Trailokya Bauddha Mahasangha, Sahayak Gana activists to work towards a time when "all India will be Buddhist," the quote provides a stark secular-focused contrast to Indian social activists' penchant for citing religious ideals in order to galvanize the identity of followers. Pantawane's conception privileges Dalit as symbolic of a post-modern identity in which caste distinctions have become irrelevant. Yet, it was the life and legacy of Dr. B.R. Ambedkar that laid the foundation for this competition to win the hearts and minds of Dalits.

As both a social reformer from within the government, and then later a cultural reformer from the outside, Dr. Ambedkar's life itself represented a balancing between these two, not incompatible, identities. While many people outside the Indian sub-continent are familiar with Mahatma Gandhi, few who live outside of India know much about Dr. Ambedkar, or about the movement he helped spawn.

Both his political significance as the foremost representative of the Mahar 'untouchable' community in Maharashtra, and the religious importance he played in changing the social identity and spiritual commitments of that particular community of Dalits through a revival of Buddhism, are unrivaled throughout India's long historical development. Ambedkar's prolific legacy culminating in his chairmanship of the drafting of the Indian constitution, as well as his call to all former 'untouchables' to convert to Buddhism has made his continued influence among scheduled castes unrivaled.

Though his life narrative is so compelling that Indians of all persuasions have appropriated his image, like other low-caste social reformers, both before and after him, Dr. Ambedkar struggled to create intra-caste bonds; bonds that were lacking even among the lowest of caste groupings who were divided and aggrieved. Dr. Bhimrao Ramji Ambedkar, affectionately known by his followers as Babasaheb, overcame the cultural and economic impasses of being born an 'untouchable' Mahar, one of three lowest-caste segments of Maharashtra society, in late 19th Century Hindu-dominated India. Breaking through countless stereotypes, Ambedkar was taught early of the importance of education, and he used the social cleavages that the British administrative policy provided to transcend his socially prescribed role. Rising to the post of Law Minister in Nehru's first independent Indian cabinet, he was appointed chairman of the drafting committee for the new constitution.

From this vantage point, Ambedkar was well-placed to destroy the legal foundations of the caste system, and in 1948 Ambedkar presented his draft of the Indian constitution, which was accepted a year later. In it can be seen Ambedkar's push to get social change codified legalistically. This part of Ambedkar's legacy culminates in Article 17 of the Indian Constitution, which states:

- 'Untouchability' is abolished and its practice in any form is forbidden. The enforcement of any disability arising out of 'untouchability' shall be an offense punishable in accordance with the law.

But despite this important legal success, Dr. Ambedkar slowly began to realise that structural reform was only one means to his larger goal of social change in India. Increasingly frustrated that change was not coming to his people fast enough, he began to believe that social revolution was necessary, which could come only from actively critiquing the cultural structure of Hinduism, as opposed to attempting to change it from within. Similar to later conflict resolution scholars, the trailblazing Ambedkar seemed to ask: "Will we contribute to harmony through conflict resolution, but do so at the cost of accepting the continuation of some injustice? Or should we pursue justice for a particular group, knowing that this pursuit may increase conflict rather than resolve it?".

Gradually coming to believe the answer to these questions was a resounding commitment to pursue justice, Dr. Ambedkar began to focus more on societal rather than structural change. By organizing political parties, educating low-caste people, and agitating for change, Dr. Ambedkar pursued broad based change by re-conceiving the meaning of justice in society, not only its structures, but also its social realities. Ambedkar's identity evolved throughout his life to one of social activist, and the evolution of his growth and thought can be seen clearly in his prolific writings. During the latter part of his career, Ambedkar increasingly began to see religion as a valuable means to realise change through socio-cultural critique.

As an answer to his discontent with the structural violence imposed by the caste system, religion provided a vehicle to restructure social discourse and remake the foundational values of the social system— two important aims of legions of young Dalit activists. It was also with a life-long desire to understand religion that Ambedkar conditioned his analysis of caste. Thus, by 1935, Ambedkar had decided that Hinduism was the root cause of the 'untouchable' problem and had resolved to change his religion as a result. This, he believed, was the best solution for the Mahar 'untouchables' that he now led. Encouraging other 'untouchables' to join this cause,

- If you want to gain self-respect, change your religion.
- If you want to create a cooperative society, change your religion.
- If you want power, change your religion.
- If you want equality, change your religion.
- If you want independence, change your religion.
- If you want to make the world in which you live happy, change your religion.

But Ambedkar saw religion as a social vehicle as much as others saw it for its soteriological commitments to explain life. For Ambedkar choice of religions was a means to social change in the present. By changing religious traditions he, as well as each individual, could change society. Thus, he waged a polemical and rhetorical war against Hinduism.

Declaring Hinduism the root cause of Dalit suffering Ambedkar challenged the orthodox beliefs of Indian culture head on, and was either reviled or loved for this audacity. These acts created support, criticism and fierce debate. Gandhi, upon hearing Ambedkar speak, was once said to have remarked, "religion is not like a horse or a cloak, which can be changed at will. It is a more integral part of one's self than one's own body". Yet, while Gandhi criticized the idea of a choice in religion, Ambedkar studied all the world's faiths in order to find the one, which would best fit his 'untouchable' communities' needs.

The act of choosing his religion was, for Ambedkar, the cement of a repositioned identity which was both personal and collective. As the answer to many of the needs of his 'untouchable' community, it was an act of social protest and self-help rolled into one. If his more outwardly social protests brought spite from Brahmins, his repositioned identity as a Buddhist would bring him deification among his own 'untouchable' community—something he himself was said to be uncomfortable with. On October 14th, 1956, on the 2500th anniversary of the Buddha's Nirvana, Ambedkar led a mass conversion of 'untouchable' Hindus to Buddhism.

This was the culminating act of his now repositioned identity and in writing his own vows upon taking refuge Ambedkar ensured that he had created what some religious scholars have since called "neo-Buddhism". Through this repositioned identity he legitimated a new social perspective and Buddhism happened to be a means to the end of creating a new worldview and social discourse. As the ultimate upaya, Buddhism itself was to give new hope and confidence to thousands of Dalits. However, as Ambedkar died only six months after his controversial conversion, it is not completely clear what form of institutionalization his Buddhism would have taken.

He nonetheless ignited a revitalization of Buddhism on the Indian sub-continent, inspiring many a social activist, and living up to his promise to not die a Hindu. The leadership narrative provides a common grounding for both secular and religiously inclined Dalit rights activists. Yet, depending on the specifics of the story that is emphasized, one can see divergences in social movement organization. Two thousand plus years of caste discrimination has left a void in Dalits' collective cultural identity, which Ambedkar attempted to fill. At the same time, future activists will continue to argue as to which void Ambedkar's narrative fills—a clarion call for secular rights or a human need for ultimate meaning? As Taylor, Bougie, and Caouette have argued, lack of a collective cultural identity is the most socially damaging and difficult to overcome aspect of a group's identity.

It seems that Ambedkar's emphasis on the role of religion in society is an implicit acknowledgment of this argument and an attempt to reconstruct a new version of this collective cultural identity. The role of cultural collective identity is not merely for group members to have a shared cultural history. As we have argued, it is a stable reference group against which the individual engages positioning processes on an ongoing basis in order to develop a healthy personal identity. Ambedkar was a pragmatist, studying under John Dewey at Columbia University, eager to develop a healthy collective cultural identity for those he considered his people—the downtrodden of society.

Religious narrative structures were used as a vehicle to attempt to redeploy a self-aware collective cultural identity. But his use of both secular and religious narrative structure as a means is telling. Ambedkar had a modern understanding of religion, which emphasized that belief was not only about ends, but also a means of social interpretation. He saw the wisdom of approaching social conflict from a position, which privileges neither simply religious nor secular explanations. Unfortunately, Ambedkar's Buddhist followers have failed to openly and fully explore the social and political resources of both the secular and religious narratives they have at their disposal.

Despite the fact that Ambedkar Dalit activists' discourse seems to strategically use one or the other these narrative structure—religious or secular—to support their cause and build support, an analysis of the social positions that each creates has been lacking. Secular attempts to focus on Ambedkar's injunction to "educate, organize, agitate" have failed to see the added value that creating a new religious identity can bring to oppressed groups' aspirations, not to mention the added value religious institutions bring to attempts at mass mobilization. Similarly, religiously inclined converts to Buddhism have failed to realise that their religious rhetoric can be exclusionary. Though preaching an inclusive and voluntary belief system, converted Dalits often fail to realise their emphasis on religious-based explanation sidelines broad based rights-based opportunities for mobilization.

Further, each side of this spectrum of activism has seen the other side as problematic for maintaining their own base of support within the Dalit community. In other words, followers of Ambedkar's religious narrative see secular rights talk as problematic since it relies too much on outside notions of liberty, democracy, fraternity, and agency while followers of Ambedkar's secular narrative see religious rhetoric as backward and pre-modern.

In order to bridge these two narratives within the Dalit rights movement their foundation, structures, and expressions have to be further explored and dissected, as both narratives provide important resources, which have the reach and impact all Dalit activists desire.

SECULAR VERSUS RELIGIOUS ACTIVIST NARRATIVES

The religious narratives of Dalit assertion focus on leaving the Hindu-fold, which is seen as the root cause of the Dalit social condition. In doing so, the individual reasserts him/her self and repositions their identity as coming from a religiously converted worldview, as opposed to coming from a certain caste which is seen as a partitioning of society that has been too long sanctified by the hierarchical system now called Hinduism.

As such, the religious framework of conversion as a means to social justice fosters a sort of dualistic identity among Dalits by empowering Dalits not only as newly self-reliant through the experience of conversion, but also as one that has been victimized in an all too recent past. As Sen reminds us "the adversity of exclusion can be made to go hand in hand with the gifts of inclusion", but this fact should not deter us from seeing that the complexity of identity highlights the difficulty inherent in mobilizing people around "identity justice". In particular, the combination of liberation and victimization is problematic for mobilizing widespread international support. Conversion as the living out of theology's connection to praxis does not have the same universal appeal as a narrative structure which equates Dalit rights with human rights. Despite a new identity as Buddhist—or Sikh or Christian—the converted Dalit cannot completely divorce him/her self from the psychological legacy and mobilizing power of past experiences of injustice.

This dual identity has both advantages and disadvantages for newly converted Dalits as they attempt to achieve social justice. Ever cognizant of which identity to engage when, Dalit Buddhist followers of Dr. Ambedkar must navigate an array of Dalit aspirations by balancing secular pragmatism with the desire to create a religious community based on Buddhist values. The secular frame of social justice, by comparison, presents a more unified conception of Dalit identity as first and foremost human. While this more materialist perspective on social justice places Dr. B.R. Ambedkar near the end of a long line of important low-caste social thinkers, it also downplays any religious proclivities as subordinate to secular humanism.

Simultaneously, this secular frame presents a belief that the problems of Dalits can only be cured with the help of the unified action of outside intervention, advocacy, and political agitation, taking the onus for change off the individual and placing it on the collective. From this view, the root causes of a lack of social justice, as contextual and unchangeable by any one individual, are confused by any attempt to focus attention on any sacred ultimate. It is as if religious commitments appear as anathema to those strict adherents of the secular rights frame.

It is therefore, assumed from this secular perspective that the root causes of a lack of social justice must be approached from a religiously neutral position of secular re-humanization of the oppressed. As a consequence the concepts of reconciliation and healing are often overlooked by these secular humanists in a rush to realise the equitable society. In addition, the secular activists adherents' post-enlightenment aversion to religious discourse seems to run counter to the local cultural norms and history. Religion as a constituent part of the South Asian historical and cultural milieu is de-emphasized in favour of a perspective of global interdependence.

SECULAR NARRATIVE OF DALIT ACTIVISM: THE CREATION OF A TRANSNATIONAL VOICE

The secular narrative and social position of Dalits as oppressed victim predominates among Dalit social actors partly because of the slow, but steady, success of this narrative structure's ability to build transnational support and advocacy networks. Bob argues convincingly that "organizing" and "rhetorical" changes among Dalit activists led to increased success of a Dalit rights as human rights frame of contention in the late 1990s.

But what has this increased reliance on a narrative structure of victimization cost the Dalit rights cause? As Polletta explicitly argues: while "personal stories chip away at the public indifference" and "elicit sympathy on the part of the powerful," it is also evident that "narrative comes with risks as well as benefits".

While the secular narrative structure has allowed activists to conflict Dalit rights with human rights, it has also disempowered many religiously inclined Dalits through its aversion to religious language and frames. Further, since transnational advocacy often does not respond effectively to local needs, many disenfranchised Dalits are turned off by a secular approach to organizing that sees personal belief systems as irrelevant to mobilization success.

In short, there is a cultural divide between Western post-enlightenment rights thinking and traditional thoughts rooted in local contexts that value ritualistic and institutional expressions of culture. This is not to say that the dialectic between secular versus religious narratives can be explained simply by arguing that a post-colonial clash of civilizations or cultures is either the genesis of the divergence, or the solution to unifying these different worldviews. Rather, noticing this cultural divide does signal the risky footing one stands on if advocating either a strongly secular narrative structure to combat caste or a strongly religious one. As Ganguly concisely puts it: "The modernizing desire to first reify caste as a relic of times past, and then to annihilate it, is truly alive and well".

This secular bias away from the traditional is neither the best nor most effective way to create social change. Instead, it often leads to sensational excitement outside of India, while faltering in the local context. The bias among secular Dalit rights organizations, which disregard the conversion perspective so prevalent among Indian Ambedkarite Buddhists, serves as a case in point.

During the recent, and first ever in the Unites States, Dalit Studies conference, an academic panel on the "Paradox of Religion" failed to raise this issue of religion's relation to traditional manners of thought, much less address the Dalit rights movement from a perspective that privileges religious conversion as a crucial factor in the identity of low-caste groups. Beyond the academic community, however, a secular rights-based focus also creates a number of limitations and paradoxes for activists.

DANRIA, the organization portrayed in the second short vignette that began this piece provides a prime example of the dialectical problems that secular activists face in approaching their religiously-grounded counterparts. The DANRIA leaders desire to engage Ambedkar Buddhists, but within a frame of the strictly secular.

At a DANRIA planning meeting in May 2007 Ambedkar Buddhist representatives from the TBMSG attempted to develop linkages with the work and resources of DANRIA members, and DANRIA members continually made it clear that their work was to support secular Dalit education and empowerment. Partly due to how religion is understood in a postreformation West, such interactions revolve around a judgment that equates support for religious-based organizations as support for the propagation of that religion. It is the old stigma of religious proselytization; no matter what good work an organization may be doing it must always be scrutinized upon the backdrop of its religious commitments and the assumed privileged priority of those commitments. In this dance of assumptions and commitments, Ambedkar Buddhists try to re-frame their contention to fit the desires of secular activists, while secular activists assume religious organizations' exclusive goals and underestimate their ability and opportunities to mobilize. Secular narrative structures of Dalit contention present benefits to go along with the limitations, which they pose.

They bring pragmatism to an often-disorganized array of activist decisions and goals. Through an unequivocal support for humanity and secular humanism these narrative structures provide grounding for international mobilization which bridges religious and cultural difference. The International Commission for Dalit Rights' mission statement demonstrates this tendency to both symbolically and pragmatically bridge these aspects of difference within the Dalit movement: "Eliminating rights-based human need and fulfilling freedom and democracy is necessary to achieve effective national and global development policies and programmes, and to alleviate discrimination and extreme poverty."

Sufficiently secular such a statement allows for the possibility of religious responses to lack of freedom, discrimination and poverty. In place of a strong religious commitment, the secular narratives that such organizations profess, are often founded on an enduring faith in ideology. In interviewing Chadra Bhan Prasad, the only Dalit writer for a major Indian weekly and a Dalit rights activist who tends towards the secular end of the Dalit movement's narrative structure, it was immediately evident that he was not even familiar with TBMSG, one of the major purveyors of the religious narrative of Ambedkar and Dalit rights in

Maharashtra. Though at first surprising, this observation seems more understandable given that Prasad, a native of Uttar Pradesh who is based in Delhi, is a strictly secular Ambedkarite who sees Ambedkar upon the backdrop of a Marxist analytical ideology of change.

Now arguing that capitalism is the only thing that will save the Dalit, Prasad draws an interesting comparison to the Ambedkar Buddhist activists of the TBMSG who see the solution for Dalits as coming through the dharma. This secular narrative structure implies that religious commitment can be sidelined in favour of an underlying, and more basic, commitment to humanism—an assumption, which runs deep in the Dalit rights movement.

One ICRD Dalit activist even stated: "Despite the fact that many different Dalit groups employ different strategies, our goal is the same." The idea that Dalit activists' deploy diverging strategies despite common goals posits not only that Dalit activists have one collective identity, but also that this collective's social justice concerns are all the same. Such broad assumptions, however, limit the effectiveness of Dalit organizations by disempowering the potential to reflect on real difference.

RELIGIOUS NARRATIVES AND DALIT ACTIVISM

- The religious-based narrative and social position of Dalits as actualized adepts and citizens has limited religious-based ability to build transnational support and advocacy networks. The following narrative transcript from a Dalit Buddhist activist leader of the TBMSG is telling of the frame acrobat. He was opposed to any ideal system which was based on any scripture.
- So he said that democracy has to be based on the individuals
- That there should be equal respect in the society for all beings.
- And he gave a formula sort of thing

- He said that 'One man, one value' is the most important.
- Instead of we have a system where we have one man one vote, but more than that what is important is one man one value.
- And he promoted that form of system, from early on.
- And he had to fight very hard with the established elite Indians.
- For example Gandhi who was adopted in the form of governance based on the Hindu scripture, kind of a very utopian and ideal form of society, which was based on the Hindu scriptures... like Rama Raja, the kingdom of Rama and that frightened the minorities in India, for example the Muslims.
- And... ahh... like in that... ahh... particular concept of an ideal society there was a kind of... ahh... strong support for the caste system... and another thing he noted is that there has to be a system, that there has to be a kind of... ahh...ahh... a method to secularize the society, because the religious concept when they dominate the human mind they do not let to the... like many a times
- Like what that happens in India is that people will have a deep belief system which they will not be ready to test in the light of the scientific methods...
- So for example if there is... ahh... say for example a Test Tube Baby some innovation happening in the Western world
- Hindu maximalists, the Fundamentalist tradition, they will try to say that particular innovation or discovery was already there you know with us... but if you poke further and ask for the method they will not have any...
- So it is like trying to take the scientific language in order to prove what is not there.
- So this kind of superstitious ideas like at one point of time some Hindu Fundamentalists they will

claim that the caste system is the best form of organizing the society it is the best form some people has to be lower, some people has to be... and they will then try to support this system in terms of the food chain the big fish ate the small fish kind of a very crude form of social Darwinism...

- A very crude form of social Darwinism.
- So we try to challenge those ideas, the 'so-called' religious ideas which like kind of fit into the system and try to enslave the human mind.
- And Dr. Ambedkar was very keen on promoting the scientific culture in India like what's the intellectual side of that like how we can challenge the concepts that are detrimental to the growth of the human personality. ...which are detrimental to growth of human society.
- That is one of his strategies and he started a political party in order to really... ahh... ensure the similar political rights for the people who were classed as the 'untouchables.'

Mangesh's sincerity and commitment to social justice through building a peaceful community in which everyone has the ability to reach their potential, is not simply lipservice to a vague altruism—it is lived.

His Buddhism is more humanistic than sectarian or scriptural; more philosophical than overtly spiritual. Yet, the inclusiveness of the TBMSG family of organizations is not simply an expression of pragmatism.

The members who carry the mantel of the TBMSG movement are, first and foremost, believers in dharmadatu and this belief provides philosophical grounding for an egalitarian social prescription aimed at redefining karma in the Indian society as scientific and not supernatural. As an Indian, but humanist above all else, Mangesh is representative of a young generation of modern Indians who are both newly curious about the world outside of India and armed with the means to explore it.

Eager to integrate Western political ideals, such as rights discourse, with Eastern conceptions of the examined life, these modern Ambedkar Buddhist activists see themselves as "the fruit of the movement." In other words, the beneficiaries of their parents' conversion and insistence on following both, their father and mother's example as well as Ambedkar's call to education. Mangesh believes full-heartedly that focusing on inner change is a priori to attempt at social justice and peace-building. Therefore, teachings of the practice of Buddhism are crucial to the community that he aims to assist. This is a rational, not spiritual belief and the Buddha—from the Ambedkar Buddhist perspective—provided guiding principles to achieve inner change.

Yet, this insistence on rationalism and pragmatism is where a certain bias threatens to stunt the full potential of the TBMSG movement. The symbolic use by movement members of ritual and stories can, and does, get lost when a rational problem-solving approach to the world is privileged. This is not to say that Mangesh's commitment to social change is weak or even unjustified by experience, but rather that a combination of both inner and outer change can be problematic.

Exclusively focusing on rational approaches to problems solving can limit TBMSG's ability to affect lasting change of the local level; while a focus on inner-change marginalizes strong believers in other religious and normative systems and simultaneously decelerates the pragmatic realization of TBMSG's wider social justice ideal. That sustainable social change can only come with inner-change may be a truism, but it also places limits on TBMSG appeal and deftness to claim secular support or argue for symbolic senses of meaning. This poses a number of pragmatic problems for the movement. For one the narrative represents a normative assumption that rationality always explains moral justifications. Mangesh's positioning of Ambedkar Buddhists as consistent believers in scientific processes—while exposing the rational assumptions involved in narrating justice—also acts as an attempt to justify a moral stance via delegitimizing the other.

MacIntyre would label such a process as falling within "the When men and women identify what are in fact their partial and particular causes too easily and too completely with the cause of some universal principle, they usually behave worse than they would otherwise do. In reference to this particular narrative, it is not presumed here that it engenders bad behaviour among movement members, but rather that it misses an important realization of the potential for destructive behaviour created by the identity it enforces. Positioning Ambedkar Buddhists as rational humanists and all Hindus as superstitious anti-rationalists only concerned with pleasing the gods, Mangesh is unconcerned with his own moral denigration of the other and the processes of positioning this type of delegitimization models to others.

Mangesh's ascription of unscientific characteristics to others that are associated with under-education, or lack of intelligence, positions Ambedkar Buddhists as freed from the fear of superstition through education and Buddhist practice. This freedom is seen as liberating not only in the sense of being based on methodological reliability, but also in a sense creating an epistemological freedom. Furthermore, Mangesh's own relived experiences of this anti-rationalist thinking provide an emotional energy which legitimizes Mangesh's speech.

Paying attention to the uses and processes of social positioning within Mangesh's attack on fundamentalist Hindus as superstitious provides a means to understand the TBMSG social justice narrative upon a spectrum of interconnected meanings. Coming in the context of Mangesh's description of Ambedkar's sociological analysis of the caste system, this narrative transcription exhibits an opposition between rational and ideal conceptions which is immediately apparent in line one.

Positioning Ambedkar as opposed to any ideal system based on scripture, Mangesh develops the image of Ambedkar as an egalitarian freedom fighter. The ideological other becomes the antithesis to actualizing liberty, fraternity, and equality. More than simply pejoratively categorizing mythical or idealistic social constructions, privileging the rational as normatively more valuable and as implicitly congruent with equality has the effect of positioning the superstitious as irrelevant and undemocratic. Anti-rationalists are thereby equated with anti-democracy's proponents, while simple minded ideologues are de-legitimized.

Invoking Gandhi in line 9, Mangesh is drawing attention to the unacknowle-dged role of Ambedkar in the independence movement; yet at the same time branding Gandhi as advocates of future aspirations ungrounded in reality. Such utterance implies that if these future aspirations are ungrounded in reality, then they are bound to produce unjust social relations and structures. By contrast, the TBMSG ideal is grounded in a scientific methodology, which is attainable from a pragmatic view.

Unaware of the full spectrum of needs in society these Gandhians are utopian thinkers with little by way of concrete analysis and/or proscription for creating their utopia. In citing examples like Rama Raj and test-tube babies Mangesh is essentializing all Hindus as superstitious—equating Gandhi followers with Hindutva nationalists or extreme fundamentalists. Though subtle this positioning process is intentional. Creating a sense of us versus them such crude associations have the effect of reinforcing a TBMSG belief in social uplift through the personal empowerment of education and Buddhist practice.

In the context of this speech act, Mangesh is positioning himself and his movement as the original purveyors of Indian democracy and scientific rationalism. To an audience of foreigners, the Ambedkar Buddhist is positioned as providing a logical method for explaining the world and therefore proscribing change; while the Hindu is the cause of the stereotypical view of India as nonsensical and mystical, thus making them incapable of instituting equitable change. Nuanced and multi-faceted, Mangesh's narrative holds multiple levels of meaning, aspects which are often overlooked by both movement members and outsiders. On the deepest level this transcribed narrative is an attempt to position

Hindus as falling outside the Western scientific community—as pre-modern and mythical in their worldview. But as Cassirer has argued "mythical and verbal thought are interwoven in everyway". Only through metaphor, Cassirer argues, is one able to see the "unity" and "difference" of the verbal and mythical worlds. Mangesh uses an evolutionary metaphor, "the big fish ate the small fish," to explain the Hindu justification for caste.

This metaphor is then discredited as "a very crude form of social Darwinism". Since social Darwinism has a negative connotation, the use of this metaphor is aimed at further discrediting the non-rational un-methodological approach of the other.

It provides another example of caste Hindus attempts to justify the inequities of the Indian social system as having a rational basis, but by de-legitimizing it as social Darwinism Mangesh repositions the view as unscientific and a-historical. In cycling through orienting the listener developing complicating actions and evaluating the situation, Mangesh is positioning unscientific culture as detrimental to society and an Ambedkarite restructuring of society as the only prescription able to correct this flaw.

This has the dual effect of legitimizing secular humanism and Buddhist practice. Therefore, only through seeing the failure of current social constructs can change become possible and an Ambedkar Buddhist analysis provides the best lens to identify this failure. In this context, it is also insightful to return to this narrative paying close attention to pauses and other aspects of speech processes in Mangesh's talk. Such analysis not only tells us more about the speaker, but also about the "reflection-in-action" aspects of scripting the talk to his specific audience.

Speaking in English is harder than speaking in his native Marathi dialogue and periods of pause are undoubtedly periods of actively choosing specific words and word phrases suitable for the context and the audience. Invoking Gandhi—a well-known figure to the American audience—provides a means to understand Mangesh's own identity as inter-related with his minority sense of nationalism. After debunking the ideal of the Rama Raj, Mangesh—having equated this idea with the father of Indian nationalism—seems to stumble in finding an adequate example to show the superstitious nature of the castebased ideal, which underpins this idea.

Mangesh is jumping between various examples to orient the listener and provide evaluative statements in order to develop a complicating action these listeners can clearly understand.

In setting up the Hindu nationalist ideal—exemplified by the well-known personage of Gandhi—Mangesh then challenges this ideal as scientifically un-grounded and superstitious and casts the work of TBMSG as attempting "to challenge those ideas, the 'so-called' religious ideas". Essentializing the idea as ideal, he struggles to find adequate language to express these ideas.

Forced to explain through example and analogy, Mangesh invokes a traditional ideal, a modern discovery, and a scientific theory as tools to expose the injustice of an irrational social stratification system.

His pauses represent rhetorical reassessments of his context and audience, providing a passion and gravity to his speech that mere words could not accomplish. From a Lobovian perspective these pauses represent the struggle to adequately express evaluative statements. The prosody of these adds legitimacy to his evaluative statements and helps to play on the Western scientific worldview.

There is nonetheless a sort of revivalist, or anti-modern, element within TBMSG movement narratives. Though they are harkening for a modern scientific worldview, they are also invoking a revival of anti-traditionalist tendencies within the Indian society.

Embracing modernity and technology, TBMSG always draws its' narrative back to the historical Buddha—placing the genesis of their thought in a time of antiquity. Such a recourse to an idealized past can be very effective in mobilizing support, as many religious movements have noticed. In this sense, TBMSG's approach is not revolutionary. Mangesh's words, as well as the processes through which they evolve into a narrative construct, provide a window into the identity and sense on injustice that TBMSG members feel. By recourse to a constructed past ideal and an unrealised future implementation of that ideal, such speech acts are the foundation of the TBMSG movement. Simultaneously alienating and cohesive, such speech acts provide the foundation for a reconstructed identity that is coextensive with a sense of injustice. The reconstructed identity acts as a means to express injustice.

THE FUTURE OF DALIT ACTIVISM

Inherent in the promise of these two worldviews is a sort of grounded pragmatism. The mobilization experience, social networks, and common purpose of religious activists, is something that secular Dalit right activists can and must tap into. Conversely, the rightsbased language of secular Dalit rights activists can provide social justice ends that are less ambiguous than the rigorous spiritual practice of individual self-attainment.

The following reaction to the celebratory Buddhist conversions of October 2, 2006 by a keen observer of the Ambedkar movement underscores the issues at stake when this connection between secular and religious narrative structures goes unattended and unanalysed:

- 'What do they mean: All India will become Buddhist?... These people need to live in a world with Muslims and Hindus and all the rest. Dr. Ambedkar wanted to reconstruct the Buddhist tradition so it met the needs of his time. But can the Ambedkarites do the same with Ambedkar's own ideas? Nagaloka should be teaching comparative religion... They need to say what they are for, and leave aside what they are against.'

The seeming incongruence of Dalit identities as either victim or as self-aware Buddhist leaves conceptions of social justice, citizenship, and community vague and unbounded. Hence this lack of balance cries for a syncretism between these often competing narrative frames of social justice—an integrated religious/secular focus on individual rights that does not overlook the importance of individuals' spiritual worldview in creating social justice.

As Dalit activists strive for a society open to pluralist ideals they must practice pluralism in the narrative constructions that they deploy. Such a mix of transnational and local strategies for contention redefines the transnational and highlights the need to critically analyse the role of such activists' narratives in the wider global society.

5

Ambedkar's Legacy to Dalits

AN OVERVIEW

DALITS, meaning 'broken' or 'oppressed', is a synonym for the 'depressed classes'. Both these terms are now too loosely and indiscriminately applied to an assortment of social groups, variously labelled as oppressed, deprived, downtrodden, disabled, disadvantaged, weaker parts, other backward classes, minorities, scheduled tribes, untouchables, scheduled castes, Harijans, and so on.

The lumping of all these groups and the use of the terms DCs and Dalits as 'catchall' categories are for at least two reasons: First, the failure to grasp the magnitude of the disparate socio-cultural, educational, and economic conditions of these groups. Second, as a ploy of self-serving politicians pretending to be the protagonists of backward classes for invidiously extending the constitutional safeguards meant for the real Dalits to the less deserving groups as well. In either case the losers are undoubtedly the really deprived and disabled bottom groups which alone are Dalits.

In this connection it is pertinent to recall B R Ambedkar's usage of the term DCs. That was in the limited sense of untouchables. Among other things, in his written statements and oral evidence before the Simon Commission of 1928 and the Round Table Conferences of 1930-31 and their subcommittees he made it explicit that he was using DCs and untouchables as convertible terms. More often than not, he preferred to address the untouchables as just untouchables as though to remind them of their plight as a 'besieged', 'broken', and 'dehumanised' people. If he addressed them as DCs it was primarily because this term was already in circulation as a British officialese covering the untouchables and a few other groups such as the aboriginal and hill tribes.

But when occasion arose Ambedkar did not hesitate to condemn this usage. Thus, in a supplementary memorandum on the claims of the DCs for special representation, submitted on November 4, 1931 to the Minorities Subcommittee of the Second Round Table Conference, he made it clear that the term DCs was degrading and contemptuous, and its use objectionable to the members of the concerned class and others interested in them.

So, he demanded its substitution with the less derogatory 'noncaste Hindus', 'protestant Hindus', or 'nonconformist Hindus', or some such appellation. In his note on the untouchables, submitted on May 1, 1932, to the Indian Franchise Committee of the same conference, Ambedkar again objected to the use of this term. He also noted that the term had led to a great deal of confusion in the census as it included other groups who were not strictly untouchables. Therefore, he insisted on describing the untouchables by the more expressive term 'exterior castes' or 'excluded castes'.

While Ambedkar had no difficulty in accepting the British officialese SCs as incorporated into the Government of India Act of 1935, he detested Gandhi's grandiloquent appellation Harijans. In January 1938 when the Bombay legislative council refused to accept an amendment for deletion of this term from the Local Boards Act Amendment Bill, Ambedkar along with members of his Republican Party walked out of the house. The reasoning of B K Gaikwad, who moved the amendment, was that through several conferences the untouchables had voiced their opposition to this usage. If they were people of god, that is Harijans, were the touchables monsters, he asked.

In view of the fact that untouchables have been the largest category and the most depressed and downtrodden of all the bottom groups of Indian society, and in keeping with Ambedkar's usage of the DCs only with reference to the untouchables, the term DCs as well as its vernacular equivalent Dalits is used here in the limited sense of untouchables or their constitutional equivalent SCs. Such a restricted usage also assumes significance because of Ambedkar's role as the greatest of all the hitherto leaders of the untouchables, who launched a life-long crusade for their liberation from centuriesold enslavement and ostracism.

Ambedkar contemplated various means for liberating the Dalits. However, it was primarily through the numerous safeguards incorporated into the Indian constitution, of which he himself was the chief architect, that he hoped to arm them with political power, to improve their socio-economic, educational, and cultural conditions, and to actualise their gradual deliverance from rhetoric to reality, from deprivation to development, from social stigma and suffering to social respect, solace, and equality.

As Ambedkar's legacy to Dalits is thus primarily the constitutional safeguards for the SCs, the celebration of his birth centenary year should at least serve as an occasion to take stock of the fate of his legacy, and to ascertain if the nation has really honoured it or reneged on its promises to honour it. This calls for an examination of the performance of the various measures undertaken in pursuance of these safeguards.

CONSTITUTIONAL SAFEGUARDS

The specific constitutional provisions intended to safeguard the interests of the SCs are on the abolition of untouchability and prohibition on its practice in any form; prohibition of 'begar' or forced or bonded labour, consideration of the claims of the SCs in appointments to services and posts in connection with the affairs of the union or a state; and reservation of seats in proportion to their numbers for the SCs in the Lok Sabha and in the Vidhan Sabhas.

Some of the other provisions also reinforce the status of the SCs as a 'protected weaker part'. They include the departures from the anti-discriminatory and formal equality provisions of the constitution, empowering the state to make any provision for the advancement of any socially and educationally backward class of citizens, and for the reservation of appointments or posts in favour of any backward class of citizens which in the opinion of the state is not adequately represented. They also include the directive in Article 46 that the state shall promote with special care the educational and economic interests of the weaker parts of the people, and, in particular, of the SCs and the STs, and shall protect them from social injustice and all forms of exploitation.

For analytical purposes the measures undertaken in pursuance of the various constitutional provisions for the SCs may be treated under three broad categories, namely, protective, developmental, and preferential. Abolitien of untouchability and the disabilities arising out of its practice in any form, and prohibition of bonded labour come under the first category.

Various educational schemes such as post-matric scholarships and girls hostels under the central sector, and pre-matric stipends, reimbursement of tuition fee, book banks, and hostels under the state sector, special component plans of the centre and states, special central assistance, and the SCs Development Corporations are of the second category. Legislative, educational and employment reservations are of the third category. Of these, the effective implementation of the measures of the first two categories is a precondition for actualising the measures of the third category. However, the implementation of these measures hitherto has been too ineffective to achieve their intended objectives. This has been brought to light time and again by a number of studies, and in particular, by the commissioner for SCs and STs.

PERSISTENCE OF UNTOUCHABILITY

The Untouchability Act of 1955 was intended to wipe out untouchability and the social disabilities arising out of it, by making its practice in any form punishable under law. But, the total number of cases registered with the police from 1955 to 1970 were only 6778 for the country as a whole, with only 1779 or 26 per cent of them ending up in conviction. As this act proved to be too weak and inadequate to meet the constitutional requirement, in November 1976 it was amended and amplified as the Protection of Civil Rights Act, 1955, with the resolve to totally eradicate untouchability within five years of its implementation. But, even this act has not fared any better.

Data on PCR cases indicate the persistence of untouchability in virtually all the states. This is especially so in Andhra Pradesh, Gujarat, Karnataka, Madhya Pradesh, Rajasthan, Tamil Nadu, and sadly enough, even in Ambedkar's home state Maharashtra. The only state reported to be relatively free from untouchability is West Bengal.

Of the yearly average of PCR cases from 1977 to 1985 only about 62 per cent of those registered with the police were 'challaned' or filed before the courts; only about 31 per cent of those before the courts were disposed of; and only about 20 per cent of these disposals ended up in conviction. Stated differently, of the total cases registered with the police on an average not even 10 per cent ended up in conviction.

If this all-India pattern is any indication of the poor performance of the PCR Act, data available for some of the states indicate that the variations at the state level have been mostly for the worse: Despite a relatively higher percentage of 'challaning' by the police in at least two states and despite a relatively higher percentage of disposals by the courts in at least one of them and two others in all the states most of the cases have ended up in acquittals. Stated differently, only less than 9 per cent of the cases before the courts and only less than 4 per cent of the cases registered with the police have ended up in conviction. The relatively smaller proportion of cases 'challaned' by the police and the smaller proportion of disposals by the courts tend to magnify the proportion of convictions in Rajasthan.

While the large number of cases pending with the courts is a reflection of the tardy judicial process, the larger number of cases ending up in acquittals is for other reasons as well. As the reports of the commissioner for SCs and STs indicate, these include the weak socio-economic condition of the victims and their witnesses, defective investigation by the police, ineffective or indifferent handling of cases by the prosecution staff, victims yielding to pressures, promises, allurements, or intimidation, and the long drawn out trials which alone can discourage any victim from pursuing the case effectively.

Though the some idea of the persistence of untouchability, they are too inadequate to bring out the real magnitude of this evil. For, more often than not most of the cases go unnoticed and unreported. The seventh report of the Commission/ er for SCs and STs noted that quite a large number of the victims do not seek legal redress, and that though in states like Bihar and Orissa the problem of untouchability is acute, they have been reporting significantly lower number of cases compared to states like Tamil Nadu, Maharashtra, and Karnataka. The reason for this is not far to seek. Economically the SCs are still dependent on caste Hindus, and as such they do not risk approaching the police.

A survey by the All-India Harijan Sevak Sangh conducted about a decade ago in 1,155 village spread over 12 states, clearly brought out the widespread practice of untouchability in the rural areas in terms of denial of access to the SCs to wells, temples, hotels and restaurants, barbershops, laundries, and so on. That this evil practice still persists unabated in many areas is evident from the subsequent reports of the Cornmission/ er for SCs and STs. Stating that untouchability persists in one form or the other, particularly in rural areas, the eighth report of the Commission for SCs and STs brought to light instances of discrimination against the SCs even in urban areas, especially in Andhra Pradesh, Bihar, Karnataka, Madhya Pradesh, Orissa, Rajasthan, Tamil Nadu; and Uttar Pradesh.

PERPETRATION OF ATROCITIES

Closely related to the persistence of untouchability is the perpetration of atrocities against the SCs. The atrocity cases registered have continued to be relatively more in Bihar, Gujarat, Kerala, Madhya Pradesh, Maharashtra, Rajasthan, Tamil Nadu, and Uttar Pradesh. Of late, there has also been a considerable increase in the number of atrocity cases in some states, especially in Gujarat, Madhya Pradesh, Rajasthan, and Tamil Nadu. Of the different types of atrocity cases registered in the whole country at least one-fourth have involved grievous hurt, followed by arson, rape, and murder. The nature of disposal of these cases has not been any better: Data available for some of the states indicate that of the total atrocity cases for disposal by the police during 1985 only about 53 per cent were 'challenged', that of the total cases for disposal by the courts only about 5 per cent were disposed of, and that of these only about 34 per cent ended up in conviction.

Stated differently, of the total cases for disposal by the police not even 10 per cent ended up in confusion. The performance was especially poor if, Karnataka, Madhya Pradesh, Orissa, Punjab, and Tamil Nadu. These cases again do not reflect the magnitude of atrocities; more so when contrasted against the recurrent press reports from different parts of the country about the crimes on the SCs. The reasons mentioned earlier for the PCR cases also apply to this and to the large number of cases pending with the courts and ending up in acquittal.

As atrocities against the SCs are closely related to untouchability, their perpetration has to be partly explained by the persistence of untouchability and by the increasing resentment of the SCs against the social indignities emanating from its practice in different forms. These include denial of entry into public places of worship, discrimination and differential treatment in hotels and teastalls, refusal of service by washermen and barbers, and restriction on movement in certain localities, on wearing sandals, riding horses, and leading marriage processions through certain caste-Hindu localities.

The other major factors listed in the various reports of the Commission/er for SCs and STs include envy of the caste-Hindus for the various welfare measures adopted by the government to ameliorate the socioeconomic conditions of the SCs, the wide economic disparities arising out of landlessness, wage labour, bondage, nonpayment of fair share of agricultural produce to the SC sharecroppers, forced harvesting of crops, forced eviction of the SC ₹ from their land and house-sites, dispute over non-payment of minimum wages prescribed by the state, and land disputes, especially as a result of land reforms and the redistribution of surplus lands.

The reports also reveal that of late many of the atrocities committed have been by some of the affluent parts of the middle caste peasantry—the so-called backward classes—,who have been the major beneficiaries of agrarian reforms and other rural development programmes and of the resultant changes in the economic and political structure in the villages. It is important to note that, as observed in the seventh report of the Commission for SCs and STs, the incidence of atrocities is relatively lower in states where literacy rates and economic development of the SCs are relatively higher.

ABETMENT OF EXPLOITATIVE BONDAGE

Closely related to the persistence of untouchability and atrocities is the existence of SCs as bonded labourers. As the second report of the Commission for SCs and STs noted, "bonded labourers represent the extreme situation of abject prostration of landless agricultural labourers in the rural economy". The 21st report of the commissioner for SCs and STs described the bonded labour system as follows:

- The prominent feature of the system is that a man pledges his person or sometimes a member of his family against a loan. The pledger or his nominee is released only on its discharge. Until then the man himself or the member of the family is required to work for his creditor against his daily meals. Since he gets no money, he has to depend upon someone in the family to procure the sum required for his release and this, of course, is rarely available. The relationship lasts for months and sometimes years, occasionally for an entire life time and not infrequently follows the male heir.

The Bonded Labour System Act of 1976 is intended to abolish this evil practice, and identify, free, and rehabilitate its victims of whom at least 80 per cent are reported to be SCs and STs. But its implementation has not served this purpose so far. For one thing, under this act the term bonded labour itself is defined in a limited sense.

Of this the fifth report of the Commission for SCs and STs wrote: The very definition of the term 'bonded labour' restricts its meaning so much that its connotation excludes many who are virtually compelled but may not be forced to work as bonded labourers. It is particularly difficult to establish the element of force applied by the creditors with the result that many labourers are excluded from the meaning of the term though their condition is by no means better than that of others. Because of the apparent loophole in the law, in states like Bihar systems like "attached labour" cannot be brought under the purview of the Bonded Labour System Act, 1976.

Terms like "attached labour" are nothing but a euphemism for bonded labour. For another, the implementation of the act has been far from effective even to release and rehabilitate those bonded labourers who come under its purview. Consequently, in practice the system still persists in some form or another in many parts of the country. Data available in the eighth report of the Commission for SCs and STs reveal that as on March 31, 1986 only about 2 lakh bonded labourers were identified and freed, and of them only about 1.6 lakh were rehabilitated.

But, if the estimate of bonded labourers in the country at about 22.4 lakh as made by a survey conducted in 1978 by the Gandhi Peace Foundation in collaboration with the National Labour Institute is any indication, by its implementation the act has so far only scratched the surface. Even going by the conservative estimate of 3.4 lakh as made by the 32nd round of the NSS, the implementation of the act has to cover a lot more ground. What is more, due to inadequacies in the rehabilitation scheme and lack of follow up action, even the freed bonded labourers are either back in or on the verge of further bondage. Of this, the fifth report of the Commission for SCs and STs wrote.

- Rehabilitation measures in many cases do not appear to be sufficient or are adopted unimaginatively. One of the reasons for unimaginative rehabilitation is that, due to poverty, illiteracy and economic backwardness, freed bonded labourers are not in a position to exercise option and preference for a particular scheme of rehabilitation. In such a situation the field functionaries have to decide for themselves the role of freed bonded labourers, taking a decision about what would be the form of rehabilitation.

As examples the report pointed out that in certain land-based schemes the agricultural land allotted was too inadequate for the maintenance of a family, and that sometimes such land itself was fallow and unfit for cultivation.

ECONOMIC DEPENDENCE

That many of the social disabilities of the SCs are because of their continuing existence as the poorest of the poor is stating the obvious. Available data also point towards this. In 1982 the SCs owned only about 8 per cent of the total land owned in the rural areas in the country as a whole, though their households accounted for about 20 per cent of the total rural households.

The index of their access to land ownership reveals that the land owned by them was virtually nil in Haryana and Punjab, and that the ratio of percentage of land owned to the percentage of households was not even one-fourth in Kerala and Bihar, was only between one-fourth and one-half in Gujarat, Andhra Pradesh, Tamil Nadu, Maharashtra, Uttar Pradesh, and Himachal Pradesh, and only between one-half and two-thirds in Karnataka, Madhya Pradesh, Orissa, Rajasthan, and West Bengal.

This low access to land, the principal resource and the main source of power, dominance, oppression and exploitation in rural India, has several implications: First, the higher percentage of landless households among the SCs compared to the rest of the population. This is so in virtually all the states, in particular in Bihar, Gujarat, Haryana, Rajasthan, Kerala, and Madhya Pradesh. Second, the smaller area of land owned by most of the SC land owning households. In most states the SC households are conspicuous by their absence or negligible presence in the large ownership category, and by their concentration in the marginal ownership category. In Andhra Pradesh, Bihar, Haryana, Himachal Pradesh, Kerala, Orissa, Punjab, Tamil Nadu, and Uttar Pradesh between 72 per cent and 92 per cent of the land owning households among the SCs were in the marginal ownership category as against only between 39 per cent and 58 per cent of the non-SC households in all but Bihar and Kerala.

That the area of land owned by the SC households in the marginal category is too inadequate for their economic use should be only too obvious from the average size of their holdings in all the ownership categories combined. At the all India level, it is only about one-third of that among the non-SCs.

At the state level it is even less. This is especially so in Punjab and Haryana, followed by Kerala, Bihar, Gujarat, Andhra Pradesh, Tamil Nadu, and Uttar Pradesh. In fact, even most of the SC households coming under the marginal ownership category should be treated as landless, inasmuch as a large number of the landless SC households have been pushed into this category consequent on the distribution of the often barren surplus and government waste lands. This is especially so in Tamil Nadu, where the percentage of landless households among the SCs appears smaller than that among the non-SCs.

Third, the greater incidence of poverty among the SCs, and their greater deprivation by and dependence on the caste-Hindus. As the Planning Commission's Working Group on SCs and STs reported, the SCs have few assets; "are generally unable to avail themselves of the new employment opportunities generated through various economic development programmes", and "are in fact caught up in a vicious circle in which they are dependent upon their exploiters for their sustenance and are largely denied opportunities to develop the capabilities of attaining an independent livelihood". Fourth, in the absence of access to land, as either owners or protected tenants, the SCs are forced to eke out a living mostly by working on the land of others as agricultural labourers on daily wages, by attaching themselves to landlords or cultivators, and as bonded labourers, and partly by pursuing their traditional 'unclean' and socially 'low' occupations of sweeping, scavenging, carrying 'nightsoil', leather work, and mat weaving.

The 1981 Census, cultivators accounted for only about 28 per cent, whereas agricultural labourers accounted for as much as 48 per cent of the total working population among the SCs. The corresponding percentages among the general population were 42 and 25 respectively. The composition of the SC workforce in Andhra Pradesh, Gujarat, Karnataka, Maharashtra, Orissa, and Tamil Nadu was more or less of this all-India pattern.

In the remaining states, with the exception of Himachal Pradesh and to some extent even Madhya Pradesh, that is, in Bihar, Haryana, Kerala, Punjab, Rajasthan, and Uttar Pradesh, the proportion of cultivators among the SCs was much less and that of the agricultural labourers much more than the corresponding proportions among the general population. Between 1971 and 1981 there was not any drastic change in the composition of the SC workforce in most states. The only exception is Kerala, where the percentage of SC cultivators dropped from about 21 in 1971 to just 2 in 1981, and of agricultural labourers from 66 to 50, with many persons moving into the category of 'other workers'.

In Kerala there was considerable fall in the percentage of agricultural labourers in the general population as well from about 31 to 20. The fragmentation of agricultural holdings and their uneconomic nature, especially after the decade long land reforms implementation of the seventies abolishing landlordism and tenancy, conferring ownership rights on cultivating tenants, and distributing part of the surplus land, and the increasing scarcity of water for agricultural purposes, probably caused this major shift.

EDUCATIONAL CONDITION

As the SCs can take advantage of the measures of the third and most important category of safeguards, especially of employment and educational reservations, only with educational advancement, and educational advancement can come about only with socio-economic advancement, their educational condition can be a crucial indicator of their overall status as beneficiaries of the implementation of the various constitutional provisions.

No doubt, there has been some progress in the growth of literacy among the SCs; In 1961 the literacy percentages among them and the general population including them were 10.3, and 24, whereas in 1981 these were 21.4 and 36.2 respectively. Compared to the general population the increase is relatively more significant in Kerala, Himachal Pradesh, Maharashtra, Gujarat and Tamil Nadu. Despite this increase, the SCs are still far behind the general population in most states.

This is especially so in the case of women. While the male literacy among the SCs itself is much lower than that among the general population, female literacy is much more so. In fact, female literacy among the SCs is virtually nil or negligible in Bihar, Madhya Pradesh, Orissa, Rajasthan, and Uttar Pradesh, only about one-third of their male literacy at the all-India level, and only less than one-half in all but Kerala, Himachal Pradesh, and Maharashtra.

At the all-India level female literacy among the SCs is only about three-fourths of the female literacy among the general population. At the state level, it is even less. Only in Gujarat, Kerala, Himachal Pradesh, and Maharashtra it is above this all-India rate. What is more, literacy, understood in the census' sense of mere ability to read and write, is at best only the base of the educational pyramid, and any growth in it assumes meaning and significance only if it is sustained at the higher levels.

But, this has not happened among the SCs. The available data might give the impression that in the primary stage the SCs have almost caught up with the general population. But, this may not be true even with a steady increase in enrolment over the years. For, enrolment is just the first step in the educational process. The report on the programme of action on national educational policy, rightly pointed out that "enrolment by itself is of little importance if children do not continue education beyond even a year, many of them not seeing the school for more than a few days". The report noted that nearly 60 per cent of the children drop out between classes I-V and 75 per cent between classes I-VIII and that nearly 22 per cent of the enrolled at the primary stage are outside 6-11 age group, mostly overaged.

For obvious reasons the corresponding percentages among the SCs must be still higher. This is partly evident from the lower enrolment ratios of the SCs at the middle stage. Here again there is considerable interregional variation. If the available data are any indication, the position is far from satisfactory at least in Andhra Pradesh, Bihar, Haryana, Uttar Pradesh, and West Bengal.

As the SCs move up further in the educational ladder, their enrolment ratio also shrinks or their drop out rate increases correspondingly: As the first report of the Commission for SCs and STs noted, for a population of about 15 per cent, at the all-India level the percentage of SC students in professional and other educational courses was only 4.3 in 1964-65, and only 5.7 in 1974-75. At the state level, it was only in Maharashtra that their enrolment as percentage of the total enrolment in high school, undergraduate and postgraduate equalled or exceeded their population percentage in 1976-78.

In virtually all other states it was below their population percentage at all the three stages. In the high school itself the position was very bad in all but Gujarat, Kerala, and Tamil Nadu, while in the UG and PG it deteriorated even in these states. The position was especially bad in Andhra Pradesh, Bihar, Karnataka, Orissa, Punjab, Rajasthan, Tamil Nadu, Uttar Pradesh, and West Bengal in the case of both UG and PG courses. While there might have been some change in these percentages in the subsequent years as well, it would not have been so dramatic as to equalise the educational status of the SCs with the general population. The access of the SCs to higher education is further reduced by the fact that the instructions issued by the government of India for reservation of seats are not followed by a number of states.

REPRESENTATION IN PUBLIC SERVICES

If the SCs are thus still far behind the general population in their educational attainments, it is only to be inferred that they are more so in their representation in public services. The representation of the SCs in the central services has increased over the years in all the four classes of jobs, it is only in class 4 that it has been adequate In classes 1 to 3, especially in classes 1 and 2, it has been far below their population percentage.

Comparison of the data on the representation of the SCs in the services of the states for the earliest and latest available years reveals similar shortfalls, despite an increasing trend over the years. It is only in Maharashtra that the representation of the SCs has been adequate in all but class 1; and it is only in Gujarat, and Rajasthan that it has been so at least in classes III and IV.

In all other states their representation has been well below their population percentage. Their representation in classes 1 and 2 has been especially poor in Haryana, Himachal Pradesh, Madhya Pradesh, Orissa, Punjab, Tamil Nadu, Uttar Pradesh, and West Bengal.

LIMITATIONS

As the data thus portray a dismal picture of the nation's efforts in honouring Ambedkar's legacy, there is urgent need for streamlining the implementation of the various provisions. For doing this, some of its present limitations have to be borne in mind.

These limitations stem from at least nine sources:

- The continuing absence of social conscience, a condition so necessary for the implementation of the programmes aimed at eliminating the disabilities of the SCs. In this context it is pertinent to recall Ambedkar's observation that "rights are protected not by law but by the social and moral conscience of society", that "if social conscience is such that it is prepared to recognise the rights which law chooses to enact, rights will be safe and secure", and that if the "rights are opposed by the community, no law, no parliament, no judiciary can guarantee them I in the real sense of the word"." It is in this sense that the repeated pleas by the Commissioner for SCs and STs for creating awareness among the masses and for involving them in the implementation of the various constitutional provisions have to be understood.

- Lack of an appropriate machinery for effectively enforcing the various measures. The official status accorded, and the facilities and personnel made available, to the Commissioner for SCs and STs appointed under Article 338 have not been commensurate with the nature of his responsibility and the enormous magnitude of the problems concerning the SCs and STs. Consequently, he has not been able to function as a 'watch-dog' agency as envisaged in the constitution. It is as though realising this, and under mounting pressures, that the government of India set up the high-level commission for SCs and STs in 1978. But, as a parallel agency so far it has tended to duplicate the work of the Commissioner for SCs and Sis, who incidentally is also its ex-officio secretary. That apart, this commission itself has observed that it is greatly handicapped in performing its functions effectively as it does not enjoy any constitutional status, that its role has been purely recommendatory, which has made it at times 'a helpless spectator of non-performance and non-compliance'. Though economic development of the SCs is well recognised as a precondition for overcoming their social disabilities, neither of these agencies is given a clear mandate in this regard, and matters pertaining to policy issues involving the SCs are hardly ever referred to them. Though both these agencies are expected to monitor the implementation of the various safeguards, even the mere monitoring has been wellnigh impossible for them, and their reports deplore time and again their inability to get the required information from the administrations in the states and union territories even after repeated reminders. The effect of their inability on the SCs is confounded by the long delay in preparing and placing their reports before parliament, leave alone any serious debates on the contents of these reports. Very often the reports themselves are very shoddy devoid of systematic presentation of any complete, reliable, and uniform data so necessary for an overall assessment of the performance of the concerned programmes.

- The *ad hoc* formulation of development schemes for SCs and STs without any long-term perspective and an operationally integrated strategy, as observed by, among others, the Planning Commission's Working Group on SCs and STs and the Commissioner for SCs and STs. Though the special component plan introduced since the Sixth Plan is expected to fill this lacunae, so far it has not made much headway.
- The meagre and woefully inadequate budget allocations in the successive five-year plans for the programmes covering the SCs. As the first report of the Commission for SCs and STs noted, during the first 30 years of planning the SCs and STs were all along left out on the fringe, and the paltry provisions made under the sector of 'welfare of backward classes' hardly accounted for 1 to 2 per cent of the total plan outlays. The situation might not have changed dramatically in the last one decade. In this context the failure of the overall developmental efforts, problems and politics of scarcity, and like Buridan's

ass the state's dilemma of choosing between its alternatives, all call for some serious rethinking.

- The misconception of the constitutional provision for taking into account the employment claims of the SCs 'consistently with the maintenance of efficiency of administration'. For preventing the abuse of this efficiency clause, the Planning Commission's Working Group mentioned earlier recommended the deletion of the clause itself. That is, however, only a desperate remedy. Consistency with efficiency has to be construed as equipping the disabled well before and even after their entry into services, to work with others on equal footing through a package of practices. The absence of such a package or its weak and inadequate presence, and the official attempt to arrive only at a crude statistical equality devoid of the much needed socio-cultural vitality which alone can eventually, if at all, equalise the social life of the SCs with that of the mainstream groups, have reduced the special safeguards to tokenism and mere concessions. In the long run the nemesis of such concessions, as Tawney rightly stated in another context, is death by dilution, if not for the administration which in any case is too big to be swayed or swatted by the small number of SCs, at least for the SCs themselves by indirectly arresting their growth potential for want of motivation and morale.
- The 'higher-echelon' nature, of the benefits and the lack of access of the SCs, especially those at the lower levels, to the administration, to the political system, and to the judiciary.
- The absence of any mechanism for gradually excluding individuals or groups from claiming the benefits of the constitutional provisions for special dispensation once they have attained measurable self reliance in terms of inter-generational socioeconomic, educational, and occupational attainments or

mobility. Such exclusion will prevent the present concentration, and result in the diffusion, of benefits, and gradually even phase out these provisions.

- The absence of any mechanism for providing special attention to the most needy by disaggregating the individual beneficiaries into groups most deserving, least deserving, and so on.
- The failure of the provisions, especially those for employment and educational reservations, to penetrate private institutions.

6

Ambedkar: Dalit Culture and Civilization

THE MAHAR MOVEMENT'S MILITARY COMPONENT

Dr. Bhimrao Ramji Ambedkar, is famous for being "the most highly educated Untouchable in India." His education, encouraged and financed largely by the Gaikwad of Baroda, led to his role as the Untouchable's chief spokesman, the founder of a political party for Untouchables, and the moving spirit behind organizations, schools, and colleges established for their uplift. One of Ambedkar's final acts was the initiation of a Buddhist conversion movement that ultimately attracted more than 3 million Untouchable adherents.

This part of Ambedkar's story is well-known. However, his family's military service in the British Raj is not widely acknowledged for creating an environment that laid the foundation for his later success. Eleanor Zelliot, an expert on Dr. Ambedkar and the Mahar movement, maintains, "[T]he hundred year period of Mahar recruitment into British armies may well have been the single most important factor, aside from economic reasons, in producing the Mahar movement." This substance examines the importance of military service in improving the social status of Ambedkar's caste, the Mahars of Maharashtra.

The focus is on their relationship with the British. The Mahars benefited from their participation in the British Army in a number of ways. First, military service became "a significant part of caste élan and mythology." The first part provides the historical evidence they use to establish their credentials as a caste with martial traditions. The documents detail the advantage, especially education that accrued from military service and discusses their access to the government that otherwise was unavailable to Untouchables.

The final part discusses the British decision to recruit only "martial races," in which the Mahars were not included, for the British Indian Army and the Mahars' efforts to gain reinstatement in the Army. The substance does not focus exclusively on Dr. Ambedkar, but uses him as a point of reference for many of the examples given.

EARLY MILITARY PARTICIPATION

Eleanor Zelliot explains that the British gave Mahars the opportunity to seek different occupations from their traditional role as a village servant. She explains that before the arrival of the British,

- Mahars had no special skill or craft, but performed necessary duties for the village as watchmen, wall-menders, street-sweepers, removers of cattle carcasses, caretakers of the burning ground, servants of any passing governmental official.... Mahar service was essential for the village; his status was low, his work menial, but his place was secure. With the coming of the British and the spread of new ways of administration and communication, the Mahar place in the village grew less important.

Military service provided Mahars with the opportunity to move beyond their traditional social position in the village. In fact, the Mahar tradition of being in armies precedes the British Raj. The recorded history of the Mahars' military achievements dates back to Shivaji's Army in the 1600s. Cynthia Enloe, a noted sociologist who has written extensively on ethnic-military relationships, states, "The best of all militaries in the eyes of a state elite is one in which the most competent soldiers are also the most politically reliable, because they have the greatest stake in the continuation of the current system." The Mahars met this condition just as to descriptions of their loyalty. Colonel V. Longer, author of Forefront Forever: The History of the Mahar Regiment, states:

- There were a number of useful functions which the Mahars performed. Their Argus eye; their daring tenacity and determination; their faithfulness, loyalty and honesty; their courage and candour, were inestimable qualities which were always held in respect and were for ever utilized to advantage by the village.... In course of time, their voice carried great weight when there were disputes over property as their evidence was considered most accurate, intimate, and trustworthy.

This sense of loyalty and trustworthiness led Shivaji to include Mahars as a vital component of his army. Shivaji, leader of the Maratha nation, fought for a Hindu empire, but using Untouchables did not bother him. He "found the Mahars useful, for the wily Maratha chief realised that the best way of obtaining the maximum results was to mix up various castes in his garrison forces." He used the Mahars "to watch the jungles at the foot of the hill forts, act as scouts and [they] kept the forts supplied with wood and fodder."

This was the first exposure of the Mahars to an organized army that provided its soldiers with steady pay and benefits. After Shivaji's death, Mahar units continued to serve his descendants throughout the 1700s. Their experience with Shivaji and others encouraged them to seek similar employment as sepoys of the British East India Company. Ardythe Basham, in her detailed examination of the Mahars and the military, found the perceived early martial history to be an important part of Mahar identity.

She concludes, "Whether or not these incidents are historically true, they are widely accepted by the Mahars as part of their tradition, and now form part of the official history of [today's] Mahar Regiment." The Mahars have often used this martial identity, rooted in the 1600s, to legitimate their continued presence in the military. Mahars began their service with the British in the 1750s. Stephen P. Cohen, an expert on the Indian Army, discusses the importance of Mahars in the Bombay Army in his seminal work, The Indian Army: Contribution to the Development of a Nation. He writes that Mahars were a sizeable portion of the armies of the Mahratta chieftain Shivaji, served as hereditary local policeman, and were thus a "natural" martial class.

Heavily recruited in the premutiny years, the Mahars constituted a fifth to a quarter of the entire Bombay Army. In addition to the size of the Mahar contingent, they were also praised for their conduct as soldiers. The Mahars rewarded the British with the same loyalty that Shivaji had enjoyed. The Bombay Army fought in several battles, and in most, the Mahars were recognized for their skills. Longer proclaims:

- Much praise was showered on the Mahar Sepoys of the Bombay Army who endured the rigours of difficult marches when rations were low and disease was high among men and animals. Whether they were charging ahead or were besieged or taken prisoner-of-war, whether they were storming fortresses or making tactical withdrawals, they always stood steadfast by their officers and comrades, never letting down the honour of their Regiments.

The recorded history of their exploits, especially prior to the mutiny of 1857, supports this effusive adoration. Basham located evidence of Mahar participation in the Second and "Third Anglo-Maratha War, the Second Anglo-Sikh War and the Second Afghan War." The Mahars' exploits in these conflicts form an important part of their military lore. The Mahar participation in the battle of Koregaon on 1 January 1818 is the most famous, and also the best documented, action involving Mahar soldiers.

This battle gave the British the advantage in the Third Anglo-Maratha War. The successful defence of Koregaon by a small force of 500 men... under the command of Capt. F. F. Staunton fought without rest or respite, food or water continuously for twelve hours against a large force of 20,000 Horse and 8,000 Infantry of Peshwa Baji Rao II who was threatening the British garrisons at Kirkee and Poona. Mahars dominated Staunton's unit. The Peshwa's troops inexplicably withdrew that evening, despite their overwhelming numbers, giving the British an important victory. The men of the 2/1st Regiment Bombay Native Infantry, including many Mahars, who fought in this battle, were honoured for their bravery.

The official report to the British Resident at Poona recalls the "heroic valour and enduring fortitude" of the soldiers, the "disciplined intrepidity" and "devoted courage and admirable consistency" of their actions. Further, the action is commemorated by a monument, with the names of twenty-two Mahars killed there, erected at the site of the battle and by a medal issued in 1851. Today, the monument still "serves as a focal point of Mahar heroism." Similar anecdotes are recorded in the written histories of the Mahar Regiment and Bombay Army. All demonstrate that most Mahars soldiers were dedicated and courageous.

In addition to Army units on land, the Mahars formed a vital component of the Bombay Army's Marine Battalion. This unit's history is well documented and provides numerous examples of Mahar actions, including several acts of bravery by Mahars in the battalion. In September 1810, during the Second Maratha War, several Mahars proved their loyalty when captured by the French Navy. The French tried to induce their prisoners to enter their own service, a practice which enjoyed some success with Irish, Madrassi and Bengali troops. On this occasion, the Bombay sepoys were shown the captured Bengal and Madras Sepoys dressed in French uniforms and enjoying considerable privileges and luxuries, whereupon the Bombay Detachment started abusing them as being dead to all shame that they could forget the oath and desert their colours.

The upshot was that they were very roughly treated and some were severely wounded. To the seventeen survivors who reached Bombay a special medal was given and of this number twelve were Mahars. This is just one of many cases where Mahars distinguished themselves as a part of the Marine Battalion and is another part of the martial history that the Mahars used to legitimize their important role in the British

Indian Army. But, in the wake of the 1857 mutiny and threats from Russia, the British reexamined their recruitment policies. The Mahars were a casualty of this new thinking.

THE MAHARS DELISTMENT

Despite the Mahars' long martial history, the British ceased recruiting them in 1893. The Bombay and the other Presidency Armies were reevaluated following the 1857 mutiny. The Peel Commission first examined class composition of the armies in 1858. One report to the Commission "emphasized that 'we cannot practically ignore it, so long as the natives socially maintain it.'"

This led to the discrimination against the Mahars and other low-caste groups as well as some Brahman castes which were considered unreliable. General Lord Roberts, while not originating the concept of martial races, was instrumental in implementing a strategy of building "class regiments." Recruiting policies were rewritten, and the Bombay Army "was notified that the Mahars, together with a number of other classes of the Bombay Army, would no longer be recruited to the Army." Lord Roberts recorded his rational in his autobiography, Forty-One Years in India.

He writes:

- I have no doubt whatever of the fighting powers of our best Indian troops; I have a thorough belief in, and admiration for, Gurkhas, Sikhs, Dogras, Rajputs, Jats and, selected Mahomadans; I thoroughly appreciate their soldierly qualities; brigaded with British troops, I would be proud to lead them against any European enemy.

Roberts thought that the first step to making the Indian Army was "to substitute men of the more warlike and hardy races for the Hindustani sepoys of Bengal, the Tamils and Telagus of Madras, and the so-called Mahrattas of Bombay."

He was convinced that:

- In the British Army the superiority of one regiment over another is mainly a matter of training; the same courage and military instinct are inherent in English,

Scotch, and Irish alike, but no comparison can be made between the martial value of a regiment recruited amongst the Gurkhas of Nepal or the warlike races of Northern India, and of one recruited from the effeminate peoples of the south.

The Mahars believed that their martial history demonstrated their abilities as warriors, but the British had made their decision. Mahars could only enlist as bandsmen or clerks. This would not provide the same opportunities for promotion, and allow little change in their social status. As expected, the Mahars felt the British had betrayed them after over 100 years of loyal service to the British Raj. Throughout India, there was controversy about which groups should remain in the Army.

The Mahars had support from some British soldiers, including three commanders who recommended their continued service. The commander of the 2nd Grenadiers argued that 'the Parwari is of far better fighting material than the Deccani Mussulman," and suggested that the Marine Battalion might be made a class regiment of Parwaries. The commanding officer of the 9th Bombay Infantry thought that a regiment of Parwaries, especially from the Deccan, would "give a very good account of itself." The Commanding officer of the 19th Bombay Infantry stated that:

- "They are possessed of as much soldierly quality as many

However, their assistance was not enough to overcome the sentiments of Lord Roberts and other senior officers of the British Indian Army. Longer provides an excellent commentary on the impact of the decision on the Mahars.

He writes:

- The excellent system with its cosmopolitan composition, which had worked out over the years, was dismantled and destroyed. The Mahars, who had proudly carried the Colours of various Regiments of the Bombay Army, were crestfallen and heartbroken. For years they had provided abundant evidence of their courage, resolution, perseverance, constancy,

> and fidelity. When they bade farewell to arms there were eight Subedar-Majors, 62 Subedars, 34 Jemadars, and a host of Non-Commissioned Officers and Sepoys of the Mahar community who had served with distinction in the Bombay Army.

The Mahars would continue to fight for the right to re-enlist in the Indian Army. They were loath to lose the benefits that the military provided. Furthermore, the education provided to the soldiers had created an educated cadre that would transfer their skills into political action. However, there were few Mahars left in the Army by the beginning of World War I.

BENEFITS OF MILITARY SERVICE

Eleanor Zelliot notes that the "emergence of Mahar leaders and a new spirit of militancy in the 19th century was due in large measure to the influence of education acquired in the military." The result was that

- During the 19th and 20th centuries, a substantial number of Mahars removed themselves from their traditional village servant role. The establishment of British rule in Bombay Presidency provided Mahars with the opportunity for service in the army, employment in cotton mills, ammunition factories, railroads, dockyards, construction work, and as servants in British homes. The 1921 Census records that only 13.5 per cent of the Mahar working force of nearly 300,000 were employed in their traditional occupation even though most Mahars maintained strong ties with their ancestorial village.

The Mahars' ability to work among the British exposed them to Western ways, and helped them to realise that their status as Untouchables did not keep them from working in successful and satisfying occupations. They aggressively used the advantages provided by their relationship with the British. Military service provided important benefits to its soldiers. The benefits include "pay and pensions, access to education and/or specialized training, preferential access to employment, enhanced social status, and personal satisfaction." For the Mahars, the access to education and increased social status was the most important benefits. The best example of their results was Dr. Ambedkar.

Zelliot writes that Ambedkar's experiences were "[f]ree from the traditional village role, his early life was spent among educated ex-army men, imbued with the pride of soldiers and acquainted with a more sophisticated Hinduism than that found in the village." In fact, Ambedkar extends much of the credit for the start of the movement to improve the Untouchables' place in society to contact with the British Army.

He maintained:

- Until the advent of the British, the Untouchables were content to remain Untouchables.... In the army of the East India Company there prevailed the system of compulsory education for Indian soldiers and their children, both male and female. The education received by the Untouchables in the army... gave them a new vision and a new value. They became conscious that the low esteem in which they had been held was not an inescapable destiny but was a stigma imposed on their personality by the cunning contrivances of the priest. They felt the shame of it as they ever did before and were determined to get rid of it.

It is indisputable that this access to education was helpful to Ambedkar, and therefore, to all of India's Untouchable communities. Ambedkar's family had extensive links to the military. Additionally, his mother's "father and her six uncles were all Subedar Majors in the Army," the highest rank that Indians could hold. Ambedkar's father also was a Subhedar Major and

- a full-fledged teacher trained at the Normal School then established by Government for turning out teachers to impart education that was then compulsory for the children as well as both male and female relations of the military servants. For fourteen years Ramji Sakpal served as Headmaster in the military school.

Undoubtedly, the accomplishments of this family were exceptional. Nonetheless, the availability of education had a positive effect on all members of Mahars in the military, including women. Consequently, Basham concludes, "The loss of this education option with the loss of their right of enlistment was therefore a real blow, not merely the loss of a theoretical benefit which few actually received." The quality of life for soldiers and their families suffered because of the loss of educational opportunities available through participation in the military. Mahars joined the military with the intent of improving their social status. They were successful in this regard.

As Basham explains:

- Within the closed circle of the regiment, caste prejudice was, if not actually absent, at least officially discouraged. Army regulations no distinction was made between soldiers on the basis of their caste or community.... Mahar officers were able to command men of other castes apparently without difficulty.

After growing up in this environment of equality it was a shock for the Untouchables to travel and live in situations away from the military cantonments. Ambedkar's biographer, Dhananjay Keer, writes of young Ambedkar's shock the first time he travelled outside the military environment while he was in school. He and his brother were travelling to meet his father in a distant village. At the railway station, they hired a bullock cart to take them to the village, but

- hardly had the cart gone a few yards when the god-fearing touchable Hindu cartman, to his wrath, came to know that the well-dressed boys in his cart were the accursed Untouchables! In a fit of rage he threw them out on the road as one overturns the dust bins;for he felt they had polluted his wooden cart and destroyed the purity of his domestic animals!

This was Ambedkar's first experience that forced him to confront his status as an Untouchable. Life in the military cantonment had sheltered him from the prejudice and discrimination for the early part of his life. After retirement, there was a period of adjustment for Mahars who lived outside the cantonment. Basham concludes:

- As nearly as can be deduced from rather limited information, it would seem that while actually in the army, or after retired or taking other employment, while in contact with British employers and officials, the Mahar soldier was not treated in any way differently from a soldier of higher caste. Once retired and living in his native village, a Mahar soldier, although he might have a relatively high status among the Mahar community and even among caste Hindus, would nevertheless once again have to accept his untouchable status.

The important point is, even after retirement, Mahars with a military background still had access to the British government. The retired military officers were an effective lobby for Mahar rights. Retired officers also created a group of political leaders with access to the Indian government. This was especially true near military cantonments in Poona, Satara and Ahmednagar. Basham relates an incident where Mahar children were not being offered equal educational opportunities.

Local caste Hindus and low-level British education officials refused the Mahar demands for Mahar boys to be integrated into classes with caste-Hindu boys. The dispute was resolved in favour of the Mahars. Basham argues that this demonstrates they were seeking not just education for their sons, although this was obviously important, but also an improvement in their social status.

The fact that many of these parents were retired officers, and therefore could legitimately make a claim on the attention to government officials, indicates the value of military service in this respect. Clearly, the type of access available to the soldiers, active or retired, was unavailable to most Untouchables All the benefits the Mahars received were the result of their ability to develop a link with the British. This helped them overcome the obstacles erected by the Hindu social system. Zelliot observes:

- It was their entry into the British army which proved significant for the subsequent history of the Mahar movement. It is important to gauge this significance. It consists not in any automatic elevation in the social hierarchy through military service, which indeed is ruled out in a hierarchical system governed by considerations of ascriptive status and ritual purity. It rather consists in the fact that military service at such an early date exposed them to British institutions much before the dissemination of western culture took place on a large scale.

Such an exposure socialized them sufficiently early to the new political order so that when new opportunities and alternatives became available, they were found prepared to use them more effectively than those groups which did not have this opportunity. Following the delistment of 1893, the Mahars would need all the access and knowledge they had gained to overcome the impact of being refused service in the Army.

THE FIGHT FOR RE-ENLISTMENT

The Mahars did not give up their positions in the Army easily. The British decision of Mahar "[d]elistment in 1893 had been a severe blow to them as a community, not only threatening their economic status, but also giving official sanction to caste Hindu discrimination against them." Overcoming both of these threats was the focus of two different efforts to petition the Government of India to reconsider its decision between 1894 and the start of the first World War.

The Mahars used two different strategies to influence the government; with both they tried to regain enlistment privileges in the army and an improved social status. Zelliot maintains that these efforts "show the importance of army service to the Mahars. This was clearly the beginning of their efforts to induce government to intervene on their behalf, and their questioning of their traditional inferior status." In both instances, the movement was led by educated, former military officers. The first organized attempt was in April 1895. Some of the details of the petition drive presented by Zelliot and Basham are speculative. Basham, who has completed the most recent study, states it was originally presented to the Viceroy, but was later returned for resubmission through the Bombay Government.

It appears that the petition was submitted by Gopal Baba Walangkar, a retired military officer, on behalf of the Anarya Doshpariharak Mandali, the non-Aryan committee for the rightings of wrongs, an Untouchable organization. Dr. Ambedkar, following the death of his father, found a copy of the petition in his documents. Ambedkar "believed that his father had obtained the assistance of Justice M. B. Ranade in preparing the petition."

The petition compares Mahar actions to those of the higher castes and requests reinstatement in the military. The petition's pleas were simple. The Mahars believed that, in 1859, the Government had declared that the castes who fought loyally for the British were to be given due preference for military enlistment. Therefore, they demanded:

- In view of that promise, Government should employ in civil, military and police department without any discrimination these faithful and honest persons. They should also be given education and proper opportunity for suitable posts in the department.

The case they presented for reinstatement was more complicated than their demands. Much of their argument attempts to demonstrate that their identification as Untouchables was a mistake. The 1895 petition argues that the Mahars as a group who are actually of the Kshatriya caste. This represents the Mahars attempt to change their position in the caste structure by "Sanskritization."

The petition states:

- Our ancestors were Kshatriya. In about the year 1396 there was a great famine for about 12 years which was called Durhavedi famine. That time our ancestors survived by eating whatever they could find. Therefore, they were considered low case under the Peshwa rule.

It continues by attacking the legitimacy of the higher castes. It claims, "The so called high caste and pure people's ancestors were as degraded as our people and were used to eat flesh of cow and beef. They wrote their own religious scriptures." Finally, the petition provides a "creation myth" about the high castes.

It maintains:

- The high caste people of the South are progeny of Australian Semitic Anaryas and African Negroes whereas the high caste people from North are mixture of several castes.... Several castes of foreign origin became high caste Hindus by giving up beef-eating.
- The Chitpavan Brahmins of Konkan came from the Jewish race. They fled from Africa for fear of their lives by the invaders and their ship was wrecked nearby Malabar coast. Their children and women drown and died in the sea. Those men who survived, married the native low caste women.... [W]hen they became rulers, they called themselves Brahmins.

The document's tenor shows the importance of military service to the Mahars and the use of Sanskritization tactics to show they were at least equal to the alleged high castes. This campaign was unsuccessful. The Mahars were unaware of the debate "over recruitment policy or the acceptance of Lord Roberts views on martial races" which was the prime component in the British decision.

However, Basham shows "the government of India took the petition seriously enough to request information about the Koregaon monument from the government of Bombay. Eighteen months after the initial submission of the petition, the Indian government replied that it was "unable to rescind the orders which have been issued regarding the castes to be admitted to the Bombay Army." Shortly after the turn of the century, a second attempt was organized. The second major petition was submitted to the government three times between 1904 and 1910. The document's "signatories included forty-two military pensioners" including Dr. Ambedkar's father. Basham's research found that "[s]everal of the signatories had also written letters to newspapers or had signed at least one other petition, suggesting a long-term commitment and a willingness to agitate for change." This petition had a broader base of support than the one in 1895.

This campaign was more sophisticated than the first. The spokesman, Shivram Janba Kamble, spoke English. More importantly, the petition's "appeal for consideration was not on the basis of the Mahars' having been demoted from Kshatriyahood, but on the grounds of former service, English justice and human worth." This pragmatic approach attracted greater support than the earlier petition, and used arguments that were later refined by Dr. Ambedkar. In fact, Ambedkar took over leadership of the Mahars from Kamble.

The 1910 petition was more polite and less argumentative than the 1895 petition. The document states, "We do not aspire to high political privileges and positions, since we are not educationally qualified for them, but humbly seek employment in the lowest grades of the Public Service, in the ranks of Police Sepoys and of soldiers in the Indian Army."

It continued:

- We are making no new demands; we do not claim employment in services in which we have not been engaged before. Indeed, some few of our people do still hold positions in the Police Force, and have acquitted themselves most honourably. So also have our people been employed in the Indian Army from the very commencement of the British Raj in our country, and they have risen to the highest positions by their valour and good conduct.

Despite the reasoned arguments, this petition demands, like the first, were denied. The manpower demands of World War I had a greater effect, and beginning in 1914 Mahars, again, were recruited into the Army and given their own Regiment, the 111 Mahars. The Regiment's three battalions "were formed the towards the end of the war, but they did not see action and their martial qualities were untested." Shortly after the war, the Regiment was disbanded by the British "on the excuse of the economy." More important, however, is that the petition drives provided an organization for Dr. Ambedkar to use after the war to improve the social status of Untouchables. Basham correctly concludes:

- Military service had been a significant factor for the Mahars in two respects. Education and skills acquired through military service created a class of community leaders, and the wish to retain the social and economic benefits derived from military service was a powerful incentive to organize behind these leaders and work for a common goal. A high level of organization and political activity in the Mahar community by the 1940s was therefore at least in part a consequence of their military past.

The long association with the military gave Mahars an issue to organize around and the movement then worked to achieve more substantial achievements than just military service.

NOW WE CAN SAY

The 120 years of service in the British military gave the Mahars excellent skills.

Basham concludes:

- Mahar soldiers were able to establish a link with the most powerful institution in India—the British Raj—and in some instances to use that link to bypass local authorities. Military service was also a way to sever the ties of village customary law which maintained the inferior status of the Mahars. Other forms of employment could take the Mahar out of the village, but none offered long-term financial security in the form of pensions.

This case study shows how military service has assisted the Mahars to fight the stigma of untouchability. Their positive experiences fighting with Shivaji encouraged them to seek similar opportunities from the British. It is clear, that in their service they received their most tangible benefits. Before delistment, Mahars in the Bombay Army received a steady wage, housing, and education. With this, many were able to retire with a pension, which, often, eliminated the need to return to the traditional Mahar occupations following their military service. These obvious benefits were eliminated following the 1893 decision. However, military service still influenced Mahar life following delistment.

As Basham argues:

- If the army system of education had produced no effects for the Mahars other than to provide an appropriate environment for Ambedkar's early life this in itself would be a significant impact on the Mahar community.

Furthermore, the petition drives provided political organizations to press for overcoming the stigma of Untouchability. There were other benefits that were accrued, even if their requests for reinstatement were refused until the beginning of the war. Kamble's work in Poona that formed the base for Ambedkar's later political movements is the best example of this. Therefore, even after military service was taken away from the Mahars, the traditions and accrued benefits continued to be an advantage to this Untouchable community.

UNDERSTAND BAHUJAN PHILOSOPHY INSTEAD OF PROLETYSING

INDIAN HISTORY

This is in response to letter from Dr. Choudhrie in DV of Sept. 1-15. I am glad to know that he is trying to study Ancient Indian History. Not only it is illuminating, but it throws ample light on the happenings of today. One finds that from times immemorial, the struggle between the so called upper caste savarnas on one side and the rest of population on other side is going on. It had assumed different names, shapes and forms during the course of different periods of history, and the history of India is nothing but the history of conflict between these two ideologies, as is well demonstrated by Dr. Ambedkar. The present name for this is bahujan-vad and bahujan-virodh-vad. The present day protagonists of these are Phuley, Shahu and Ambedkar on one side and Tilak, Gandhi and Golwalkar on the other. All the leaders of christians and muslims need to understand this point and explain it to the gullible ignorant and illiterate christian and muslim masses, instead of thinking in lines of proletising Dalits. These are the only two ideologies in present day India, and sooner the people understand this, earlier they will be freed from their slavery.

UNCHRISTIAN SIDE OF THE INDIAN CHURCH

In his rejoinder to Dr. Chaudhrie's letter, VTR has very aptly described the situation. If I remember it correctly, he had commented that the missionaries are educating the children of oppressors, who tomorrow will come to power and see that these very schools be closed.

It is like feeding milk to the serpents' offsprings. He had also suggested that at least 50% of seats in all christian convents must be given only to SCs and STs at no charge, and the deficit be made good by charging double fees from the children of oppressors.

AMBEDKAR'S ADVICE TO CHRISTIANS

I like to make all conversant with one of the speeches of Dr. Ambedkar, during the period of active consideration of choice of religion to adopt. May be, this might clear doubts, if any. The speech delivered to Indian Christians of Sholapur. Published in 'Janata' of 5.2.1938, reproduced from 'Dnyanodaya' "From the available religions and personalities in the world, I consider only two - Buddha and Christ for conversion. We want a religion for me and my followers which will teach equality freedom among men, and how man must behave with men and God, how child should behave with father etc. "Missionaries feel they have done their duty when they convert an untouchable to Christianity. They do not look after their political rights. I find this is a big fault in Christians. Because they have not entered into politics up till now. It is difficult for any institution to survive without political support. We, Untouchables, though are ignorant and illiterate, we are in movement. That is why we have 15 seats in the Legislative Assembly. Students are getting scholarships, there are government hostels. Such is not the case of Christian students. If an untouchable student getting scholarship get converted, his scholarship is stopped though his financial status remains same. If you were in politics, things would have been opposed.

"Your society is educated. Hundreds of boys and girls are matric. These people have not agitated against this injustice unlike the uneducated untouchables. If any girl becomes a nurse or any boy becomes a teacher they are involved in their own affairs, they do not get involved in public affairs. Even clerks and officers are busy in their work, he ignores the social injustice. Your society is so much educated, how many are District judges or magistrates? I tell you, this is because of your neglect towards politics, because there in nobody to talk of and fight for your rights...."

BSP AND KANSHIRAM

To relieve the humanity from suffering, in India, the remedy is to develop the spirit of Bahujan Samaj. We cannot progress by merely "Dalit Unity", or by only "Dalit Muslim Unity", or by only "Dalit Christian Unity", we have to build a Bahujan Samaj, which is not an easy task. One has to understand the mechanics of Bahujan Samaj. There are many misconceptions about BSP, Kanshiram and Mayavati, purposefully spread by vested interests. One has to understand Bahujan Philosophy with all its intricacies. It is pity that Dr. Choudhrie could not get time to understand BSP while he was in Punjab. I hope he will have ample opportunity to understand it in M.P, where there is remarkable influence of BSP. BSP is not merely a political party unlike many others; it is a movement. One must read Phuley, Shahu Ambedkar and follow it with reading about Kanshiram and BSP.

SOCIAL SERVICE AND SOCIAL TRANSFORMATION

This is the important point which one must understand. Medical ethics says, prevention is better than cure. Instead of curing a disease give more attention to its prevention. To mend a fracture is social service, to create environment so that fractures do not take place is social transformation.

To give vitamin pills to malnourished Adivasi children is social service, to give their parents employment so that they can buy wholesome food for their children is social transformation. To give charity to a beggar is social service, to create social atmosphere so that nobody has to beg is social change. To give rice at ₹2 per kilo when market price is ₹7/- is social service, to raise the income of the person so that he can buy the rice at market price is social change. To feed the hungry is social service, to create situation where nobody remains hungry is social change. To teach an illiterate is social service, to destroy the social structure which made him illiterate is social change.

To open a new school in thee vicinity of an illiterate poor colony of zopadpatti could be social service, to motivate the poor hungry and illiterate man to send his child to school walking five kilometres away even on an empty stomach is social transformation. To protect a weak person by giving him weapons is social service, to make him strong enough to let him manufacture and use his own weapons is social change. To teach an egalitarian prayer to a school child may be social service, to dynamite the scriptures spreading inequality among human beings is a social change.

To assure protection to scared minorities may be social justice, to give them power so that they can defend themselves is social transformation. I have great respect for missionaries who did a tremendous amount of good work. If there were no missionaries, there would have been no Phuley, no Shahu and no Ambedkar, let alone Kanshiram and Mayawati. In my humble opinion, missionaries in India are doing social service, and are the very best at that. But still it is not social transformation. I think here lies the importance of BSP, which is not a political party alone but a movement which stands for not social service or social justice alone but for social transformation and economic emancipation.

THE NATURE OF DALIT MUSLIM UNITY

This is in response to substance by Adv. Md. Karim. It was a great misfortune that Dr. Ambedkar and Br. Jinnah could not work together, Adv. Karim says. He says Azad was a stooge. He says the anti Muslim activities are a symptoms and not a disease. He says Muslims are not a minority. He believes that population of Muslims could be more than presumed 15 per cent. He also quotes authorities to show that Islam is an egalitarian religion.

All this need not refuted and any Bahujan can agree with all these points. He avers that Muslim masses in India are in a need of allies to fight the existing system under the guidance of Islam He advises his Muslim brothers to help the Dalits in all spheres, and keep good contacts for future interaction. This is quite correct. But the main point is, what kind of unity is sought for.

He says: "The future of India lies in the unity of Dalits and Muslims - not under the banner of this party or that because no party is aiming at providing an alternative to the existing social, political and economic setup but under the invigourating and revolutionary message of Islam..." Why no political party is thought to be neccesary? Is it an invitation for the Bahujans to adopt Islam?

Is it a proletising work? If it is, well and good; nothing wrong in that; only that perhaps DV is not a forum for it. Our experience of mixing religion with politics is always counter productive. The combination does neither promote the religion nor the politics. The political meetings of RPI used to start with Buddhist prayers, the non Buddhists in the party, gradually, faded away.

The religious sermons to Budhists used to end with request for support to RPI work, the non-RPI Buddhists stopped comming. I feel the two must not be combined, the religion and politics. I hope Adv. Karim does not wish to propagate religion from political platform.

WHAT IS THE SPIRIT OF ISLAM

Do the Muslims consider Dalits as non-hindus? I think, it is the first neccesity that they must make a distinction between "Hindus" and Dalits. Dalit leaders have time and again declared that. Leaders of all Dalit parties, of all shades and colours. But Muslim leaders do not think about this. I think this is the main hurdle. No doubt, Islam is a great religion. Also it can not be gainsaid that meeting of Ambedkar and Jinnah could not bear fruits.

If the unity has to bear any fruits, today, it has got to be based on secular points. The basis has to be non-religious. It should be purely on political ideology. What is that ideology? I believe, that ideology could only be Ambedkarism. Our Muslim brothers have got to get themselves aquainted with Spirit of Ambedkarism, which is different from Spirit of Buddhism

HINDU MUSLIM RIOTS AND DALITS

A letter by Dr. Ambedkar sent from England at the time of Third Round Table Conference published in "Janata" of 24.12.1932, "When Hindus and Muslims fight among themselves, the Untouchables tend to incline towards Muslims. They feel, they would be benefitted if they develope friendship with Muslims. But Untouchables should keep in mind that it is not all that true as it appears and so they should be very careful. What I experienced at the time of Sarada Act about the Muslim policy, can not called satisfactory.

I got first severe jolt when I found that almost all the Muslims got ready to oppose the essential Act like Sarda Act along with the obsolete and puranic, fundamentalists and revivalist orthodox Hindus. And at the time of Round Table Conference, I got second experience now that their attitude can be how narrow and retrograde, like that of sanatani orthodox Hindus.

A special telegram from the Brahmin President of Varnashram Brahman Sangha was received recently by a Muslim delegate, Mr. Gazanavi. It was a message that Muslims should cooperate with orthodox Hindus in opposing the

Untouchables temple entry movement. It was also suggested that, if India gets freedom, it would be dangerous to the religion of both Hindus as well as Muslims, and so the religious Muslims should be careful about the swaraj like religious Hindus. The sanatani brahmins also requested Mr. Gaznabi to put forward the side of sanatani Hindus by the Muslim delegates in the RTC! Thus, it could be said that these arthodox brahmins have materialised the proverb that 'we are orhtodox brahmins and our relatives are muslims'. Mr. Gazanabi has published this telegram in 'Times' here. The fact, that the orthodox Bengali Muslim like Mr. Gaznabe should be entrusted the job of preserving the religion of Hindus, by the orthodox Hindus, and that he should accept it, should be borne in mind by all the reformists in India.

It is an execlent example of how an orthodox sanatani Hindu is ready to pray even an 'yavan' or a 'mlenchha' when he finds the life of his 'dharma' is in danger. And the 'dharma' of Hindus is such a provokative one, that whenever any thing new happens, or due to time any change takes place in traditional customms, they shout that, dharm' is in danger. Just like a sanatani Hindu, the Indian Muslim also is a strange object. He is averse to all social reforms. His corelegionists outside India have turned to be social revolutionaries.

A Muslim patriot like Kemal Pasha has quashed all customs and traditions which are hurdles against the progress of nation and human life. I have great respect and affinity for Kemal Pasha. But the Indian Muslims, even the patriots and nationalists like Shaukat Ali, do not like Kemal Pasha and Amanullah. Because they are reformists, and in the eyes of a Indian Muslim, reform is a sacrilege."

SUB-CASTES WITHIN THE SC/ST

This has reference to the substance on rivalry of subcastes Madigas and Malas among the SCs, and a frank debate welcomed by our editor.. Our editor has welcomed the rivalry among the subcastes in these words: "There is nothing to be ashamed of or worried about the inter-Dalit bickering. Rather this should be welcomed." This attitude is quite in keeping with his old known notion that if you could strengthen each jati and make them strong enough to demand their rightful share just as to their population from the 'evil' jati people, then the system of jatis will crash. Unfortunately I beg to defer with him. Some time back Bhoja Tarakkam from Hyderabad had argued that it is against Ambedkarite principles to think of strengthening any jatis. I fully agree and endorse his view. Dr. Ambedkar had specifically advocated that the process of abolition of castes must not start with abolition of subcastes. He averred that if the process stops at that level, as suggested, end up by strengthening the caste system. What applies to subcastes equally applies to castes within the SC/ST group. Annihilation of castes was what Dr. Ambedkar wanted.

It could only be achieved through social amalgamation by inter caste marriages, and to promote that the sanction behind the sastras must end. This was what was intended. Your contention is that, when castes, individually, become strong enough, will fight with BSO and get their rightful number of positions, and thereby reduce the power of BSO. Unfortunately this does not happen in practice. When Ambedkar said educate, agitate and organize, he meant agitate against BSO oppressors.

We took it to mean struggle amongst ourselves. We fight amongst ourselves for every thing and we beg for favours from others. We have become subservient dummy stooges of others, popularly termed 'chamchas'. Though we do not have enough strength to get elected in Parliament, we rush to the feet of men in power, and that too individually and separately, ignoring the so called unity, and beg for a berth in ministry for self and get kicked out. All our self respect vanishes that time. This is the state of affairs. How do you expect that such a people will be able to fight with the oppressors for the rights of masses, they can only beg for self prosperity.

First we have to increase our strength, then and then alone we can bargain. Power is something that can not be obtained by begging, begging only budgets petty alms. Why some castes among the SC/ST could not progress? This is the question one must answer with some clear vision and self introspection. It must be agreed that, in spite of equal opportunity given by the reservations which started at the same time for all SC/STs, the progress made by different castes among the SC/ST is not uniform. There are many reasons, which must be understood before we devise ways and means to bridge the gap of disparity among the SC/ST castes. The main point is that, Dr. Ambedkar had given a call to denounce old ways of earning a subsistence and embark on mass scale education. Some people followed his ways were Ambedkarites, and some followed Gandhi's ways and were called 'harijans'. They did not change.

Those people who abandoned their ancestral calling and gave up the dirty means of livelihood, which they were ordained to follow by the Brahmnical social order for centuries, progressed faster and those who stuck to their old professions lingered behind. Why there is dissatisfaction? The main reason is that there is supposed to be a restriction imposed by Supreme Court to limit reservations to 50 per cent.

Under what circumstances Supreme Court has given this ruling and what are legal ways to counter it, must be debated by the legal luminaries from among the bahujans and people should take steps legal or legislative to amend the constitution, if needed, to ensure that every caste must get their rightful share in running of government, *i.e.* in legislature and executive, including judiciary, as Kanshiram says "jisaki jitani sankhyaa bhaari, usaki utani bhaagidaari". I consider this is the only method, by which dissatisfaction among the various castes can be reduced. When there is enough for everybody, nobody should grumble.

There is now grumbling because share of 50 per cent people is appropriated by 15 per cent. Reservations must not be on economical grounds Shri T.P.Kamala- nathan has given, in the same issue of DV, the instances of people against caste based reservations. Everybody knows that manuvadis are behind this. Unfortunate part of this is that, even the OBC people, who are co-sufferers, are brain washed to support this argument. They are made to believe that the OBCs can't get jobs because of SC/ST reservations. They should be explained that 1. Even after half a century, SC/ST strength is not complete as per their quota, and SC/ST are not responsible for grabbing OBC's share. 2. OBC's share is grabbed by those from 15 per cent, who rightfully deserve only 15 per cent and are now holding about 70 per cent. 3. We find even today it is not very difficult for higher caste people to obtain a certificate of being SC/ST by corrupt means. When they can obtain false caste certificates, how much easy it will be to obtain a false income certificate of low income for these people, and how much corruption will be there to prevent SC/ST poor people from obtaining their rightful share. The question of enlightenment of OBCs is rather crucial.

They have been brain washed by upper castes for centuries to be against Dalits. Their ignorance is phenomenal and their prejudice is outstanding. In spite of countrywide movement by BSP for Mandal Commission, there are many among OBCs who believe that it is something which is meant for upliftment of Dalits alone and not of OBCs. If we succeed in convincing the OBCs that caste based reservations are good for them, most of bahujan's problems will end and a strong bahujan samaj will emerge.

What is our aim? Our editor is fighting for Dalit Muslim BC unity for a long time. This is same thing what Kanshiram calls bahujan samaj taking this word from old Buddhist literature. It is simple formula of 85 per cent versus 15 per cent. But what is the meaning of unity. When different groups live in physical proximity, and have desire in them to come closer and unite, the ultimate step is social unity where whole society becomes one and there is full harmony and rapport with matrimonial relationships between groups which were differing to each other and may even be antagonistic.

This is the ideal state and should be the ultimate aim. That is annihilation of castes, as Dr. Ambedkar envisaged. But it takes centuries to achieve and has to pass through various stages. Religious harmony is an earlier stage, and that also takes tremendous will power to unite and strong urge for it and is also a lengthy process. The first stage is, of course, political unity, which must be achieved before there is any kind of dialogue possible within the groups. When we talk of unity, we only mean political unity at this early stage of understanding. If we can develop among all these groups goodwill and friendship even on only political lines, it will be a great achievement.

At the movement these groups are warring groups, there is not even a dialogue, let alone sense of common belonging. On 14th October 1956, Dr. Ambedkar converted half a million Dalits to Buddhism. Next day there was a meeting of selected workers only in Hotel Shyam in Nagpur where Babasahib was staying, and I was fortunate to be present there as one of the three student workers. That was Babasahib's first speech in Hindi, I heard. He expressed his anguish for infighting among the workers and expressed his desire to launch a party which will have people from all castes.

He asked the workers to develop readiness to work in association with others. Also on his last day, he wrote some letters to leaders like Lohia and P. K. Atre etc. But we find that, the party of his vision, could not go beyond its scope of one single caste. Even whatever people from other castes were in the party, they gradually left and now it has an image of one caste party. Hopes and aspirations expressed by our saviour are shattered to make a united party. Only hope now seems to be Kanshiram, who has not only paved the way of political unity among the various groups but also started a campaign of jati todo samaj jodo and tried to assimilate people of different castes, an aim which was very dear to our beloved saviour Dr. Ambedkar.

What is to be done? One must accept that when schedules of castes and tribes were made to be incorporated in the constitution, there was a tremendous hurry. Many were left out and many were superfluous. This was known to the founding fathers of constitution, so an arrangement was made to review the schedule periodically. This should be taken in spirit of adjustment and not of antagonism. But at the same time we should prevent categorization within SC/ST. I endorse the view of D. Venkateswarlu that this will weaken the masses and perhaps that is what the BSO wants. We must not play in their hands. We get only those reservations which are pleasing to BSO For decades RPI was demanding abolition of political reservations of SC/STs. But they are forced on us. Whereas nobody demanded reservations for women, but they are granted in a hurry and when some people wished to link caste based questions with it, the bill is shifted to select committee. We, thus get what is good for them, without any consideration for what we want. For last fifteen years or so Kanshiram has brought forward the theory of 15 per cent versus 85 per cent. You yourself have sup- ported this theory many times. Now if you advocate different castes among these 85 per cent to get consolidated separately instead of together, then how are we going to struggle against the 15 per cent. After all, at this stage of our development we are not asking for social unity, we are not asking for religious unity, we are asking only for political unity.

BAHUJAN SAMAJ AND THE EUROPEAN KNOWLEDGE

India lost these Equality and fraternity also.

The learned author points out:

- " At a still later point of time, in the long meandering course of our history, the society got divided into innumerable castes and sub-castes. The evil of discrimination as high and low among men, on the basis of birth, hereditary avocations and other considerations raised its head and the pernicious practice of untouchability with all its degrading implications."

After the demise of Equality and fraternity in India it took its birth in Europe. The rights of citizens mentioned in the preamble of the Constitution are taken from the declaration of the rights of Man pronounced by the French Constituent Assembly. The concepts of three varieties of Justice, Liberty, etc were also foreign to the caste-ridden society of India. The principles of socialism were borrowed from the economic and political thoughts of the West and USSR.

So much was the debt of the nation to European knowledge, not to speak of European Science and Technology. How did India come in contact with the European Knowledge? As in other parts of the world enquiry in this part of the world was also speculative. The attempt was to explain the reasons for various occurrences in nature. It was observed that there were evil effects during solar and lunar eclipses. Why? It required an explanation. It was attributed to the emission of poison of the snakes, which was swallowing the Sun or the Moon. Similarly Aristotle wanted to explain why the fire when it was lit went up and the stones thrown up returned to the Earth. Aristotle every object had its natural resting-place and it desired to go to its resting-place, whenever it was displaced. Heaven is the resting-place of fire and therefore whenever fire was lit it went up.

The stones had the Earth as its resting-place. So whoever it is lifted returned to the earth. The intensity of the desire of an object to go back to its resting-place depended on its size. The greater is the size the stronger is its desire of an object to come to its resting-place. So bigger objects returned earlier than smaller object. Galelio wanted to know whether it was really so. He climbed Leaning Tower of Pisa and dropped from there two objects of the same material but of different size and observed whether it fell simultaneously on the ground or whether the bigger one due to its stronger desire to come to its returning place fell earlier than the other.

He found that two objects fell simultaneously on the ground disproving the Aristotelian concept. This type of activity led to the growth of a new branch of knowledge. The specialty of this type of knowledge was that it could be tested by anyone anywhere in the world and its truth could be established beyond any doubt. This knowledge attained universal acceptance. This type of experimental knowledge came to be known as science and it made rapid progress encompassing all departments of life and natural phenomena. Europe was the centre of this activity. It had its impact on India also. During the first half of nineteenth century, in the field of education, there were two schools of thought in India;

one wanted only the traditional education in Arabic. Persian and Sanskrit and the other advocated elementary education in vernacular and higher education in English. It was at that time MACAULAY reached the shore of India. It marked the turning point of India's intellectual progress. On 10th July 1833 speaking on the India Bill in the House of Commons MACAULAY said "It may be that the public mind of India may expand under our system till it has outgrown that system; that by good Government we may educate our subjects into a capacity for better Government; that having become instructed in European knowledge they may, in some future age, demand European Institutions.

Whether such a day will come, I know not. But never will I attempt to avert it. Whenever it comes, it will be the proudest day in English history." MACAULAY came to India as Law Member of the Executive Council of the Governor general of India. He in his celebrated minute dated 2-2-1835 placed before the Supreme Council strongly defended those who advocated English education. His arguments were supported by the following two illustrations.

- "The first instance is the great revival of letters among Western nations at the close of the 15th and the beginning of the 16th Century. At that time almost everything that was worth reading was contained in the writing of the ancient Greeks and Romans. Had our ancestors acted as the Committee of Public Instruction has hitherto acted; had they neglected the language of Ciero and Tacitus; had they confined their education to the old dialects of our own Island; had they printed nothing and taught nothing at Universities but the chronicles of Anglo-Saxons and romances in Norman-French, Would English have been what she is now? What Greek and Latin were to the contemporaries of More and Ascham our tongue is to the people of India."
- "Within the last hundred and twenty years, a Nation which had previously been in a state as barbarous as that in which our ancestors were before crusades,

has gradually emerged from the ignorance in which it was sunk and has taken its place among civilised communities. I speak of Russia. There is now in that country a large educated class, abounding with persons fit to serve the State in the highest functions and in no way inferior to the most accomplished men who adorn the best circles of Paris and London_ How was this change effected? Not by flattering national prejudices, not by filling the mind of the young Moscovite with old woman's stories which his rude fathers had believed—But teaching him those foreign languages in which the greatest mass of information had been laid up and then putting that information within his reach. The languages of Western Europe civilized Russia. I cannot doubt that they will do for the Hindu what they have done for the Tartar."

The Government of India accepted the view of MACAULAY and on 7th March 1835 announced that "The Great object of British Government ought to be the promotion of European Literature and Science among the Natives of India. "Prsuant to this declaration three Universities were established in 1857 one at Bombay and others at Calcutta and Madras.

Within a period of about 30 years the new system of education produced highly educated Indians and a desire for better existence generated in them. It was at that time that Allan octavian hume took initiative to establish an organisation came to be known as the Indian National Congress. Here again it was left to a European to take the lead.

He wanted the most highly educated of the nation to meet each year and chalkout programme for the purpose of securing greater freedom, more impartial administration and a larger share in the management of the country. The first session of Congress was held in Bombay in the year 1885. The Indian intellectuals started comparing the administration of India with that of England and started feeling dissatisfied with the shortcomings in Indian administration. They started demanding European Institutions culminating in a movement for independence and ultimately asked the British to QUIT INDIA. At last India became free. The proudest day of English history as Macaulay said in 1833 dawned on 18th July 1947 when the Indian Independence Act 1947 was passed by the British Parliament as follows:

- As from the fifteenth day of August, nineteen hundred and forty-seven, two independent Dominions shall be set up in India, to be known respectively as India and Pakistan,
- The said Dominions are hereafter in this Act referred as "the new Dominion", and the said fifteenth day of August is hereafter in this Act referred to be as "the appointed day".

The Indian National Congress had passed resolutions to reorganise the states on the basis of languages. But after independence the Government of free India run by the Indian National Congress did not evince much interest in the formation of linguistic states.

Therefore, late P.Sriramulu started his fast unto death demanding formation of states on the basis of languages in accordance with the resolutions that had been adopted by the Indian Congress. He was not satisfied by the oral assurances given to him and he continued his fast and sacrificed his life.

Immediately after his death the Jawaharlal Nehru Government at the centre announced the constitution of a State Re-organisation Committee for the demarcation of the States based upon various languages spoken in different parts of the territory of India and as per its report the linguistic states were formed on 1st November 1956.

The regional languages became the official languages of the respective states and it gave tremendous impetus and encouragement to the regional languages for it's all round developments. 42 long years have rolled by after the formation of linguistic states. But the Indian languages are yet to attain the standards of European Languages in so far as science and technology are concerned. There is no progress except in collaborating with European countries. The question therefore is whether it is time to discontinue the education in European literature, science and technology, which brought about so much of revolutionary changes in all departments of Indian life. No doubt for administrative expediency the states have been reorganised and linguistic states has been formed.

Does it mean that thereafter all educations must be only in regional languages? Will it elevate the knowledge of the people to the international standard or will it draw them back to pre-MACULAY period? The Bahujan samaj has a great stake in this matter. The European educated Upper Castes led the Independence Movement and secured freedom from the yokes of the British.

It was the European education that helped them to achieve it. What about the Bahujan Samaj, which is still suffering under the iron yokes of the Upper Castes? They too will require European education to free themselves from the yokes and shackles of those who enjoy freedom today so that they may also live human beings with dignity and self-respect. Every year there should be a meeting of highly educated intellectuals belonging to the deprived and neglected parts of the people as what the Indian National Congress was doing before independence.

These meetings should consider how to shape the destiny of their people, how to alleviate their sufferings and how to take them to a prosperous new life. There should be a Second Independence Movement for the purpose and it should be the responsibility of the highly educated intellectuals of these communities to lead such a movement.

SOCIAL STATUS QUO

In June this year, a Dalit panchayat chief, Adiamma was removed from her office in Karnataka. Her only crime was that she continued with her toilet cleaning job even after becoming president of the panchayat. A few years back a Dalit youth was forced to swallow human excreta in a Karnataka village. Similarly, in southern Tamil Nadu, a Dalit MLA was shoed away, abused and humiliated publicly, when he visited his constituency, simply because he was a Dalit and yet he had audacity to visit his constituency and hear people s grievances. In most parts of rural Andhra Pradesh, Tamil Nadu, and Karnataka, hotel/tea shops maintain two-glass system one for Dalits and other for non-Dalits. In all the three States, practice of untouchability is rampant in its crudest form, uncomparable to rest of the India.

The pattern of violence in this part of India contains medieval era characteristics, and is comparable only to the pattern of violence in western UP, Haryana and parts of Rajasthan bordering UP. A few years back, in district Mathura of UP, a Dalit youth and Jat girl were hanged from a banyan tree. This gory crime occurred in day time, witnessed by some 20,000 people.

Their only crime was to enter in a wedlock, defying the caste norm. About an year back, Gujjars of district Dholpur, Rajasthan caught hold of a Dalit youth, punctured his nose, and put a thin rope, meant for stitching jute bags, through it. The bleeding victim was paraded in the village streets. The victim, Rameshwar Jatav ran a small grocery shop, and had demanded Rs 50 from Kamlesh Gujjar, who had bought items on credit.

There is no dearth of such incidents to show the point. Every year, during the marriage season, we come across news items how a Dalit bridegroom was attacked for riding a mare. Also, the Dalit panchayat chief elected from reserved seats in this region, face similar social handicaps as witnessed in the southern States. What is common to both the regions? Climate, cropping pattern, language, dress and food-habits are all radically different.

It should have been only natural that the pattern of violence in both the regions was either radically different from each other, or similar to the pattern as witnessed at all-India level. Contrary to that, both the regions have a distinctly similar pattern of violence, distinctly dissimilar to the rest of India. Why? If there is any commonality in the two regions in question, distinct from the rest of India, it is the social composition of the ruling castes. In both the regions, Brahmins have a thin presence, and Kshatriyas are virtually non-existent. Traditionally, the upper Shudras have owned agrarian assets, but were subjected to politico-cultural dominance of Brahmins. In post-Independence period, slowly but steadily, they consolidated their political power as well, replacing Brahmins decisively. Despite that, at cultural level, their dominance lacked socio-cultural legitimacy, neither Brahmins and nor Dalits, for their own different reasons, accepted them as the ruling castes. Traumatised by this unique varnal-caste logic of power and legitimacy, the upper Shudras tended to invoke fundamentals of the Chaturvarna value system, as it existed earlier.

Since a social order of the medieval era cannot be enforced today, it only adds to frustration. In order to gain an upper varna-like dominance, violence is the most reliable and the final tool that the upper Shudras know. In both the regions in question, there exists a parallel system of governance, where regulatory authority of the modern State is subjected to the antiquated laws of Chaturvarna order.

If in a couple of decades, migration of upper Varna population from rural India to urban India is accomplished, and the upper Shudras take full control of rural India, the Italian fascists, in their graves may feel ashamed of being amateurs. The Dalits and the artisan OBCs, who together constitute about 57 per cent of India's total population, and who are the real proletariat, have a tough task at this juncture of history. While the struggle for a democratic social order has to fight the upper Shudras in rural India, it has to oppose the upper Varnas in urban India. As if that is not enough, its also has to fight the intellectual hegemony of both the ruling social blocks.

And the progressives expect the people to believe in the following:

- That it is not the social conflict or varna/caste dominance which is the fundamental crisis of Indian society, but the religious conflict;
- That the varnashram system is not a social order, but a religious system called Hinduism, and a party

like the BJP, by invoking Hindus religious passion, is planning to install communal fascism, which we must prevent by bringing the Congress back to power;

- That an upper varna party like the BJP will use violence as the political weapon to suppress opposition, and the upper Shudras parties, will use democratic methods to deal with opponents and;
- That fascism as a political doctrine, as it evolved in Italy, can be more atrocious, more violent, more vicious than the ideology of the varnashram social order, and therefore we must all adopt a new phrase of fascism to define the anti-democracy doctrine. The intelligentsia of the country must understand that this is not the closing years of 18th century when a Shankaracharya would come and redefine charging elephant as mithya, and the people of India will lap it as reality. Much changes have occurred during past over one millennium. There is Amedkarism also for the Dalits to shape a vision. When Dr BR Ambedkar was raising the caste question, he was being told that Independence of the country was more important than the social question, and once freedom was accomplished, the caste question would be addressed. When Independence was achieved, Dr Ambedkar joined the Nehru Cabinet with the hope that the caste question will be addressed then. But he was told then that national reconstruction was more important, and once this was achieved, the resolution of caste question would be accompanied.

More than five decades have passed since then, but the varna/caste dominance remains. Once again, when the question of social transformation is being raised, people are being told that they must join secular brigade first to defeat communal fascism ; probably they mean that the social questions can be tackled later. This is unacceptable. One cannot fight something which does not exist. The varnal-caste conflict is the fundamental question of India, and the agenda of communal fascism is only a mischievous construct, scripted only to retain the varnal-caste hegemony, and to ensure the social status quo.

SUB-CASTES AMONG DALITS

INHUMAN QUALITIES OF HINDUISM

Graded inequality, Ban on inter dining, forced endogamy, polluting touch, and restriction on occupation are enumerated as evils of Hindu caste system, and it is claimed that these are absent in castes of SCs, STs and BCs. Dr. Ambedkar's theory of "Genesis of Castes" is quoted to support this view. Bojja Tharakam has dealt with this at length.

Let his 'tributes to DV' be construed as a courtesy and not as change of his views. In any case, I feel, to concentrate on genesis of caste, is to divert our attention to a wrong direction. The main question is whether the castes among avarnas and savarnas, today, belong to different categories. Unfortunately, the features are seen also in avarna castes. Avarna castes are no less dangerous to society than savarna castes. And Ambedkar's Annihilation of Castes applies equally to both.

KANSHIRAM'S WORK

The rosy picture painted by the editor about chamars of UP is, I am afraid, not all that true. Whatever is achieved politically is not because of strengthening of chamar jati, but due to cooperation of all the various small castes. You only have to see the caste structure of seats of MPs contested by Kanshiram during last Loksabha elections, or for that matter even in recent Vidhansabha elections. Kanshiram and Mayavati have not tried to strengthen only chamar caste, as is presumed by our editor.

They have asked to strengthen all bahujans to come together and work for common good of all bahujans including dalits. They never worked for "separate but equal" castes. Neither Dr. Ambedkar, nor Shahu, nor Phuley worked on the lines mentioned by our editor. They always worked to bring all together, demolishing walls among the castes, never

ever, they advocated salvation of any individual caste or that of an individual person within a caste.

WHAT IS KANSHIRAM'S 'JATI TODO SAMAJ JODO'

Dr. Ambedkar confirmed in 'Annihilation of Castes', that the sanction behind the sastras must end. He had given special emphasis on the 'Manu' a smriti said to be written by a brahmin pundit Sumati Bhargava at the time of counter-revolution started by Pushyamitra Shunga about 185 BC. This is the main book, Dr. Ambedkar attacked. It must be understood that though it is said to be religious scripture, Dr. Ambedkar considered it to be a political book, rather a law book, or you may call it the Constitution of Ancient and Medieval slave India.

Only in Ambedkar's India a new Constitution is provided to this country, and that too not entirely to the satisfaction of its maker. So the fundamental way is to make the bahujan samaj understand that they are not Hindus and hence they must stop considering themselves as Hindus. They shall not follow the tenets of Manu smriti. This is happening gradually, You find that the Adivasis, though they are being coerced by the manuvadis into believing that they must follow Hindu gods and Hindu religious worship etc, are talking freely of Ambedkarism and are turning gradually away from BSO. This process is the process of 'Samaj jodo'.

This can be attributed to the work of Kanshiram in post Ambedkar era. Again I have to make it clear that at this stage, without jeopardizing stand for religious and social unity, we can only strive for political unity; the religious and social unity will have to wait. I feel, our editor, also means to achieve only political unity at this time, when he says, "What we need is not the 'unity' that destroys any identity, but an understanding and harmony which would help maintain and foster such identities to fight the oppressor."

DALIT UNITY IS NOT ENOUGH

Without in any way denigrating the efforts of those who are striving for Dalit Unity, I feel, even if all the Dalits of

India, of all castes, shades and colours, unite, they cannot achieve any power without the help of other oppressed castes, as they are only about 16% or so. And if there is no power, caravan of Ambedkar will be on retrograde journey. Many non-dalit castes are realizing the mischief done by Caste system, they are having dialogue with Dalits and uniting with them, as is seen in North Indian states. To think that those who talk of 'Unity' belong to a 'dominant caste' and so have an unfair vested interest in 'unity', will rather be an injustice to their efforts. The dominance they achieved is not the cause of their 'Unity talks', but it is the result of it. Before Phuley, Shahu and Ambedkar thought of Unity, the condition of all dalit castes was more or less same, none was dominant and all were subservient to BSO.

SHOULD WE NOT DESTROY OUR IDENTITY?

Are various leaders ready to give up their identity on argument that Dalit liberation must get priority over all other demands? One does not have to give up ones identity, if we are talking at this stage of only political unity. But if we unite only politically at this stage, a time will come, when we have to unite religiously and socially also. At that time, I would like to ask these leaders, "Can they afford not to dissolve their identities?" If they did, their castes would be wiped out by the BSO. One has only to see the way these sub-castes are fighting among themselves just for crumbs, they have forgotten that their real enemy, BSO, is safe and secure in its own citadel. Even at this stage, infighting among the sub-castes is counter productive and injurious to the interest of their own caste. It is the leaders of BSO, who make them fight by showing a carrot to the stooges. It is a post Poona pact situation of proliferating chamachas, big and small. The members of Ambedkarite public have by now acquired enough knowledge and experience to identify these stooges and keep away from them. If some one likes to remind the people of this situation, let him not be labeled as selfish and his warnings condemned as being of "educated- meaning brain washed", person of a 'dominant' caste.

7

Ambedkar and Dalit Education

INTRODUCTION AND PURPOSE STATEMENT

From the moment a Hindu child is born in India, his or her opportunities for social and religious freedom are shaped through the influence of the caste system despite laws passed 50 years ago to abolish such discriminatory practices. Many children at the bottom of this caste system face a future of poverty, unemployment, illiteracy, abuse, sickness, and for girls, even rape and prostitution. Stemming from its 3000-year-old origins, the caste system is one of the world's longest surviving forms of social stratification.

People are divided by birth just as to one of four main castes, with yet another estimated 200 million categorized beneath this caste system. Many in society consider these people to be unclean and unworthy of basic human rights and label them "The Untouchables" or Dalits. In 1955, the Indian Parliament passed the Untouchability Offences Act, making the practice of castes illegal, however, it may take generations to remove the stigma and change the views and traditions of an entire society.

This lack of social justice for many, coupled with the desire to promote fair and equal treatment of the people within a country that is quickly gaining influence in the global market and economy, has made this topic one of extreme interest. Although many of these longstanding traditions continue to hold fast, India has also experienced significant changes during the last several decades. With the advancement of technology, some researchers no longer consider India to be classified as a developing country, but as a newly industrialized country. This classification includes several nations, such as Mexico and Thailand, with economies more advanced and developed than those in the developing world, yet without the full indicators that would classify it as a developed country.

With the rapid increase of major global corporations choosing to outsource large portions of high technology jobs to India, the need for quality English medium education is vital if the country intends to continue to compete in that particular market.

Yet India continues to struggle with the needs of its individuals, especially in rural areas, with limitations that inhibit the ability to make the desired changes in a timely manner. Not only has the current government been unable to increase the number of schools and teachers needed to rectify the situation, but society itself has been resistant in some areas to the change of the social order embedded in the caste system. In an effort to affect change in a social structure that consists of an interdependent set of roles and norms, Dalit leaders have joined forces to demand what they refer to as a holistic reformation for their own people.

They describe this as a concern for the whole individual's physical, mental, emotional and spiritual development through education, economic support, health aid, and legal advocacy. By accepting the outside resources of International Non-Governmental Organizations, they feel they can make the changes necessary to reduce the educational and socioeconomic gap between the castes.

The Dalit Empowerment International, a Non-Government Organization based in the United States, formed in 2002 in response to this corporate uprising of the Dalit people. The Dalit leaders at that time challenged the organization with a twofold request: to offer their children an English medium education, and to include Christian principles in the hope of transforming their worldview to one based on human dignity and self-worth, in an effort to create a new future. Working together with the already established

All India Christian Council and other partners, the DEI uses its resources from the United States, Canada and the United Kingdom, to educate the western world about the situation of the Dalits and to gather financial and human resources to support ongoing work in India.

The AICC is a coalition of over 3,000 Indian organizations and federations and proactively protects the interests of Christians, Muslims, Dalits, Tribals and Backward communities. Also, by joining together with AICC as well as another national overhead organization with four decades of educational experience, they feel they can use the expertise and experience to make a significant impact. Having volunteered with several non-profit and faith-based organizations, studying education and its societal role around the world has become an area of extreme interest for me. I chose to study the field of international comparative education in order to examine the effectiveness of such programmes in diverse cultural contexts.

Having met the president of the DEI at a symposium in the United States, I was intrigued by the overall approach and methods of their model. The organization situates the educational component within a framework of three other elements, human rights advocacy, health and medical needs, and economic development. I wanted to study in depth the effectiveness of this approach, and specifically this programme, and its religious implications within the established caste system. A substantial amount of research has been done to define quality education to confirm the educational inequities within the caste system and to acknowledge the addition of many INGOs in the global effort to create access to quality education for all.

However, little research examines the effectiveness of faith-based INGOs and their impact on an educational situation that is affected by another religious system. This study will add to the current literature by providing an evaluative look at one particular programme, which can add to our understanding of how such educational faith-based programmes could aid disadvantaged and stigmatized groups.

In order to gain insight into the strategies of this organization, I used qualitative research methods including ethnographic evaluative techniques to conduct a formative programme evaluation. A programme evaluation of this sort seeks to appraise the quality of the education and the achievement of the stated goals, which is not only useful to the DEI programme administrators, but to other programmes as well. The purpose of a formative evaluation is to examine each of the components of a programme in such a way that specific changes could be made to enhance the programme, not to judge the overall worth or value of the programme.

My role as an evaluator is to present the specific findings to the leaders of the organization such that the appropriate stakeholders and decision makers can use it to guide future implementation.

Using the following questions, I evaluated four out of the DEI's 62 schools:

- How does this education programme plan to improve the future quality of life for Dalits?
- Does the DEI programme meet its proposed goals?
- What further areas of research will address the long term societal change that will be necessary for this programme and others to be effective?

To be as objective in my evaluation as possible, given the timeframe, resources and the fact that I would be the only evaluator, I used methodological triangulation by interviewing administrators, teachers and students, reviewing the program's literature and observing in the classroom. This process allowed me to compare the goals with the actual implementation practices in order to examine effectiveness of the programme in the schools observed.

This study focuses on both the practical application and logistics of this education as well as the religious aspect. Introducing educational practices which promote religious choice and enhance India's efforts towards a worldview of human dignity may be of key importance in providing information for future aid in the urgent educational needs within India today. The following parts present the research and the findings. To begin with, the background surrounding the disparity in education for the Dalit child, as well as the governmental policy, anti-conversion laws, and the specific goals of the DEI are described. Next, a series of questions that guided the research are discussed. Following this is a review of current literature on subjects that formed the foundation for this evaluation.

This includes topics such as the inequities in education, NGO involvement, the use of English medium, the future implications of education for the Dalits, the paucity of similar studies evaluating other programmes, and finally educational programme evaluation theories. This is followed by a detailed explanation of the data collection and methods that were used to gather the information to evaluate the programme. The findings are then analysed and the results of the evaluation are discussed. In the conclusion, the findings are summarized such that programme developers can use this material in the future to benefit the programme, as well as to inform readers of the issues and future implications of this research.

BACKGROUND

UNDERSTANDING CASTES

The plight of the Dalits must be understood, in order to have the cultural sensitivity needed to bring in an outside organization and use the resources effectively. The goal of closing the gap in education, so entrenched in thousands of years of religious or cultural practices will require time and skill, and much of it will have to do with teaching from a platform of education based on human rights. As I began this study, it quickly became obvious that I could not ignore the religious element of the education, as it is so enmeshed in the cultural differences and discriminatory practices which lead to such a gap in achievement and attainment in the first place. As one director in India said:

- In the United States, you had discrimination between blacks and whites, and it was a social justice issue, which can be changed by laws over time. People were free to choose to be Christians, but were discriminated against because of their colour. In India, though, it is far deeper. It is a religious issue, if people remain Hindu, they are discriminated against, if they convert, they are fined and even persecuted. To try to change the discrimination, one must face the religious issue of caste.

It is historically understood that Hinduism was first established by an amalgamation of three different religious sects, Arayanism, Dravidianism and Animism and the four caste levels were a method of establishing social order, whereby each person had an occupational function. Traditionally, for example, the top level, the Brahmins, were considered the highest level and held the positions of priests and teachers. The next group included the Kshatriyas, who held positions as the warriors and royalty.

Then, the Vaisyas were given positions as moneylenders and traders. Finally, considered the lowest of the four levels, the Sudras carried out the menial jobs in society. The Dalits, or untouchables, or ati-Sudras were actually considered beneath all of these levels, performing the jobs that other members of society would not. To be touched or even crossed by the shadow of a Dalit made any other caste member unclean and ritualistic cleansing was required.

Though much of this structure has changed over time, as governmental order and economic models changed, the concept of social stratification has remained, in some areas more so than others. Through several grass roots efforts to empower individuals, the Dalits are now seeking societal change. The DEI, as one of these efforts, feels that by eliminating discriminatory practices in the classroom, and changing the beliefs within the family and the community, there can eventually be actual change at the government and societal level. From their literature, they intend to be involved at all of these levels:

- Serving as an international advocate for Dalit rights is the heartbeat of the Dalit Empowerment International. Beginning with the United States government in Washington DC, DEI seeks to bring an end to caste-based discrimination and the resulting oppression the Dalit community experiences. DEI also represents Dalits internationally in the United Nations and at major conferences on human rights and religious liberties. Additionally, DEI seeks funding to underwrite legal fees for Dalits actively pursuing political and social change through the Indian legal system and all necessary constitutional means.

Therefore, educational practices can become a crucial part in this path towards change.

GOVERNMENTAL VIEWS

The people of India respect Gandhi as the founding father of the modern Indian nation. However, there is controversy as to his approach to try to abolish the caste system. Some feel that he merely tried to eradicate the practice of untouchability but did not do enough to touch the foundations of the stratification of caste. He believed that "caste as it exists today is no doubt a travesty of the original fourfold division which only defined men's different calling". Gandhi attempted to teach by example that doing the menial labour of a Dalit should be considered as honourable as any other trade.

It was actually Dr. Bhim Rao Babasaheb Ambedkar, a former Dalit, who founded the Indian Constitution in 1949 and attempted to abolish the foundation of the caste system itself in an effort to bring about the commitments made in the Constitution to promote equality. Despite the strong beginnings, Dr. Ambedkar expressed his concerns that such an undertaking may seem impossible without a change in the thinking established by caste when he stated:

- There is no doubt; in my opinion, that unless you change your social order you can achieve little by way of progress. You cannot mobilize the community either for defence or for offence. You cannot build anything on the foundations of caste.

> You cannot build up a nation, you cannot build up a morality. Anything that you will build on the foundations of caste will crack and will never be whole. The only question remains to be considered is ... How to abolish caste? This is the question of supreme importance

Other countries, though not affected by caste, also recognized the need to change societal norms and in 1974, UNESCO began to lay the foundations for human rights education.

By 1978, the participants in the International Congress on the Teaching of Human Rights created specific and practical definitions by stating that human rights education and teaching must aim at:

- Fostering the attitudes of tolerance, respect and solidarity inherent in human rights
- Providing knowledge about human rights, in both their national and international dimensions, and the institutions established for their implementation
- Develop the individual's awareness of the ways and means by which human rights can be translated into social and political reality at both the national and international levels.

Following these efforts more than forty years after the creation of India's constitution, the UN Decade for Human Rights Education began in 1995 and has been influential in raising global awareness of educational inequities. It will continue to take time, however, to create curriculum based on practices that will change the thinking of the individual as well as the society.

The DEI intends to support his effort. India has become a central focus as various countries attempt to eradicate discriminatory practices through these educational efforts. For example, the United States House of Representatives just passed House Concurrent Resolution 139 on July 23, 2007, that addresses the ongoing problem of untouchability in India. The resolution is the first of its kind from the United States Congress and the DEI has been involved at several levels of global awareness. Juxtaposed with this global awareness, however, is the continued effort by the Indian government to implement more anti-conversion laws in order to protect people from coercion and manipulation by what is considered any minority religion in India. Anti-conversion laws have been passed through much controversy in eight of the 28 states and the specific language states:

- No person shall convert or attempt to convert, either directly or otherwise, any person from one religion to another by use of force or by inducement or by any fraudulent means, nor shall any person abet any such conversion.

Although these protective efforts are well founded due to past practices by different religious groups pressuring people to convert by way of inducement through education or medical aid, they create a dichotomous message that goes against the Constitution's Article 25 that promises free choice:

- Freedom of conscience and free profession, practice and propagation of religion.- Subject to public order, morality and health and to the other provisions of this Part, all persons are equally entitled to freedom of conscience and the right freely to profess, practice and propagate religion.

Though it is too complex a topic to discuss in this document, as the debate over coercion and choice through new knowledge can be subjective, one must be aware of the conflict in attempting to use any other religious educational foundation within various states in India.

GOALS OF DALIT EMPOWERMENT INTERNATIONAL

From the literature established by the DEI and through interviews with individuals involved in the education, it is clear that their goal is to accomplish each of the human rights agendas by including the egalitarian practices of Christianity as they build their curriculum. With this in mind, this study will attempt to compare the following mission statement and all of its underlying elements with the actual practices. Their holistic efforts focus on four main areas.

- Education through English-based curriculum with trained national teachers
- Medical resources of vaccinations, healthcare, and medical interventions
- Economic Development by offering micro-loans and vocational training programmes
- Human Rights and Social Justice by serving as an international advocate for social change and new governmental policies

To incorporate each of these areas into the development of a community, the DEI establishes what it calls Community Education Centres as a central location for all four aspects of their charter. Though each of these areas is crucial to the advancement of developing societies, this document will focus specifically on the educational efforts. For the purpose of this document, the term CEC or DEI school will be interchangeable. To date, 62 CECs have been established in 13 states, serving over 10,000 students, through DEI's efforts to coordinate a global interest in the situation of the Dalit people.

The DEI provides an excellent example to use for this study, because, unlike several other faith-based organizations such as World Vision and Compassion International, the DEI focuses strictly on the needs of the Dalit people. The DEI also has many collaborative sources with churches and other organizations within India. These organizations are in agreement as to the strategic importance that an English and faith-based education brings to the Dalits, as a gateway to eradicating injustice, illiteracy and overcoming poverty.

They have determined that some of the greatest opportunities for education and employment within India and around the world are given to those who are literate in English as well as their own state language. Also, since one of their main charters is to teach from a worldview based on human dignity and self-worth, the issue of faith is a key component in this study. Dalits are choosing to convert primarily to the egalitarian beliefs of Buddhism, Islam and Christianity as a way out of a system that still holds great power, not only in India, but in other countries as well. The regions for developing schools are selected through careful research conducted by the DEI national leaders to locate areas of Dalit majority with the greatest needs, where no other comparable facilities exist, and no other full time holistic development projects are functioning. The schooling is subsidized by the organization, but a nominal fee is charged to create a sense of ownership and accountability for the students and their families.

DEI's child sponsorship programme brings in funds from around the world to provide the uniforms, books, a meal where needed, and to cover the teacher's salaries, the cost of the facility and other administrative costs. I was told that, "Many of these children are introduced to education for the first time, and the enthusiasm spreads as they take home what they have learned and share it with their families." A statement from the literature given to me by the director explains:

- To teach a Dalit is social service, but to destroy the social structure which made him illiterate, is social transformation. To open a new school in a Dalit village is a social service, but to motivate the Dalit hungry and illiterate parent to send his child to school even if it meant less income for the household is social transformation. To provide free food to a Dalit is a social service, but to educate and empower him to earn his own food is social transformation.

This document will evaluate the DEI's approach of holistic transformation within a group of people in order to shed light on the goal of accomplishing global awareness and support for the struggle for freedom through education.

CRITICAL LITERATURE REVIEW

In order to lay the foundation that guided the planning and design of this research, the following part will review current literature on four essential subjects. First, it discusses established discrimination and inequities in education for Dalits and the need for human rights education. This is followed by studies about involvement of INGOs and their participation in education or social justice worldwide, as well as the paucity of studies evaluating similar programmes. Third, it discusses global debates over whether to teach from an English medium of instruction. Finally, it establishes the framework of educational ethnography and programme evaluation theories that were used as the foundation of this study.

DISCRIMINATORY PRACTICES AND THE NEED FOR HUMAN RIGHTS EDUCATION

Numerous studies have been done to understand the level of disparity between the treatment of the Dalits and their upper caste peers. Education inequality is merely a portion of the complex nature of what Prime Minister Singh acknowledges as "India's hidden apartheid". Despite the Constitutional Directive of universal elementary education and Education for All goals, the gap in educational access and achievement between the Dalits and the general population in India is still quite large and continues to increase, which is of great concern in the globalizing world today.

Dalits, also referred to in the Constitution as the Scheduled Castes make up approximately 16.2% of the population of India, yet only 41.5% of Dalits in rural India were considered literate compared to the national literacy rate of 64.8%. Using econometric estimates on data gathered from 16 states and 33,000 rural households, in 1765 villages, Borooah and Iyer found that Dalit enrollment was lower than for Hindus for various reasons such as income, psychological factors, and access. For Hindu boys and girls, the enrollment rates were 84% and 68% respectively, but for Dalit boys and girls it was 70% and 55%.

Parent and community attitude, as well as religion and caste, are intertwined and have much to do with a child's education. Even though states such as Kerala have been involved for years with anti-caste reform, findings show that there is still statistically significant disparity between the Scheduled Caste and Scheduled Tribe groups and all other groups, suggesting the continued existence of an elite group despite years of effort to eradicate the discrepancies. In an effort to uncover the reasons behind the continued disparities, a group of researchers began a first-ever study examining the practice of untouchability in 11 states, specifically in 565 rural villages between 2001 and 2002. Investigators conducted an 18 month survey, spending several days in each village using observations, interviews and focus groups to gather their data. Though there has been improvement over the past decades, they found that practices of untouchability and discrimination do indeed still exist, though at different levels in each state and region. For example, one third of the villages still keep separate glasses and plates for Dalits, and refuse them entry into the shops. Purchases must be made from outside, without touching or examining the merchandise.

They found that 64% are not allowed in public places of worship, and 48% are not permitted to use the village water facilities for fear of their contamination. In order to understand the level of degradation many of the Dalits still face today, it must be noted that investigators found that "in every state, despite legal bans, Dalits continue to manually remove human excreta from public and private latrines, often with their bare hands". Most often, they are required to perform tasks that relate to human waste, and death, all without pay, as an expected role in their existence. In terms of educational practices, Nambissan and Sedwell state that "the perspective within which the educational concerns of Dalit communities should be addressed must be one of social justice as Dalit communities have suffered from social discrimination and have traditionally been denied access to learning."

They contend that unless the discrimination is acknowledged, and confronted by teachers, parents, community leaders and educational institutions, the gap will continue to widen. For example, currently 38% of the village schools practiced separate eating arrangements, and 22% separate seating arrangements in the classroom. Shah found that "rural schools impress upon young minds and bodies the principles of segregation and discrimination, reproducing the hierarchies of caste and untouchability." Many feel that these practices must stop in order for the message of equality to be heard and incorporated into the thinking of the individuals. If the community, and society at large, does not change this way of thinking about Dalits and other marginalized groups, merely creating more sensitized teaching practices and more educational opportunities may not be enough. Studies show that despite the increased sense of dignity that education alone can bring, many still have a difficult time converting this cultural capital into actual long term employment due to discrimination within the job market. These studies depict a new crisis, where Dalit youth are becoming frustrated due to their lack of opportunities, even if they are educated, and parents are becoming less willing to invest in the education they thought would make a difference for their whole family. If education access does increase, yet society does not accept the change in thinking of these Dalits, then developmental initiatives simply focusing on increased formal education may not be as successful as hoped in raising the social standing of the Dalits.

Therefore, if outside organizations enter into a community, some find that it may be important that they teach not only with a cultural sensitivity, but with the goal of diffusing egalitarian thinking and practice throughout the entire community in order for long term effects to take place. Although such debate over the best approach cannot be examined fully in this document, these issues do become foundational in this programme evaluation as it examines both the implementation of the goals of the DEI schools, as well as how these schools are situated within the current efforts for societal changes.

Analysing the efforts towards creating quality education, taught with a holistic approach through a faith-based egalitarian foundation of human rights could be an important starting point as India attempts to educate the next generation.

NON-GOVERNMENTAL ORGANIZATION

As a newly industrialized country, India's government has found it difficult to keep up with the demand for quality education. Each state within India has widely disparate needs in educational funding, but for most, bringing in outside resources by working together with NGOs becomes a key factor in advancement for the people. Obtaining additional sources of financial aid, as well as creating effective ways of expending them, becomes even more critical if a society is expected to improve and develop. This especially becomes significant with the growing trend of dissatisfaction with the poor quality of education offered through the existing government schools.

Dalit parents have dreams for their children to become engineers, doctors and government officials, yet they realise that quality education is necessary to achieve these dreams. Many are turning to an alternate private schooling for their children. In this "differentiated demand" for education that is considered of "good quality" this began a mushrooming increase in private unaided schools in the past decade alone. However, quality becomes difficult to maintain here as well, as many of these private schools hire poorly trained teachers, with lower pay, creating schools for the Dalits that are of substandard nature with a poor reputation.

It is also difficult to gain official statistics on private schools in India, and the affects of NGO involvement, as many private schools are not granted official recognition by the government for a variety of reasons. Singh's initial studies show through preliminary tests of achievement, that performance of children in the PUA unrecognized schools did not differ much from the scores of children studying in the government schools.

Current research is needed to examine these trends and possible progress over time. With both international and national NGOs willing to step in to help fill this demand, evaluating specific programmes to determine the quality and type of education provided and whether it is effectively implemented is essential if funds are to be used to their fullest potential. Although there is plenty of literature discussing the need and involvement or NGOs, there is a paucity of literature studying the effectiveness of specific programmes and practices. With India's goals of Education For All, NGOs will continue to play an important role, working along with the government to come up with creative ways to motivate people towards further education, with a holistic approach, but without creating dependency, ultimately effecting a change in society.

ENGLISH MEDIUM OF INSTRUCTION

Even if funding and other resources are available, however, there is still much debate over the pedagogy and curriculum that must be chosen by the key actors. Currently, there is global discussion over whether classes should be taught in the more traditional style of rote learning and classroom order, or in the more recent trend towards child centered pedagogies, with interactive classroom involvement. Also included in this debate for India is the question of whether classes should be taught through an English medium of instruction, the native language of each state, or the national language, Hindi.

These decisions are being made on a state-by-state basis within India, which has 22 state languages, and continued controversy over whether Hindi should still be considered the national language as the Constitution allows for the use of both Hindi and English in varying circumstances. As an example of the difficulties in these decisions, the state of Kerala began to make some of these changes in style and curriculum in 1998. The state planned to adopt a new experimental approach that was designed to be "child-friendly and to deemphasize rote learning lectures in favour of guided learning and playful interaction".

This District Primary Education programme met with controversy, however, as people feared even further stratification between the Kerala students: those who would be able to afford to choose private schools, or those who would become "guinea pigs" in the government schools under this new method. Along with changes in style not English. Although the native tongue of Malayalum was already being used for instruction after a controversial decision to drop the universal English medium in 1987, it was still a difficult transition to make. Some continue to pose that teaching in the mother tongue or first language for most of the day with English being taught as a separate subject is the most effective method, as children will understand the subject matter better. Others feel that by starting English younger, the children will become more proficient and will catch up with the subject matter as needed. Although the controversy continues, it must be noted that Kerala, due to a variety of factors, does hold the highest literacy rate in the country at 90.9% compared to the national rate of 64.8%.

The dilemma in this decision is that although each state is requiring that all government schools will teach using the local language up through the 10th grade, all testing and education after that is in English. Thus, children who go to the local government schools, especially in rural areas where no English is used, are by default eliminated from attending upper education that would qualify them for the jobs being reserved for them under affirmative action laws.

Also, without quality English education, these children cannot compete for the jobs in the rapidly growing sectors of the Indian economy, such as technical support and sales for major corporations. Although it is not within the purview of this document to determine the positive and negative ramifications of these decisions, it helps to provide a foundation for the decisions that organizations such as the DEI must wrestle with in determining what they consider to be best educational practices for the Dalit children.

EDUCATIONAL ETHNOGRAPHIES AND PROGRAMME EVALUATION

In order to evaluate an educational programme, such as the DEI provides, it is important to understand first the terminology as well as the overall intent. Popham to evaluate something is to appraise its quality and ultimately, to determine its worth. One approach in educational research is to focus on quantitative measures, such as achievement, assessments, levels of attainment, and so on. Although I did query these particular areas, and future long term studies would be necessary to discern improvement and success, this study will use qualitative ethnographic methods, focusing on the purpose of the education, the effectiveness, and its position within a view towards societal change. Using ethnographic methods allows a more descriptive approach, seeking to understand actual situations in context, providing the reader with a far more "meaningful picture of educational undertakings than would be possible from a more traditional scientific paradigm".

As Cronbach so eloquently puts it, "Intensive local observation goes beyond discipline to an open-eyed, open-minded appreciation of the surprises nature deposits in the investigative net". It is understood that, with the ethnographer as the human instrument, there will be some influence by the personality and background of the ethnographer. Being able to study a situation in its natural context, and gather data from a range of sources such as observations, and conversations with key actors to gain their perspective, brings together a valuable collection of information.

This approach is usually accomplished in a less structured way, and the analysis of the data involves interpretation through descriptions and explanations, with any form of quantifiable analysis taking a supportive role. One of the differences in most ethnographic educational evaluations, is that there is less time spent on site than a typical ethnographic study because so much is already known about the expectations of an educational environment. Also, for the purpose of this study, there are a few differences between research and evaluation that require clarification.

Although both seek to gain new or additional knowledge, a researcher aims to reach a conclusion, and evaluators are more interested in affecting decisions, whether made by the evaluators themselves, or those who have requested the evaluation. Also, generalizability is a crucial difference between the two. Ideally, results from research can be generalized to fit a larger scope of similar situations that are being studied. However, educational evaluations tend to focus on a specific educational programme with no intent to generalize to others. The gathered knowledge can be useful to the stakeholders and key decision makers as they seek to improve the programme. Since DEI, working with the AICC, intends to expand these 62 schools to 1,000, placed all over India, the information gathered in this method, can be useful to a larger scope within the organizations and even other organizations evaluating similar issues in their programmes.

One difficulty in any kind of evaluation stems from determining the level of judgment the evaluative ethnographer can or should make in assessing the results of his or her study, what Scriven refers to as the recommendation problem. Theorists do not agree as to whether an evaluator should simply present the findings and leave it up to the programme administrators and decision makers to take it to the next step of modifying policy or implementing change, or whether the evaluators should be the ones to lay out a series of recommendations based on their findings.

Cronbach's approach would be that of a minimalist, holding to the first view that an evaluator should collect the facts about the programme being evaluated, but not place any sort of value on the results, leaving that to the programme administrators. Others, such as Scriven, would take it further, making actual judgments on "value, merit or worth" and using a team of experts to make specific recommendations that could be implemented. Finally, the term formative evaluation must be clarified. Once again, different theorists disagree on the role of the evaluator.

In 1967, Scriven created the terms formative and summative that are currently used today to distinguish two specific roles in educational evaluation. Formative evaluations apply to programmes that are still capable of being modified. That is, they are still malleable, and even slight modifications to different components can be made as the programme continues to be implemented. If there are some components that are considered deficient, they can be improved upon towards a better overall programme.

Summative evaluations on the other hand are generally focused on more complete and established programmes and are being assessed as to the overall worth of the programme and whether it should continue. This type of evaluation has more of a final judgment approach, versus the modification approach of formative evaluations. This concept is useful in understanding the overall intent and expectation in any particular evaluation.

Having reviewed the various approaches, I have chosen to use qualitative ethnographic methods to conduct an educational formative programme evaluation using a minimalist approach. To begin with, though I have background in education, and have studied the situation with the Dalits, I am not an expert nor am I fully knowledgeable in the cultural context.

As such, the value judgments should be made by both the national and international elected and paid officials of the programme who are held accountable to the budgetary considerations as well as overall strategy and outcomes. Also, there is not enough time in this study to delve fully into the data gathering phase in the field to make necessary recommendations.

This study can be useful however, as I am coming in with as objective an eye as possible, knowing that I am not a stakeholder, but am interested in the global efforts to affect change in a society through education. With this approach, I can collect data at the micro level and present this information to the programme developers of the DEI to discuss some of the changes that could be made, and how these changes would affect the overall programme. In summary, there has been much research on the educational gap, and discriminatory practices against the Dalits, and the need for quality education based on equality and human rights.

However, little research exists that specifically evaluates the various approaches of NGOS such that best approaches and methods can be implemented by others. Specifically, there is little research, if any, that evaluates faith-based NGOs as they work within a delicate balance between conflicting worldviews, societal norms and government policy. This document will add to the future foundation for such in depth research on various programmes that could aid other organizations in the continued quest to eradicate the gap in education for the Dalit children.

DATA AND METHODS

The purpose of this formative educational programme evaluation is to examine each element of the programme, focusing on individual aspects of the intended goals and actual implementation. Looking at these elements at each of the four individual sites allows for separate examination as well as some comparison and vision towards future implementation. Even though the time frame was limited to only ten days in Andhra Pradesh, I used qualitative methods, drawing largely from the ethnographic tradition of in-field research, gathering documentation, conducting interviews and observing the situation in context.

Ideally, I would have had access to some of the typical quantitative information such as test scores, attainment, and teachers' experience levels that can be used to support the findings. However, due to time constraints at each site, I had to limit the investigation to the self-report of the participants, combined with my own observations, understanding that much of this involves individual perceptions. As an evaluator, I will present the findings in such a way that they can be used by the programme developers for the purpose of shaping and refining the programme, as well as guiding further research.

Many of these findings will involve fiscal decisions, and strategic plans for future implementation, which are beyond the role of the evaluator in this case. The following four parts clarify the various points of how the data was collected as well as the methods used. The first part describes the preparation prior to departure which is followed by the in-field set up and constraints. The third part describes the interviews and limitations of this process, followed by an explanation of the observation methods.

PRIOR TO DEPARTURE

Several months prior to departure, in preparation to conduct this evaluation, I briefly outlined the intended purpose for my study and contacted the DEI in the United States to discuss feasibility of this type of research over a ten day period in the spring. The United States based administrators contacted the programme directors in India and gained permission for me to travel to Andhra Pradesh in March, 2007, to observe in classrooms and interview various programme participants at multiple sites.

Although the DEI has established schools in 13 states, this location was purposely selected by the DEI for its easy access to transportation and lodging as this area contains a college campus of a partner organization, as well a medical clinic. It was also centrally located to four different schools, one in an urban setting, and three others in surrounding rural villages which added to the diversity of the sample. I recognize that this is just one region and these schools may not be indicative of the overall programme, however, safety, cost and time were constraints that made some of the other schools too difficult to consider.

The DEI was supportive and eager to have this programme evaluated. Even though they clearly believe in the effectiveness of their programme, they encouraged having an outside observer review it from an academic perspective. Also, these particular schools have been established for at least three years, and they felt that they were stable enough to be implementing the original objectives, yet far enough along to look for continued improvement, creating a perfect opportunity for a formative approach. One of the constraints that I faced was the confidentiality issues that needed to be addressed before permission could be granted to conduct interviews and, more importantly, write up the findings to be available on the internet.

Along with the typical anonymity of the participants, I needed to commit to the leaders of the DEI schools in India that they would have permission to read the material before it became available to others to help avoid any risk of exposure to individuals. Although each school is recognized by the government and has permission to function in full academic capacity, families in these Dalit communities still suffer from discrimination and outright persecution from those in society who either do not want them to receive equal rights and quality education, or to be attending a school with faith-based ideology. Thus, any identifying details of the organization, leaders, students and locations had to be removed, including references to their website.

To begin the evaluation process, I reviewed the goals as stated in the DEI documentation and on their website and then formed semistructured interview questions that would allow the programme implementers and participants the opportunity to confirm effective implementation, and suggest improvement. This would also allow flexibility in the interview process to follow up on topics that the participants found important to discuss. Due to the time constraints and expense, I was not able to conduct a pilot study, so I discussed and revised the questions several times with the DEI administrators, as well as colleagues who received their prior education in India.

Both suggested adjustments to the questions that would help the participants better understand the questions without my leading them to certain answers. Next, a particular advantage in programme evaluation is for the evaluator to have background knowledge and some level of expertise in order to more accurately observe and document what is seen, as well as probe deeper through the interview process. To prepare for this, I read a collection of essays and written by the president of the organization to better understand the background and issues that the families face, as well as the overall goals of this organization, and its partnership with established organizations in India.

I watched their DVD and read newsletters, and other documentation. Reading news articles about current discriminatory practices as well as academic journal articles discussing the educational gaps faced by Dalits also helped to gain corroborative evidence of current difficulties that are not just the opinions of the DEI leaders. To gain a better understanding of India's historical context and current practices, I also read parts of the Indian Constitution, the Affirmative Action Laws and Anti-Conversion Laws. Rounding out this preparation was my own background teaching and volunteering in classrooms from kindergarten to 12th grades in the United States, observing first-hand the classroom environment and the expected ability levels of each age group. As Wolcott states, "we know the school setting so well that, unknowingly, we become our own best informants".

IN THE FIELD: INTENTIONS AND PRACTICAL CONSTRAINTS

Having prepared through readings and communication with the field, I then traveled to India to begin the interviews and observations. Originally, the DEI coordinator in India had committed to introducing me to the principals of the schools for interviews followed by a "snowball method" to select further participants. That is, the staff would ask for volunteers, and those who participated would recommend more volunteers, and so on. In order to maintain as much validity as possible, I had intended to interview both students and their parents as well.

Also, to avoid selecting only avid supporters, I intended to ask to interview people who may have some negative views about the education, teachers and school, as this could lead to clarification and a balance of perspectives. Typical of many evaluations, things did not go smoothly in the field. When I arrived in Andhra Pradesh, I found that the key actors who would be coordinating all of the interviews had not been notified of my plans, or the purpose of the study.

However, one advantage of the individual sites not being notified in advance was that it added a level of credibility to what I observed in that they did not have time to prepare or alter the situations in any way that would place them in a more favourable light. This lack of preparation, coupled with the fact that a school holiday was suddenly added to the schedule by the Ministry of Education, something that apparently happens periodically without prior notice, as well as the shift in schedules to a half day summer schedule that week, led to several changes in plans. So despite the number of days allocated for this evaluation, five days were lost due to logistical problems alone. Also, having to travel four to five hours each way to two of the schools made it such that I could only spend one or two hours at each, making it impossible to schedule meetings with the parents.

For greater validity, this study should have included several days at the same site, with the opportunity to interview parents as well as community leaders involved in establishing the programme. While waiting for the coordinators to establish plans to visit the sites, I immersed myself in the daily life of the campus, finding as many opportunities to meet with people in the community, travel in the area, experience life in India, and observe activities that would create a better cultural context for my study. I attended a college graduation which was especially interesting as many of these students had spent their internships teaching in the DEI schools and had earned their credentials with the goal of becoming full time teachers at various locations throughout India in the following year. Next, a pastor who volunteers with some of the local youth who attend the DEI schools, and one of the school managers, took me to visit an area they commonly refer to as "the slums," where a large number of Dalit families live in abject poverty. They also took me to what they call the "pipe village" where approximately 150 families live in concrete pipes joined together.

Although there was not enough time to start any interviews at this point, it gave me insight about their living conditions, and when I observed some of these children days later in their classroom, they had met me before with men they already trusted. This is extremely important in participant observer research.

INTERVIEWS

Finally, with only five days left, I was able to begin visiting the school locations and start the interviews and observations.

In order to protect the locations of each of the schools, I will identify them as School A, B, C and D. Each school has been established for a different length of time and depending on funding and site constraints, have a different number of grades from Lower Kindergarten through 8th. By the time we arrived at the rural schools A and B, there was only one hour remaining for observations before school let out at 12:30. Because of this, my original plans to interview individual teachers had to be revised to a focus group format after school hours.

For simplicity, and due to literacy and translation issues in the more remote areas, I prepared oral consent for all participants, even though all that I actually interviewed read English well. The total interviews throughout all four sites included two principals, three managers, two teacher focus groups, a 6th grade and 8th grade class focus group and finally the national administrator for the DEI schools. In India, and at these schools in particular, a manager has the role of evaluating a teacher's performance at the end of the year, and is responsible for purchasing materials, student enrollment, as well as moral training activities.

The principal is responsible for academics, government standards, time schedules, lesson plans and exams. One interesting constraint to note was that in the focus groups, each responded differently depending on whether their teacher or principal was present. For example, the eighth grade class was very formal with their teacher present. When I asked the questions, one by one, around the room, each student would stand in place and answer politely.

In some of the more subjective questions, it was difficult to know if some were simply responding to peer pressure by giving responses that others had already said or if they would have chosen the response on their own. Many times, when a student was hesitant, trying to think of an answer, others would give them suggestions. With the sixth grade class however, the teacher left me in charge and I made the mistake of trying to relax the more formal classroom standards, due to time constraints. They immediately became very animated, loud, changing seats, asking questions and so on. It took quite a while to get the class back under control, but they were candid in their responses. The teacher focus groups were at first reserved, but as I explained the purpose of the study, they became more cooperative and answered more readily, as many of them had just finished their own studies and wanted to support my research. However, when they did answer a question, the principal or manager often modified their answer, softening it, or adding to it. I was aware that I would not be able to get fully candid responses with a manager or principal present. Another reason that teachers were hesitant to open up I found, was due in part to the sensitivity of the topic of Dalit discrimination.

As an evaluator, I needed to establish a level of trust with the interviewees in order for them to be as open as possible. Though each one that I spoke with displayed a respect for my role as university researcher, I found that when I either explained my background, or that I had met the organization's president and studied the background of the Dalits, they quickly opened up with passionate enthusiasm for what they do and why. As I needed to remain as objective as possible, I did not want to disclose too much information about myself that would direct their answers, but at the same time, establishing this relaxed atmosphere allowed them to more openly discuss the children, the difficulties, or the religious element of their teaching.

Having more time to interview individuals would have allowed deeper probing of the issues resulting in more complete data. One last interview constraint is that due to schedules, many of the interviews with management had to be conducted in the car, one time with the principal himself driving through four hours in traffic that I have only experienced in India. The conversations were interspersed with horns honking continuously, cell phone call interruptions, barking dogs and shouts of children playing in the streets. The recordings were difficult to hear when I tried to transcribe the notes each night. Also, two of the interviewees said that they felt constrained being recorded, because they were self-conscious about their grammar, pronunciation and word usage, knowing that I would be quoting them in a research document. I found that they became much more relaxed, open and even fervent about their goals and implementation without the recordings. Therefore, most of the quotations are paraphrased from my notes.

OBSERVATIONS

As I did not know in advance exactly how many schools I would observe, or what the age levels and abilities would be, I did not develop a formal observational protocol with a list of specific events or behaviours that I intended to analyse. My observation methods were therefore unstructured, and because there was no way to observe the students completely unnoticed, I conducted my sessions as a participant-as-observer interacting with the children, tape recording and writing notes as often as I could using a journaling method.

Two of the schools, with a one day warning of my arrival, prepared a formal greeting with the traditional flower lei and special presentations, greeting me in the language of their original state as well as in English and Hindi. I was reminded of the complexity of the educational dilemmas in India. It is such a diverse land, of many languages and high illiteracy in many states, which gave me an understanding of the desire for many to learn English as a shared tool of communication and opportunity for future educational attainment.

As I was escorted through each classroom, from the Lower Kindergarten to their highest grade on campus, the students were excited and eager to welcome me and perform recitations, songs and ask questions. The children displayed their coursework, and their writings in all three languages, English, Telugu and Hindi. I spent approximately five to ten minutes in each room, as we had to complete the entire campus within an hour. I recorded the greetings, songs, and poetry, which were also performed in all three languages, as well as the questions of several of the children which I later used to evaluate the level of ability and pronunciation. After collecting the data, I read through the notes and listened to the recordings and coded for themes to evaluate the responses to the specific questions and to create as complete a picture as possible of the matching of goals with effective implementation. Although not all data that would be useful in a full educational evaluation could be gathered in a short timeframe under the various constraints, the data that was collected allows me to answer each of the research questions to varying degrees, depending on the location and the interview participants. Ethnographic evaluations begin with a desire to understand, with the next step being to appraise and assess what is understood, in such a way that the results can guide the decision making process of key actors.

FINDINGS AND DISCUSSION

An ethnographic formative programme evaluation differs from a strictly qualitative approach, in that my role as an evaluator is to examine the implementation of each of the stated goals of the DEI at the four sites, not to judge the overall values, assumptions or decisions in establishing these goals. Generally, a formative evaluator gathers information at each of the sites that can be used by programme staff to assess and improve their programme as necessary.

As the DEI did not request this evaluation, or guide the specific research questions, the overall value in this analysis rests in gaining a better understanding of the educational situation of the Dalits, such that future research can be pursued. In order to create a logical flow of the findings and discussion, I divide the following parts just as to the three original research questions. I then further separate the findings into the same categories of the DEI stated goals that I initially used to formulate the interview questions for the students, teachers and DEI leaders.

The reader throughout these finaings. It begins with the over arching question of how this programme is situated within India's overall plans to affect change for the future of the Dalits. This includes the holistic approach to addressing the needs within the local and the global contexts, followed by the specific topics of English medium of instruction and teaching from a human rights perspective based on a Christian worldview. Although economic development and health needs are addressed briefly in context of the holistic approach, the dashed arrows show that they will not be a main focus of this document. In the second part, based on the rest of the stated goals of the organization, each of the specific elements is examined to see how these goals are being implemented. Finally, the third question deals with future research to be addressed in the conclusion. Each of the findings is examined and discussed based on an analysis of the documentation, interviews and observations where applicable.

CONTEXT

India is a land of vast diversity and yet in that diversity, extreme disparity. As I rode through the streets I saw stores filled with exquisitely woven saris and expensive jewelry while children begged for coins at the corners. Oxcarts meandered through the streets next to expensive vehicles, and cows stood side by side with motorcycles, waiting to cross the street creating an interesting backdrop of both ancient and modern. From rural to urban and from state to state, there are marked contrasts that create a daunting task as India strives to educate an estimated 20 to 30 million children who are not attending primary school as the country presses towards the goal of education for all by 2015. In this type of evaluation, it is extremely important to understand the context in which each of the schools is situated as it becomes necessary in analysing the findings. For example, had I simply seen the children at each school location, well groomed, dressed in uniforms and speaking English, studying math and science, I would not have had any understanding of the level of accomplishment of the programme. These schools choose to compare their achievement levels to private schools in the area, whose children generally come from entirely different socioeconomic backgrounds and home environments. They explained that each of the schools has unique constraints that must be addressed as they make decisions on the best approach that will impact the community.

LIVING CONDITIONS

To begin with, one must understand the children's living conditions and the affects this can have on their education. As I walked through the narrow crowded streets of the slums, with over 150,000 people separated by just one wall from the airport runway, I could smell the open sewage draining in an infrastructure not designed to handle the amount of people living there.

The children clustered around wearing tattered and dirty clothing but with eager curiosity, smiling shyly and asking questions using gestures if I could not understand them. Most were barefoot and the smaller children wore no clothing at all, or simply a shirt. Stepping carefully around the pigs, cows, dogs and goats all rummaging through the trash heaps piled around the slum, I saw the "rag pickers," a name given to the women who sort through trash all day looking for glass or articles of clothing to sell.

The pastor and the school manager who were escorting me through the slums introduced me to a woman who sits all day, sorting this glass into piles for recycling. One of the families invited me into their home, which was approximately seven feet across, with a tiny door leading to another room. I was surprised by the shiny, modern looking shelving mounted on the wall for all of their neatly arranged dishware, pots, and utensils.

The pastor said it was not always this clean and orderly in these homes but that he works together with the school in their holistic efforts to teach families about hygiene, cleanliness and health, despite their living conditions. The other area that I visited prior to the school interviews was the area nicknamed the "pipe village" where people have been brought out of rural villages as bonded laborers for a concrete pipe manufacturing company.

Bonded labour is described as a "slave-like form of attachment to a particular employer, often the result of usurious personal loans". These people must stay and work for the company until they have paid off their debt. The company allows them to live in the discarded segments of pipe, where, for the past 30 years, they have built up a whole village, formed by connecting pieces of pipe and bricking off the ends and creating openings for doors. They cook outside while chickens and pigs roam freely in and out of the homes. I was told the villages used to have electricity that the company intended to be used for lighting only.

However, when people started using it for televisions, irons, radios and so on, the company considered that an abuse of the privilege and turned it off completely. Inside the pipes, it was dark and crowded, yet this is where the children read and do their homework by candlelight. Even within this village, however, there is a contrast in conditions. Walking through the village, I noticed that while one half was cluttered and dilapidated, the other half was very orderly, with cleanly swept dirt, and pipe homes lined up in rows, with all personal belongings neatly stored inside. When I asked the pastor about the difference, he said that it depends on which part of India the villagers come from.

He said that there are some stereotypical differences between the education level and hygiene of the northern and southern villagers that they see in the pipe village. We had invited one of the DEI teachers along, a Swedish intern who had not yet visited where the children lived. One little girl, excited to see her teacher in her village, motioned for us to follow her. She scampered ahead, and we could see through the opening of her five foot diametre pipe home, that she was quickly scooping up a piece of clothing from the floor and stuffing it into the corner of their neatly ordered space. She giggled at us and spread her arms in a gesture of welcome and pride to her home.

The rural areas face different types of difficulties. Transportation is not readily available and the children often have to walk for miles in the stifling heat. This affects attendance as they either arrive tardy, or end up not coming at all. Due to the types of jobs available in these areas, generally related to seasonal farming, children often either move to where the jobs are available for their parents, or some are needed to help with the family income. This affects the ability of the children to stay in school for a full year, as well as the ability of the parents to financially support any of the education on a month by month basis if fees are required. The managers said, however, that there are some positive factors in rural living, specifically that children are not exposed to "dangers and too much knowledge about life" that is seen in the close quarters of the slum areas, and they often have better access to food.

One village had small one or two room concrete homes built by the government placed neatly on individual lots. Walking past the open doors, I saw no furniture and some people were sleeping during the heat of the day on the concrete floors. I met several adults sitting on the floors hand rolling up to 1,000 cigarettes a day for a wage of approximately one dollar per day. The manager said that the DEI is working within these communities to set up training opportunities such as embroidery, tailoring, and computers and creating self-help groups using microenterprise concepts that establish cooperative loan efforts in small groups to begin businesses within the communities.

This holistic approach once again, aims not only to assist in the children's education, but to affect the community in which they live. These children, whether in urban or rural settings, have many obstacles to overcome in their path towards education. Whether it is their noisy or crowded study conditions, lack of parent education and support, distance of travel, limited days in attendance, lack of food and clothing, or even just the stress of everyday living due to limited access to water, electricity, and medical treatment, these conditions can have an overall affect on their achievement and attainment through the programmes offered.

Understanding how they live is necessary for me as an evaluator to fully comprehend the observations and interviews in context, but I recognize that it is crucial for the programme developers as well as they make decisions regarding how the funds are best spent, whether it be for curriculum, lunch programmes, uniforms, supplies, transportation, or after school homework assistance.

SCHOOL CONDITIONS

In the rural School A, the children actually meet in a condemned building while waiting for a new facility to be built. The fifth grade class is conducted outside under a tree as there is no room for a classroom and the children wanted to continue after fourth grade. Many of the rooms have no tables, chairs or play equipment for recess. There is no electricity at this school, and the water has to be carried 200-300 feet. There is also no phone service or e-mail access making it difficult for staff to communicate with other DEI locations. With no bus service, some of the children travel over six miles to get to school. They showed me the property for the new building, but the lack of infrastructure will make it difficult to build.

This adds to the time the children have to wait for better facilities and for additional grades to be added. The DEI brings in a medical clinic before school starts to assist with some of the basic medical needs within the village. They also had sewing classes for village women. School B is also in a rural setting with brightly painted murals of flowers on the front giving it a welcoming presence.

Some of the grades had desks and chairs while others sat on concrete floors. Many of the children either walked home or shared rides on the small autorickshaws that come by after school each day. The management would like to add more rooms in order to add grades to the school, as well as more rooms for the sewing classes that I visited for the women in the community. Several people referred to School C as their model and I could quickly see why.

It is also in a rural setting but the facility was markedly neat, well painted, with brightly coloured playground equipment and flowers landscaping the front. The children had desks and chairs and though they, too, would like to add more rooms, the facility was very well maintained. Instead of the typical hand printed postings on the other bulletin boards this school had computer printouts of calendars, rules and daily schedules. I visited the sewing and computer classes in session where both young men and women attend who have either had no formal education or were older than 10th grade so were beyond the formal school setting. School D, the one urban school that I observed, was located within a larger campus with other facilities nearby. In the classrooms where I conducted focus group interviews, they had desks and chairs and they did have some playground equipment to be shared by all classes.

These children have access to public transportation and several students have bicycles. They have plans to add two stories to this facility as they are limited by land space. With this foundation of context laid, the following parts present specific findings relating to the research questions. Throughout the rest of the findings, since each site is unique in its setting and stage of development, if a finding is specific to a school, I will report it separately, otherwise I will refer to overall findings on given topics.

DETAILED FINDINGS

We use tables to list the research question being addressed and the specific claims of the DEI, followed by a summarized list of the types of interview questions that I used to examine how the areas are being addressed. This first question helps to understand the overall goals of the DEI and their plans for societal change.

I found two specific areas that they address beyond the obvious educational components. One is the desire to teach English such that the children can gain access to higher education through the country's English medium universities, as well as increased job opportunities.

Although many countries struggle with the topic of how English should be taught, the fact remains that there is an ever increasing global market that requires English proficiency. The second desire is to teach a new sense of self-worth and equality that traditionally has been denied them. The organization feels that a significant way to change the thinking of the society is to teach through the children, their parents and community leaders that each individual has value, and that all should be given equal opportunity through values commonly established as human rights. Their intent is to use a holistic approach as they seek to change the future for this group of people. Although I will focus primarily on their approach to education as it interrelates with human rights and social justice, it became clear throughout the interviews and observations that they address more than these areas through economic development and medical aid in an attempt to change the framework in which these children learn.

Research shows that India has made inroads in the educational process, but the disparity still exists and simply offering education or even changing their way of thinking about their self-worth, will not guarantee a more prosperous future for these children. That is why the organization is eager to make changes at a societal level.

Though it is a very large undertaking and beyond the scope of this document, it needs to be acknowledged in order to understand how these particular schools fit into the overall framework This objective was expressed well in the conversations with two leaders. One asked me, "What do you believe, who influences the child's career most, the teacher or the parent."

I said, "I'd like to think the parent." He said, "Yes, for you, you would want that, but you are not in their world. For these children, if the parent is illiterate, the only goals will be to be the same as the parent – a street sweeper or a rag picker. At the CEC's we want to improve their education, career, and their future. DEI plans to use this education to improve the whole community." Another said, "Our duty is to help the deprived, they must have an education to be empowered, enlightened and equipped to face the challenging world." As a faith-based NGO, with a mission to aid this poor and oppressed people, they have chosen to use the egalitarian teaching of Christianity based on moral stories and concepts found in the Bible.

To examine whether the claims are being practiced, I asked a variety of questions of the children, teachers and administrators regarding the importance of English education, as well as how it is taught, what the children intend to do with the education, and how this will help reach that goal. Although the term "quality" is difficult to gauge without actual test scores and proficiency levels, I will address what was at least observable regarding this statement.

ENGLISH MEDIUM INSTRUCTION

As an English medium form of instruction, all subjects are conducted in English throughout the day, but they also learn Hindi and Telugu in separate language classes each day. Their level of achievement was really quite impressive considering that especially in rural areas, most have absolutely no access to English outside of school. Schools in the urban areas may hear it in the stores or on the streets and can practice what they learn, but in the rural areas, with no English spoken at home or in the community, there is no opportunity to hone the language skills.

In an effort to improve the children's abilities and to invest in the whole community, some of the schools are even beginning to add parents' language courses. Each of the principals and managers spoke English well, and I understood them easily, although it did take the first few days in India to adjust to the variety of accents, as many came from different parts of India, where their first language or dialect is specific to that state. Interacting with the teachers, I found some of the accents were a little more difficult to understand, but we adapted to each other quickly during the focus group interviews.

The children spoke eagerly with me in English so there was no need for the interpreter that was provided. In their villages or in their homes, they speak Telugu, as that is their state language in Andhra Pradesh. Most do not speak Hindi as I was told the southern states prefer not to use this for various reasons.

The children are not allowed to speak other languages at school at any time, either in class or on the playground. In the focus group interview with 6th grade students, I asked the children if there was anything they did not like about their school. One boy said that he did not like it when others broke the rules and spoke Telugu at school on the playground as he wanted to practice only English. Several children nodded in agreement. I did find that their accents were more difficult for me to understand, as mine was for them. One girl was explaining that her favourite subject was what sounded like "shasho shtudies."

When I looked puzzled, the teacher clarified by enunciating "social studies," and then I was able to understand more clearly their future pronunciations. They responded to their teachers' requests of them in English, showing recognition of her questions. Their written proficiency was noted as they enthusiastically showed me their notebooks filled with writing in all three languages, very neatly done, even in the younger grades.

As I observed in each classroom, the youngest children recited poems and sang songs for me in English but I was not able to assess how much beyond rote memorization they had learned yet. These children were in their first year of exposure, and the recitations as opposed to full conversations were typical of that level of achievement. The first grade class could recite the Psalm 23 and the Lord's Prayer which are both about 12 lines long, which for length alone, was an accomplishment for that age group.

In some classrooms, they had individual children recite greetings for me, and some classes chanted in unison, carrying the struggling students through it together. One thing I would like to have delved into further would be the records of the students' backgrounds before attending a DEI school. I would like to know if they learned English at another school before coming to these locations, especially those in higher grades, or if the school is solely responsible for their English achievement.

For example, several in the 8th grade at School D said they had received English education prior to the opening of this school, so I would like to have discussed this with the parents and the teachers, or be able to look at the records and create some analysis of number of years of education before attending these schools. Three in that class had come to this school for their first year with no prior English education. The teacher said they were doing very well and all students in that class were able to answer my questions, though sometimes it took two or three attempts. Another area of concern for the future for these schools is that some states are beginning to force the decision in favour of mother tongue education.

One CEC in another state for example has been warned that they have one year to stop teaching from an English medium or they will be "de-recognized by the government." This will prove to be very difficult for private schools who want to maintain government recognition, yet believe in their choice of English medium as their main form of instruction, rather than as a separate language course.

The national director said that a school would have to apply to the state to be given a "no objection certificate" and would be charged huge fines in order to maintain the Central Board Secondary Education standing within the federal government.

This is the higher standard curriculum and the one that the DEI schools would like to be recognized under. Without these restrictions, they can qualify to be recognized under the National Open Schools curriculum but they consider this a lower standard, and the DEI schools feel the quality would suffer under that recognition.

The leaders are concerned that if children have to go to the government schools which teach only in the local language of Telugu, with a small amount of English, then the issue of what will happen after 10th grade, when all tests are presented in English, has serious implications. The DEI recognizes the need for these children to continue into upper education, but feels that with the limitations on access to English will be a detriment to their future prospects.

Maintaining quality standards of curriculum from state to state while complying with government restrictions creates conflict for the leadership which will continue to be addressed under this disagreement regarding approach. With these concerns in mind, I wanted to understand the overall affect an English education had on the goals and dreams of the children. Although I had to resort to a focus group format, rather than a personal interview with individual children and their parents, I did have a chance to interact with two classes in a lively discussion about their future plans, favourite courses, and what they would do if they could not go to this school. Some of their responses reflected their desire for education in general and some pertained specifically to English.

One boy, who was still fairly new to the English language said, "It is good education in this school, I am become learned, studying English." When I asked what they would do if they could not go to this school, several said they would find another English school to go to, but two eighth grade girls, both wanting to become doctors said, "I don't know what I would do, my parents cannot send me anywhere else, and then I could not learn," and, "I would miss my education and my goal to become a doctor."

I visited the home of one of these girls the previous week in the pipe village, so I asked the manager more questions about them. He told me their scores are good and with sponsorship, they have every possibility of fulfilling that dream in the years ahead. Addressing the impediments to the quality of the English education, the director shared that it is difficult to find enough teachers who have excellent English abilities who are willing to live in such difficult environments. He said the teachers rate themselves on a scale of 1-10 at about a six or seven.

He said they cannot expect children to learn any higher than a six or seven if they have no higher example. When asking the teachers for what they wish they could have to improve their ability to teach, several of them asked for English tapes or CDs to play so that they and the children could hear clear pronunciation of non Indian English with its mix of accents from different dialects.

Since these rural locations make it very difficult to attract quality, well educated teachers, one of the ideas the leadership is considering is to offer opportunities for nine month internships for people from the United States, Canada or the United Kingdom to come and teach each age group every day, in order for them to hear it spoken by those whose first language is English. One of my particular areas of interest in this English education stems from my career as a database consultant for a major computer corporation based in the United States.

Currently working with their customer service department, which has outsourced all sales, technical support and customer service to various cities in India within the past three years, we recognize a huge demand for English proficiency. Customers express frustration when the accent cannot be understood, and corporations in India are struggling to find qualified employees with strong educational background and English skills.

Thus, both factors are important in the children obtaining higher education leading to openings in the global market. In this part, the interview questions relate to areas of human rights, current discrimination, issues of self-worth, and the situation within the community. Recognizing that there is a direct conflict between the two religious beliefs, I also examine how the DEI uses a Christian worldview to achieve these goals.

UNDERSTANDING THE GLOBAL EFFORTS

First, acknowledging the need to accomplish more than simply the education and change of thinking of the individuals, I needed to understand how the DEI addresses the issue from a macro level within the international efforts towards social justice and human rights. As the review of literature shows, even when the Dalit children do obtain an education, society will not necessarily allow them to fully utilize this and create change for themselves and their families.

I interviewed the social justice coordinator with the DEI to discuss their efforts to raise global awareness on these very issues. He explained that the DEI president travels extensively, along with other spokes people from India, the United States and the United Kingdom, in a concerted effort to advocate for the Dalit people. Using documentary screenings and research gathered from current sources, the DEI joins with others to present in committee meetings, hearings and briefings in several arenas such as the United States Congress, State Department and the United Nations. The recent passing of the US HCR 139 shows marked solidarity in the global efforts to eradicate continued discriminatory practices.

HUMAN RIGHTS EDUCATION USING A CHRISTIAN WORLDVIEW

Along with these efforts, many of the sources on the DEI's philosophy and work emphasize that social change comes not just from government rulings, but requires grassroots social activism as well. The sources further emphasize that there must be a change in thinking of the people in order for these new changes in societal order to take place.

Their mission statement asserts that "The DEI exists to empower the Dalits in their quest for social freedom and human dignity by networking human, financial, and informational resources." Acknowledging the disparate thinking between the two belief systems, I asked how they planned to teach their stated values, within the framework of the government restrictions and societal opposition. The DEI considers the education a secular education using a government standard curriculum, yet taught from human rights framework based on Christian ideology.

Their intention is to establish egalitarian thinking along with the moral principles that promote equality in society. The managers and director said that through songs, moral stories, and even some Bible verses, as well as the behaviour and expectations modeled by the staff, they feel they can help the children and their parents engage in a new way of thinking, promoting self-worth, fair treatment and future hope.

They have labeled this approach as "holistic transformational activities." However, in order to be careful to separate actual Christian doctrinal religious teaching, from the moral and egalitarian principles taught on a weekly basis, they said they also offer a traditional Christian "Vacation Bible School" during the week just after school lets out for the summer. This is an optional week, offered to the children and any of their friends who are interested. Parents choose whether to have their children attend with an explanation that it is not part of their educational curriculum but will be a series of children's activities based on Christian teaching.

This allows a careful division between the holistic transformational activities throughout the school year and specific religious teaching in the summer. Each of the leaders and managers I spoke with articulated specific messages that they wanted to get across to the children and families through their teaching which seemed to divide well into two main categories:

1. Each individual has value and self-worth
2. All are created equal, with equal rights as a citizen of India

I address each of these, as well as the use of a Christian worldview to accomplish each goal.

INDIVIDUAL VALUE AND SELF-WORTH

Effectively teaching and measuring the construct of "value and self-worth" is difficult but they feel that by daily reinforcement, encouragement and modeling, they can begin to affect change. To teach a sense of value, the staff said they find a variety of ways from the time children are in the LKG to encourage the development of their understanding of who they are as human beings.

For example, through songs and verses, the schools teach that God loves each child and values them, which differs, the director said, from the Hindu traditions that Dalits are considered God's waste product and therefore unworthy of the benefits that others receive. The president states in his writings that he would like for the children to at least hear that they are loved by God, which he feels brings a sense of dignity and self-worth.

It is typical of Dalit children, as with most children, to assume they might do the same job that their parents do some day. Only with Dalits, these jobs often entail the most menial and repulsive tasks imaginable in society perpetuating the concept that this is their only value to society. To combat this type of thinking, some of the schools hold activities such as a Career Day, where the children dress up in costumes that the school has for different career choices. These include nurses, doctors, policemen, engineers, musicians, judges, lawyers, athletes, and so on.

Not only do the children participate in this, but the parents are invited to the event, to encourage them to see the potential in their child with this education. I asked one of the managers if the parents are happy with the education, as I could not interview them directly. He said the parents at his school have expressed excitement over the changes they have seen in their children because the "growth and learning gives them hope." To follow up on this in my focus group sessions with the sixth and eighth grade classes, I asked them what they would like to do for a career when they finished school.

It is common for children to pick a goal that sounds glamorous or popular, but for these children, who have been impressed with the concept of taking on the least desirable jobs in society since birth, their responses indicated a different hope. The school said they work very hard to stress the options for their future, and these children reflected that in their responses.

Each selected specific career paths, with the most popular being "children's doctor," "software engineer" and "police officer." Although only one had actually worked on a computer they had definitely been exposed to this idea for a career. When I pressed them on some of their specific answers such as cardiologist, or eye doctor, they explained that each had family members who had benefited from these particular fields and they wanted to be able to help someone like that someday.

These results are important in that they seem to reflect that these children are not making any assumptions based on their parents' job choices, as none of the children interviewed had parents in any of these fields.

ALL ARE CREATED EQUAL AND HAVE RIGHTS

Promoting the second concept that all are created equal, the DEI said that the education is offered to all faiths, races, and genders with no restrictions or need to convert in order to obtain the benefits of education. For specific examples of how they use Christian ideology to show egalitarian beliefs, the staff said that they have moral classes on Fridays or Saturdays using commonly accepted books in India that teach moral values, and some simple biblical teaching throughout the week such as the verse, "All men and women are created in God's image".

The director said this differs significantly from the traditions of Hindu teaching that each of the caste levels stems from a different part of God, such as the Brahmin caste from God's head, down to the lowest caste from God's feet. The children recited these verses and poems for me, as well as songs about how "God created you and me."

In the hand-motions that accompany this song, the children pointed first to me - a white, American woman and then to themselves. The fact that they could perform these gestures as a perfectly natural act, without hesitation, was quite remarkable when one understands the cultural background.

Teachers and students must demonstrate this equality as well. They said they are very careful that no caste or discriminatory practices are shown among the staff, or in their treatment of the children. In School D for example, if children show discrimination in any way, they are made to publicly apologize and parents are told that if this continues, the child will be removed from the school. Each of the schools offers community involvement with the parents, such as parent meetings, parades in the community and even clean up days in one.

In order to teach these concepts to all, one school said that at each of the four parent meetings per year, they "remind the parents that each child is an Indian citizen and therefore entitled to all rights and privileges belonging to every member of society, that all people are created equal, and that no caste treatment is allowed." To continue this in the community, they held a Children's Day parade, where all teachers and children marched throughout the village carrying banners stating, "Drive out castism to open equality," and "Education opens the doors for future life."

Every two months, they hold an evaluation and planning meeting where they question how they are doing academically, and how well they did in the community at passing the vision on from the manager, to the teachers, to the children and to the parents.

As they teach these concepts, they said they are fully aware and respectful of the government restrictions on certain states, or even resistance within particular communities. For example, one of the main restrictions that some states face is the anti-conversion law discussed previously. Although the four schools I visited are not in one of these states, several of the other DEI schools are. Anti-conversion laws state that no one can pressure others with financial resources or gifts, or through threats of divine displeasure, in order to convince someone to convert.

They take several precautions in offering this education, such as clearly explaining to the parents that while it is a government recognized school it is based on a Christian worldview, as well as making sure that the community leaders are supportive of this and that there are no coercive practices. When I asked the managers if there are any difficulties with this method of teaching, which goes against Hindu beliefs, one school told me that some parents chose not to have their children attend because of the Christian influence.

He said this makes it difficult for the children as many of them want to come and be with the other children and learn, but the parents do not want them to be taught another religion. Another manager said that there was some difficulty when parents complained to the leader of the village about the Christian teaching.

He said the village leader did not want to upset the school, as he valued the education for the community, but he did not want to upset the parents, as they are the ones who elect him to office as leader. So he resolved it by reprimanding a local teacher at a public meeting, telling him not to teach these songs and verses. The manager asked the leader to encourage all parents to come to him directly in the future if they have any concerns, but he said that none of the parents removed their children from the school.

In their efforts to teach equality and human rights, several managers said they are aware that some of the children are too young to understand the concept of inequality. One said they all live in a Dalit community, so at a young age, they are not exposed to the idea that anyone is any different. However, by fourth and fifth grade the schools want to begin an active strategy beyond the daily teaching, that will engage them in awareness of their rights as an Indian citizen and to develop critical thinking skills.

One school said that they will be starting debate teams, where they divide up the upper grades into four groups or "houses," and assign them an "awareness topic" topic such as AIDS, equality and so on.

The school would assign teachers to help the children prepare and a judge for the event. The idea is to have schools join together for a special day, and have all children present so that they can learn from the skills practiced and topics discussed.

He said, "This way, their language will improve, their thinking will improve and they will learn to ask other people and prepare." Each of these collective practices is used to continue their efforts in "holistic transformation" throughout the communities.

By approaching it from both the global level and the classroom level, and even into the homes, they aim to affect change throughout India. In order to gain information regarding the vision for future schools as well as current statistics.

SELECTION OF SCHOOL SITES

So far, there are 62 CECs in 13 states with an average of approximately 200 students each. At the time that I started this research, there were 54 CECs with 7,000 students enrolled, and now, less than one year later there are over 10,000 students enrolled in the schools. The goal is to eventually have other organizations join through the AICC to establish 1,000 CECs nationwide. I was told that selecting the locations of the CEC's involves several steps. First, the DEI must be invited into the village.

"The overhead organization that the DEI works with is very popular," just as to one of the managers, and village leaders have heard that they are building schools to help the Dalits. If a leader expresses a desire to have a school built within the community, the DEI responds by sending a team to survey the area to determine whether it is a match for the criteria.

The village or area must show a specific need, that is, there must be a high enough concentration of Dalits, without a similar English speaking school within walking distance. There must also be government cooperation with vaccinations, and healthcare for the children, and finally, the leader within that village must be motivated and cooperative as he will have direct influence on the parents and the community to affect change.

The village leaders and the parents are informed that it is an English medium school, following government standards of curriculum, using a Christian worldview. Village leaders have found that the level of violence is lower with more education and they desire an opportunity to see a hope for the future of their children.

Gaining the trust and participation within the community is a key element in establishing effective intervention. The issue of anti-conversion laws is also carefully addressed in each state in order to protect the individuals from any fines.

This part lays out the quality of the education, as well as academic placement within the surrounding communities. Once again, although "quality" is difficult to measure without specific quantitative measures, I will address their goals and observable efforts.

QUALITY OF EDUCATION

Each of the schools currently has government permission to operate and recognition from the Ministry of Education. Twice a year, the ME inspects the teachers, children. From LKG to fifth grade, the schools may choose their curriculum and still be recognized, but from the sixth grade on, the schools must follow the government curriculum and timetables of testing under the Centralized State Board Exams and India Centralized Standard Education.

Board exams from the state are required at seventh and tenth grades. As one principal stated, they also give their own exams each trimester and if the students are not performing well, they approach the teacher and help the teacher with the subject matter to improve for the next testing round.

Although I was not able to gather quantitative data on test scores, and compare them to statewide results, the director said that they prefer to compare themselves to private schools which have a higher level of standard than the government schools. He said they compare very well and students from some schools are even beginning to win prizes in local extra curricular competitions for drawing, singing and sports. While I was there, an annual review was in progress, where managers and principals of all the southern campuses had gathered to discuss strategies, dreams, difficulties, goals and successes.

If this were a more complete evaluation, this would be the perfect forum where future improvements would be discussed, based on findings, especially if I were able to conduct the parent interviews, and individual student and teacher interviews.

EQUAL OPPORTUNITY FOR EDUCATION

The children and adults all stated that any child could go to the school, however, the managers and director confirmed that preference is given to the Dalit children if there is a capacity limit. Most of the schools reserved 60% for Dalits. To determine whether this was actually in practice, and to see if it appeared that many children convert either because of the education, or in order to obtain the education, I asked two of the schools if they knew the attendance rate based on religious beliefs or practices. The records from School B, the percentage of the students' faith background is 92% Hindu, 6% Muslim and 2% Christian.

School D had 10% Muslim and the rest mostly identified themselves as Hindu. Most areas, they said, have very few Muslims or Christians, which fits with their overall strategy to establish schools in the areas with the greatest need for education for the Dalits.

As these schools are at least three years old, there does not appear to be any high conversion rate, just as to their records. One of the difficulties mentioned by several with regard to allowing all children to attend is the transience of the families who work with seasonal jobs.

One school said that parents will sign their children up and begin school for the first two months, but then leave with the uniform, shoes and books, following job availability. The school does not want to turn these children away, or discriminate in any way based on what they think might happen, but at the same time, they recognize the reality that the student may leave, and take the supplies with them that would have benefited another child coming in.

Also, another school has parents who are trying to get their children into a boarding school facility, which would provide for all of their needs. As soon as any opening becomes available, they will remove their children from the DEI school. To accommodate this, one school requires a beginning of the year fee, knowing of the particular problems in that area. Then, as the year progresses they continue a monthly payment schedule.

For this subject, I discussed with the management some of the issues commonly discussed in attempting to evaluate overall quality of the teaching staff. I then questioned two focus groups of teachers regarding their educational background and years of experience. I asked the management how they train the teachers in the "holistic transformational activities." This part also discusses the teacher's level of satisfaction with the teaching experience, and what they wish they could change, as well as perceived obstacles to their ability to teach or to the overall educational experience.

ACCOUNTABILITY

A key component in the success of any educational programme has been shown to be the accountability of the teachers. One particular aspect is teacher absenteeism. Students cannot be educated if the teacher is not present, and India holds one of the higher rates of teacher absenteeism with 25% absent in government primary schools on any given day. There are several reasons for this, including the lack of repercussion if a teacher does not show up to class. The CECs address this by allowing eight "casual days" which are used for vacations and eight "sick days."

Anything beyond that, they do not get paid for. The school day runs from 8:00 a.m. to 3:30 p.m. Teachers are permitted three "tardies," but anything beyond that is disciplined by a reduction of pay or removal of a vacation day.

The principals claim that this has not been an issue with their staff, partly due to the rules and accountability established and partly due to the commitment of the teachers to help these underprivileged students.

STAFF EDUCATION

As I was not able to interview the staff at each of the four schools, I summarize the findings regarding the years of experience and education level from schools A and B. As these schools have only been open for two years and five years respectively, the average teaching time of 16 months at School A and 2.7 years at School B is low, but not surprising.

Part of this is due to the fact that the schools are very new, and part to the difficulty they have in maintaining staff in rural areas with lower pay. The four schools had an average ratio of 22 students to one teacher. Of these two schools, School A had less educational background among the staff. Three were still completing their degrees remotely, and two held

Bachelor of Science in Education degrees, one a Bachelor of Science in Education with a credential of a Bachelor of Education and two held other certifications.

School B, the more established school, had more degreed staff, three with BA or BSc degrees, five with BEd credentials in addition to their BA or BSc or MA degrees, and two with specific training in nursing and Hindi. There are several reasons that the leadership faces difficulty attracting well educated staff, however. One is the lack of equipment and materials that these teachers have been trained to expect in order to do an excellent job of educating.

They have been trained in many cases with full degrees in education, but in the rural areas, there are not enough resources for science laboratories, computers, audio visual equipment, libraries, musical instruments, sports equipment and so on.

They feel they cannot do as good a job as they were trained to do without the necessary resources. Also, as the principal reported, the living conditions are much harder than these teachers who have lived in the cities have ever experienced and being far from their families and friends creates a lonely environment.

However, those educated through a partner organization have already experienced many of these conditions because part of their education contains a service component, where they have spent as much as a year in the field, working in very difficult conditions, such as the slums or remote villages. The leadership foresees difficulties, however, in maintaining continuity with the staff in these conditions.

I asked if they ever hire teachers who are non-Christian, and the principal said it would be very rare. They want teachers to be able to teach from a Christian perspective, with the DEI's approach to holistic transformation so there is no confusion in practices.

It is hard to recruit teachers into the villages, however, as the government pays more for a BEd, making it hard to attract the quality teachers who could choose the government city jobs instead. Despite facility differences and varying educational backgrounds, one other point that was notable as I observed in these schools was the order and discipline. School A, the newest of the schools where many children are being exposed to formal education for the first time, had far less structure and order than School C, the model school. When School A lined up to greet me and have their photo taken, the children clustered close together, in no particular order while the children in School C, also with very little warning of my arrival, filed out of their classrooms in perfect order, separated by one arm's length, standing at attention, ready for the salute and pledge.

It was a very impressive sight to see each row, perfectly aligned by grade, with teachers standing in the back. Children had previously memorized greetings that they used as well as their daily pledge routines. I am told by colleagues from India that this is the standard routine for the elite private schools in India.

It was a very interesting observation to see the difference between a newly formed school, and one that is more established. It would be useful to discuss further with the staff whether these differences in the schools are due to the length of time since they were established, the expectation of the leadership, or the children's background, or a combination of the three.

JOYS AND OBSTACLES

I asked the teachers what the enjoyed most about teaching and though it did take some time at first to think of an answer, several said that they enjoyed seeing the changes in the students, and watching them learn about their rights as human beings and about Christian principles through Bible verses and stories.

After even a small amount of education, they see improvements in health and hygiene, and they hear the children speaking English in society. The teachers agreed that watching the children gain confidence as they learn provides the impetus for many of them to continue. One of the difficulties they face is that it is hard at first to get the families to take learning seriously and to cooperate together with the school, or to even have their child enroll. One school went door-to-door, explaining the cost, the value and what would be provided. Students would start to attend, but since many walked for some distance, they would often come in late.

This caused disruptions in the classroom and in their learning. Also, the children did not know how to treat a teacher, and the parents had never been to school themselves so had little expectation for their children's behaviour in school.

Recognizing this, one manager conveyed that he felt that, "Discipline comes first, then education will come out of it." To aid in this, the school created a policy for the parents, showing what was expected of the children on holidays, weekends and in the evenings, such that what they were allowed to do at home would match with the school's expectations. If the child was going to be absent for more than three days due to illness, the parent needed to show a doctor's excuse.

In order to handle the "tardies," one school warned the students and parents that they would start locking the gate when school began at 9:00 a.m. When parents and children came late, they were turned away. The manager shared that when one little boy cried and begged to be allowed to come in, it "broke his heart," and he allowed him to come, talking to him about correcting one's mistakes and learning from them. He said that after two days of these methods, none of the children have had difficulties with tardiness.

FUTURE DREAMS

Every programme has some room for improvement regardless of current successful application so I asked the managers, teachers and students if there is any one thing they would like to add to their school. Interestingly enough, their answers all coincided with similar categories.

The following is a list of the five most common answers and a summary of the participants' comments:

- *Transportation*: They would like a bus or large van

for the children, staff and even parents when they come in for meetings with the teacher. With no public transportation in the rural areas, the distance is often so far that if children walk, as was noted before, they are often late to class or do not come at all.

- *Music*: Even though most of the 6th grade focus group had already given me their answer, when one student said they would like musical instruments or singing classes, two-thirds of the class instantly raised their hands in agreement and wanted me to add that to their previous answer. Teachers also wanted to have music and to be included in the community-wide events that some of the DEI schools are competing in successfully. In some of the classes, I found it interesting that the children did not hold a tune very well, but sang in more of a chant. Although it is typical for several children out of a class of 30 to not be musically gifted, I found this lack of ability to sing to be noticeable. I asked how much exposure they have to music and I was told there is very little due to where they live in rural areas, the lack of electricity, and so on. There is little that would train their ear from a young age while forming foundational musical abilities.
- *Science Labs*: Science in general seemed to be very important to these students and their teachers. Several students said their favourite subject was science, and they listed specific topics, with ten out of 23 saying biology. Other students listed chemistry, physics and botany. Teachers wanted to be able to offer these science classes that utilized their full expertise and to include hands-on laboratory experience for the children.
- *Libraries*: Every group wanted to add a library that would be available to check out material such as history books, general knowledge books, science books and stories. Some of the schools are going to be able to add this soon.

- *Sports Programmes and Equipment*: Each school generally had one or two barrels with play equipment to be shared by all classes at recess time. In receiving the gifts sent from the United States, one teacher said, "Thank you for the gifts, you have just doubled our jump rope supply!" I had only delivered one per school. The children wanted organized competitive sports, and the teachers and managers said that having an actual Physical Education teacher would help with discipline issues as there would be an incentive to behave or else miss out on something they enjoyed. Also, they said that PE teachers are trained in techniques of order and discipline

Surprisingly, only two people mentioned tables, chairs and desks, even though many of the classrooms had no furniture. At the time, I did not think to question whether they considered this an obvious goal they were already working towards or unnecessary compared to the other items they could not substitute with any other object or method, such as sitting on the floor.

There were several other needs listed, such as manipulatives, audiovisual equipment, computers and craft supplies. In this part, I summarize the interviews with staff regarding fees that parents pay for their child to attend, and how it is handled if they cannot pay. Also discussed are the school's provision of books, supplies, uniforms and the availability of a midday meal, as well as facility issues.

COST OF EDUCATION

As is stated in their goals, and through interviews, the DEI leadership has found that having the parents pay for part of the education creates a sense of ownership and accountability.

Each of the schools charges fees on a different scale, based on the surrounding community, the average wage and availability of jobs for the parents. Once this is determined, the fee is collected from the parents on a monthly basis, with the rest being subsidized by the DEI funding. There is a problem with the transience of some families due to the type of seasonal labour they are employed in. Therefore, the fees are adjusted by school depending on these issues.

School D, for example, charges an initial fee of 50-100 rupees with the monthly remainder supplied by the DEI which covers the costs if a family leaves and takes the supplies with them. For Schools A, B and C, the parents pay fees ranging from 25 to 30 rupees per month with the remainder of the cost of approximately 75 rupees per month being subsidized by international funding through the DEI.

The managers, most parents are able to supply the fees, but if they cannot, the DEI pays the full fee. An average salary in the rural area of School A is 1,000 rupees per month which is approximately 25 dollars.

BOOKS, SUPPLIES AND UNIFORMS

Each of the schools supplies at least one uniform per student, which usually included shorts for the boys, a jumper for the girls, one shirt, socks, shoes, and a belt and tie for both. One of the schools supplies two uniforms. These children come from such poverty, that they have found that having one complete clean outfit brings a sense of pride, belonging and unity.

It also levels all sense if inequality, as each has equal opportunity to look the same at school. I noticed the children generally came with carefully groomed hair, the girls in pony tails and braids, sometimes wearing bracelets and barrettes. When one school was notified that morning that I was coming to evaluate the school, the principal, knowing it was wash day in the community, quickly sent the local children back home to put their uniforms on for their "inspection."

When I arrived, some were in uniform and some in "street clothes," and the principal explained the situation, wishing they each had two uniforms so that all week long, they could look clean and well groomed. As a way of combining efforts within the community, the women who are learning to sew, create the uniforms for the children, so it is a matter of funding more than availability. Each school, after carefully evaluating the needs within the community, supplies at least the school books required, and some schools add a book bag, writing utensils and other supplies.

The children carry an average of over 20 small text books and writing books each day, similar to the size of a bluebook used for exams. People from the United States had donated one suitcase of gifts for the schools, including Frisbees, blow up balls, pencils, vitamins, and so on. One of the teaching interns was excited about the pencils. She explained that one day, one of the young boys got up to leave the classroom after she asked them to write down an assignment. She told him to sit down and follow directions.

He said, "I can't, I have to go see my brother." She reminded him that this was class time, and he could see his brother later. After some interchange, he finally explained, "I have to go see my brother, he has our pencil!"

Most of the younger children use chalk and a slate board for in-class work such as math calculations. This school provides all the supplies needed for any science fair projects or materials needed to join in local school competitions as they have found that parents cannot afford these additional expenses.

MIDDAY MEAL

Two of the schools no longer provide a midday meal of eggs and fruit because they did not have enough resources and had determined that this was a programme that would have to be cut rather than cut resources to any other part of the programme.

One school is still planning to initiate this programme when they have a new building as there is no kitchen facility at their current site. One of the schools gives one egg per day for each student. Although the director acknowledged that research shows that children at this level of need could do better in school with a meal provided, he felt that these particular children would get some sort of a meal from home, but that parents would not be able to, or would not choose to buy books or school supplies. This decision is made individually for each school depending on the needs within that community.

FACILITIES

One of the needs most commonly mentioned is to have separate bathroom facilities for boys and girls. Several adults that I interviewed explained that these children are "exposed to way too much information about life," living in the conditions that they do. They explained that Dalits are usually expected to use open fields, or that girls, especially in the slums, are exposed to even dangerous conditions, being made to wait until evening to use the facilities, which puts them at risk of attack or even rape. By adding separate facilities, they felt they could add to the community education about health and hygiene.

Also, if a lunch programme is to be provided, they would need a room in which to store and prepare the food. Each of the schools I visited was using every room available, sometimes for multiple purposes such as after school programmes and self-help groups, with no place for teachers to store their materials, join for meetings, study or prepare. They said that all schools will need to expand, not only to supply these needs, but to even have enough rooms for each grade level as the schools grow each year to meet the demand.

Some of the most common requests for improvement that I heard were for a teachers' room, computer lab, library, science lab and enough rooms to at least go through the eighth grade. However, as one principal shared, the DEI and partner organizations are continuously putting money into new schools, which then limits the resources available to existing schools. This dilemma will be discussed in the conclusion as I look at future goals.

OVERALL SUCCESS OF THE PROGRAMME

Each of the findings show clear accomplishment of the overall goals of the DEI, with each school at a different level of achievement due to location, years since establishment, availability of resources as well as background of the children. Although there are areas that each could improve if given additional resources, seeing the difference in these children's lives, knowing the environment and background from which they approach this educational experience, is remarkable.

uIdeally, I would like to continue to follow the success of this programme over time, and to interview the parents, students and community leaders to assess the long term positive influence for these children and their whole community.

8

Dalit Events and Movements

POONA PACT

During the first Round Table Conference, when Dr. Bhimrao Ramji Ambedkar favoured the move of the British Government to provide separate electorate for the oppressed classes (Dalit), Gandhi strongly opposed it on the plea that the move would give power to the oppressed classes (Dalit). He went for an indefinite hunger strike from September 20, 1932 against the decision of the then British Prime Minister J.Ramsay MacDonald granting communal award to the depressed classes in the constitution for governance of British India.

In view of the mass upsurge generated in the country to save the life of Gandhi, Ambedkar was compelled to soften his stand. A compromise between the leaders of caste Hindu and the depressed classes was reached on September 24,1932, popularly known as Poona Pact. The resolution announced in a public meeting on September 25 in Bombay confirmed -" henceforth, amongst Hindus no one shall be regarded as an untouchable by reason of his birth and they will have the same rights in all the social institutions as the other Hindus have".

This landmark resolution in the history of the Dalit movement in India subsequently formed the basis for giving due share to Dalits in the political empowerment of Indian people in a democratic Indian polity. The following is the text of the agreement arrived at between leaders acting on behalf of the Depressed Classes and of the rest of the community, regarding the representation of the Depressed Classes in the legislatures and certain other matters affecting their welfare.

- There shall be seats reserved for the Depressed Classes out of general electorate seats in the provincial legislatures as follows: - Madras 30; Bombay with Sind 25; Punjab 8; Bihar and Orissa 18; Central Provinces 20; Assam 7; Bengal 30; United Provinces 20. Total 148.
- Election to these seats shall be by joint electorates subject, however, to the following procedure All members of the Depressed Classes registered in the general electoral roll of a constituency will form an electoral college which will elect a panel of tour candidates belonging to the Depressed Classes for each of such reserved seats by the method of the single vote and four persons getting the highest number of votes in such primary elections shall be the candidates for election by the general electorate.
- The representation of the Depressed Classes in the Central Legislature shall likewise be on the principle of joint electorates and reserved seats by the method of primary election in the manner provided for in clause for their representation in the provincial legislatures.

BATTLE OF KOREGAON

THE MARATHA WARS

While I can understand the desire of Dalits to home into that skirmish and claim that to be the be all and end all of all, skirmishes like this have to be grounded in the greater framework. The Maratha Empire brought to life by Shivaji attained its greatest strength by 1760.

And I should point out that Shivaji was not a Brahmin. While they claimed Kshyatriya status later on, there are some arguments that he was originally a Dalit, a Shudra to be precise. Finally, Shivaji's army was largely composed of people like him, so it was a Dalit Army anyway which got promoted, so to say. Then comes the first Anglo Maratha War 1777-1783 where first the Maratha's won and then the British won. In both cases, native soldiers were far too frequently Dalits. Anyway, more land was captured by the Brits and the power of the Maratha's was further reduced. Peshwa Baji Rao II and his father basically got up to no good. In 1802, BajiRao went and sucked up to the British after being defeated by Holkars in the Battle of Poona. This pissed off the other Maratha warlords and they got into a bit of a fight with the British which ended with more loss of territory for the Marathas. Then comes the crucial 3rd War which our Dalit friends might now appreciate. This relates to the 3rd Anglo Maratha War 1817-1818 or the Pindari War. The Pindari's were highly mobile cavalry units which were not on the payroll of any ruler but associated with rulers in return for protection and permission to plunder. Guess what? These Pindari's were low caste, Ladul and also had quite a lot of Muslims (mainly Afghans and Pusthun). Anyway, all this plundering was not good for the British and a really very big army of 120,000 men and 300 artillery pieces was put into gear by Lord Hastings to exterminate these Pindari's. The attacks happened from the east in Bengal, from the South in the Deccan and from the west from Gujarat and Bombay.

THE IMMEDIATE PREDECESSOR TO THE 1ST JAN 1818 BATTLE OF KOREGAON

Once the British invaded Maratha territory to go after the Pindari's, there were skirmishes between the Peshwa's forces and the British forces such as the sack of the British Residency in Pune, and then the British routed another Peshwa force at Khirki. Then the main battle was fought in the Battle of Khadki on November 5, 1817 where the Peshwa Baji Rao was routed pretty much comprehensively and then the British took over the Peshwa's seat at Shaniwarwada by November 17, 1817.

The Peshwa, by this time, was running ragged. There was another battle between the Nagpur forces and the British at Sitabalsi on November 27 1817. The next battle to be fought was the Battle of Mahidpur on 20th December where the Holkar's fought and lost to the British, after being betrayed by one of the Pindari (who killed Tulsibai).

THE BATTLE OF KOREGAON

A good description of the battle can be found here. This is a book by WC Taylor, A Popular History of British India published in 1847. Sounds like a pretty good bash. Taylor says that the Peshwa's forces numbered about 25,000 although it should be noted that counting was pretty vague at that time. Still, it wasnt 50,000. But here's the crucial thing, the Peshwa's forces then retreated not because they were defeated by Captain Francis Staunton's forces, but because they got to hear that British reinforcements were coming over. The British forces lost 200 soldiers out of 500, and 6 out of 7 British officers. Good defensive battle without food or water at this village.

THE SOLDIERS

The soldiers who did most of the dying were Mahars. And again ironically, they got their start in being soldiers by no other than Shivaji to become scouts and fortress guards. They were highly mobile light infantry, which is the reason why they were in the 2nd Battalion, 1st regiment of 'Bombay Native Light Infantry' as part of the Maratha Light Infantry. The Peshwa's soldiers were also by and large lower caste soldiers including Mahars, in any case, not Brahmins.

So the fighting basically was between lower castes, only the people who were ordering them around were the British and the Peshwas. This Mahar Regiment still exists and has provided two of the most brilliant Indian Army Chiefs: Gen (Retd) K V Krishna Rao and Gen (Retd) K Sunderji. Also, there is no caste element to the regiment from 1963 onwards and it is now a fully mixed regiment.

THE AFTERMATH OF THE BATTLE OF KOREGAON

There was another fight between the fleeing Peshwa's forces and the British at Ashti on February 20th 1818 and he remained under pressure till he surrendered to Sir John

Malcolm on June 3, 1818 and was given the pension of an annual payment of 8 lakhs rupees. The Battle of Koregaon was celebrated by raising of an Obelix which commemorated this. So all in all, I am afraid what my research threw up was in sharp variance with the mythology is being provided. It was frankly a small battle / skirmish in a much bigger war, the Peshwa's forces were not defeated in this skirmish, the British Army did not fight this battle expecting the worst because they had been winning every battle in this war, this battle of Koregaon was not really that important as fighting kept on happening for months after this battle and I am afraid there is absolutely no evidence that any kind of caste based ideology was involved in the fight. So all in all, good myth but a rather more calm reading of the historical record tells differently.

I can also see why the Dalit hotheads want to use this battle to burnish their credentials. After all, all revolutions need their battles. If they do want to celebrate the success of lower caste soldiers, they should celebrate Shivaji, the Indian Soldier, the bravery that these soldiers showed to whoever paid them.

SELF-RESPECT MOVEMENT

The Self-Respect Movement was founded in 1925 by Periyar E. V. Ramasamy (also known as Periyar) in Tamil Nadu, India. The movement has the aim of achieving a society where backward castes have equal human rights, and encouraging backward castes to have self-respect in the context of a caste based society that considered them to be a lower end of the hierarchy.

The movement was extremely influential not just in Tamil Nadu, but also overseas in countries with large Tamil populations, such as Malaysia and Singapore. Among Singapore Indians, groups like the Tamil Reform Association, and leaders like Thamizhavel G. Sarangapani were prominent in promoting the principals of the Self-Respect Movement among the local Tamil population through schools and publications. A number of political parties in Tamil Nadu, such as Dravida Munnetra Kazhagam (DMK) and All India Anna Dravida Munnetra Kazhagam (AIADMK) owe their origins to the Self-respect movement, the latter a 1972 breakaway from the DMK. Both parties are populist with a generally social democratic orientation.

THE TENETS OF SELF-RESPECT

Periyar was convinced that if man developed self respect, he would automatically develop individuality and would refuse to be led by the nose by schemers. One of his most known quotes on Self-Respect was, "we are fit to think of 'self-respect' only when the notion of 'superior' and 'inferior' caste is banished from our land".

Periyar did not expect personal or material gain out of this movement. He used to recall in a very casual manner that as a human being, he also was obligated to this duty, as it was the right and freedom to choose this work. Thus, Periyar opted to engage himself in starting and promoting the movement. Periyar declared that the Self-Respect Movement alone could be the genuine freedom movement, and political freedom would not be fruitful without individual self-respect. He remarked that the so called 'Indian freedom fighters' were showing disrespect of self-respect, and this was really an irrational philosophy.

Periyar observed that political freedom as conceived by nationalists not excluding even Gandhi and Jawaharlal Nehru did not cover individual self-respect. To him neither revival of the original spirit of Hindu religion and ancient traditions which formed part of Gandhi's conception of freedom, nor complete liberation from the British rule which was considered by Nehru to be the meaning of freedom or both of them together could ensure individual self-respect or remove the ills from Indian societies. In his opinion the task of fulfilling the need for self-respect would have to be faced whatever be the extent of political freedom gained. Pointing out that even the British monarch in a sovereign independent nation had no freedom to marry a person of his choice and had to abdicate his kingdom, Periyar raised a question whether Gandhi's vision of freedom or Nehru's concept of independence contained even an iota of individual self-respect. Periyar believed that self-respect was as valuable as life itself and its protection is a birth right and not swaraj ('political freedom'). He described the movement as Arivu Vidutalai Iyakkam, that is, a movement to liberate the intellect. The terms tan-maanam or suya mariyadai meaning 'self-respect' are traceable in ancient Tamil literature considered a virtue of high valor in Tamil society. Periyar once claimed that to describe the ideology of his movement, no dictionary in the entire world, implying that no other language, could provide a word better than or equal to suya mariyadai.

Started as a movement (Iyakkam in Tamil) to promote rational behaviour, the Self-Respect Movement acquired much wider connotation within a short period of time. Periyar speaking with M.K. Reddy at the First Self-Respect Conference held in 1929, explained the significance of self-respect and its principles. The main tenets of the Self-Respect Movement in society were to be: no kind of inequality among people; no difference as rich and poor in the economic life; men and women to be treated as equals in every respect without differences; attachments to caste, religion, varna, and country to be eradicated from society with a prevalent friendship and unity around the world; and every human being seeing to act just as to reason, understanding, desire, and perspective, and shall not be subject to slavery of any kind or manner. Equality with stress on economic and social equality formed the central theme of the Self-Respect Movement was due to Periyar's determination to fight the inequalities ingrained in the caste system and religious practices. Working on the theme of liberating the society from the baneful social practices perpetrated in the name of dharma and karma, Periyar developed the idea of establishing this movement as the instrument for achieving his objective.

ANTI-BRAHMANISM

Tamil Brahmins (Iyers and Iyengars) were frequently held responsible by followers of Periyar for direct or indirect oppression of lower-caste people on the canard of "Brahmin oppression" and resulted in attacks on Brahmins and which among other reasons started a wave of mass-migration of the Brahmin population. Periyar in regards to a DK member's attempt to assassinate Rajagopalachari, "expressed his abhorrence of violence as a means of settling political differences". Eventually, the anti-Brahmanism subsided with the replacement of the DMK party by the AIADMK.

SELF-RESPECT MARRIAGES

One of the major sociological changes introduced through the self respect movement was the self-respect marriage system, where by marriages were conducted without being officiated by a Brahmin priest. Periyar had regarded the then conventional marriages were mere financial arrangements and often caused great debt through dowry.

Self-Respect marriages encouraged inter-caste marriages and arranged marriages to be replaced by love marriages. It was argued by the proponents of self-respect marriage that the then conventional marriages were officiated by Brahmins, who has to be paid for and also the marriage ceremony was in Sanskrit which most people did not understand, and hence were ritual and practices based on blind adherence.

MANDAL COMMISSION

The Mandal Commission was established in India in 1979 by the Janata Party government under Prime Minister Morarji Desai with a n andate to "identify the socially or educationally backward." It was headed by Indian parliamentarian Bindheshwari Prasad Mandal to consider the question of seat reservations and quotas for people to redress caste discrimination, and used eleven social, economic, and educational indicators to determine backwardness.

In 1980, the commission's report affirmed the affirmative action practice under Indian law whereby members of lower castes (known as Other Backward Classes (OBC) and Scheduled Castes and Tribes) were given exclusive access to a certain portion of government jobs and slots in public universities, and recommended changes to these quotas, increasing them by 27% to 49.5%.

SETTING UP OF MANDAL COMMISSION

The plan to set up another commission was taken by Mr. Clooney and the Morarji Desai government in 1978 as per the mandate of the Constitution of India under article 340 for the purpose of Articles like 15 and 16. The decision was made official by the president on 1 January 1979. The commission is popularly known as the Mandal Commission its chairman being B.P. Mandal..

CRITERIA TO IDENTIFY OBC

The Mandal Commission adopted various methods and techniques to collect the necessary data and evidence. The commission adopted 11 criteria which could be grouped under three major headings: social, educational and economic in order to identify OBCs.

Social

- Castes/classes considered as socially backward by others.
- Castes/classes which mainly depend on manual labour for their livelihood.
- Castes/classes where at least 25 per cent females and 10 per cent males above the state average get married at an age below 17 years in rural areas and at least 10 per cent females and 5 per cent males do so in urban areas.
- Castes/classes where participation of females in work is at least 25 per cent above the state average.

Educational

- Castes/classes where the number of children in the age group of 5–15 years who never attended school is at least 25 per cent above the state average.
- Castes/classes where the rate of student drop-out in the age group of 5–15 years is at least 25 per cent above the state average.

Economic

- Castes/classes where the average value of family assets is at least 25 per cent below the state average.
- Castes/classes where the number of families living in kuccha houses is at least 25 per cent above the state average.
- Castes/classes where the source of drinking water is beyond half a kilometre for more than 50 per cent of the households.
- Castes/classes where the number of households having taken consumption loans is at least 25 per cent above the state average. Also known as "Creamy layer," this criteria of separation is ignored by the government which is known as the most controversial issue of reservation.

Weighting Indicators

As the three groups are not of equal importance for the purpose, separate weightage was given to indicators in each group. All the Social indicators were given a weightage of 3 points each, educational indicators were given a weightage of 2 points each and economic indicators were given a weightage of 1 point each.

Economic, in addition to Social and Educational Indicators, were considered important as they directly flowed from social and educational backwardness. This also helped to highlight the fact that socially and educationally backward classes are economically backward also.

It will be seen from the values given to each indicator, the total score adds up to 22. All these 11 indicators were applied to all the castes covered by the survey for a particular state. As a result of this application, all castes which had a score of 50 % (*i.e.* 11 points) were listed as socially and educationally backward and the rest were treated as 'advanced'.

OBSERVATIONS AND FINDINGS

The commission estimated that 54% of the total population (excluding SCs and STs), belonging to 3,743 different castes and communities were 'backward'. Figures of caste-wise population are not available beyond. So the commission used 1931 census data to calculate the number of OBCs. The population of Hindu OBCs was derived by subtracting from the total population of Hindus, the population of SC and ST and that of forward Hindu castes and communities, and it worked out to be 52 per cent. Assuming that roughly the proportion of OBCs amongst non-Hindus was of the same order as amongst the Hindus, population of non-Hindu OBCs was also considered as 52 per cent.

- Assuming that a child from an advanced class family and that of a backward class family had the same intelligence at the time of their birth, it is obvious that owing to vast differences in social, cultural and environmental factors, the former will beat the latter by lengths in any competitive field. Even if a backward class child's intelligence quotient was much higher as compared to the child of advanced class, chances are that the former will lag far behind the latter in any competition where selection is made on the basis of 'merit'.
- In fact, what we call 'merit' in an elitist society is an amalgam of native endowments and environmental privileges. A child from an advanced class family and that of a backward class family are not 'equals' in any fair sense of the term and it will be unfair to judge them by the same yard-stick. The conscience of a civilized society and the dictates of social justice demand that 'merit' and 'equality' are not turned into a fetish and the element of privilege is duly recognised and discounted for when 'unequal' are made to run the same race.
- To place the amalgams of open caste conflicts in proper historical context, the study done by Tata institute of Social Sciences Bombay observes. "The British rulers produced many structural disturbances in the Hindu caste structure, and these were contradictory in nature and impact .... Thus, the

various impacts of the British rule on the Hindu caste system, viz, near monopolisation of jobs, education and professions by the literati castes, the Western concepts of equality and justice undermining the Hindu hierarchical dispensation, the phenomenon of Sanskritization, genteel reform movement and militant reform movements from below, emergence of the caste associations with a new role set the stage for the caste conflicts in modern India. Two more ingredients which were very weak in the British period, viz, politicisation of the masses and universal adult franchise, became powerful moving forces after the Independence.

RECOMMENDATIONS

The report of the commission was submitted in December 1980. Following are the recommendations as stated in the report. It may appear the upliftment of Other Backward Classes is part of the larger national problem of the removal of mass poverty. This is only partially correct. The deprivation of OBCs is a very special case of the larger national issue: here the basic question is that of social and educational backwardness and poverty is only a direct consequence of these two crippling caste-based handicaps.

As these handicaps are embedded in our social structure, their removal will require far—reaching structural changes. No less important will be changes in the perception of the problems of OBCs by the ruling classes of the country.

Reservations

One such change in the attitude of the ruling elite pertains to the provisions of reservation in Government services and educations institutions for the candidates of Other Backward Classes. It is generally argued that looking to the large population of OBCs (52 %), recruitment of a few thousand OBCs every year against reserved vacancies is not going to produce any perceptible impact on their general condition. On the other hand, the induction of a large proportion of employees against reserved vacancies will considerably impair the quality and efficiency of the Government services. It is also stated that the benefits of such reservations will be skimmed off by those parts of OBCs which are already well off and the really backward parts will be left high and dry. Another argument advanced against this approach is that the policy of large scale reservations will cause great hurt burning to those meritorious candidates whose entry into services will be barred as a result thereof. All the arguments are based on fairly sound reasoning.

But these are also the arguments advanced by the ruling elite which is keen on preserving its privileges. Therefore, like all such reasoning, it is based on partisan approach. By the same token, while illuminating some immediate areas of concern it tends to ignore much larger issues of national importance. It is not at all our contention that by offering a few thousand jobs to OBC candidates we shall be able to make 52% of the Indian population as forward. But we must recognise that as essential part of the battle against social backwardness is to be fought in the minds of the backward people.

In India Government service has always been looked upon as a symbol of prestige and power. By increasing the representation of OBCs in Government services, we give them an immediate feeling of participation in the governance of this country. When a backward class candidate becomes a Collector or a Superintendent of Police, the material benefits accruing from his position are limited to the members of his family only.

But the psychological spin off of this phenomenon is tremendous; the entire community of that backward class candidate feels socially elevated. Even when no tangible benefits flow to the community at large, the feeling that now it has its "own man" in the "corridors of power" acts as a morale booster.

In a democratic set-up every individual and community has a legitimate right and aspiration to participate in ruling this country. Any situation which results in a near-denial of this right to nearly 52% of the country's population needs to be urgently rectified. Apprehensions regarding drop in the quality of Government services owing to large-scale induction of S.C. / S.T. and O.B.C. candidates against reserved posts may be justified only up to a point. But is it possible to maintain that all candidates selected on merit turn out to be honest, efficient, hard-working and dedicated? At present, top echelons of all the Government services are manned predominantly by open competition candidates and if the performance of our bureaucracy is any indication, it has not exactly covered itself with glory.

Of course, this does not imply that candidates selected against reserved posts will do better. Chances are that owing to their social and cultural handicaps they may be generally a shade less competent. But, on the other hand, they will have great advantage of possessing first hand knowledge of the sufferings and problems of the backward parts of society. This is not a small asset for field workers and policy makers even at highest level.

It is no doubt true that the major benefits of reservation and other welfare measures for Other Backward Classes will be cornered by the more advanced parts of the backward communities. But is not this a universal phenomenon? All reformists remedies have to contend with slow recovery along the hierarchical gradient; there are no quantum jumps in social reform.

Moreover, human nature being what it is, a "new class" ultimately does emerge even in classless societies. The chief merit on reservation is not that it will introduce egalitarian amongst OBCs when the rest of the Indian society is seized by all sorts of inequalities. But reservation will certainly erode the hold of higher castes on the services and enable OBCs in general to have a sense of participation in running the affairs of the country.

It is certainly true that reservation for OBCs will cause a lot of heart burning to others. But should the mere fact of this heart burning be allowed to operate as a moral veto against social reform.... When the higher castes constituting less than 20% of the country's population subjected the rest to all manner of social injustice, it must have caused a lot of heart burning to the lower castes. But now that the lower castes are asking for a modest share of the national cake of power and prestige, a chorus of alarm is being raised on the plea that this will cause heart burning to the ruling elite.

Of all the specious arguments advanced against reservations for backward classes, there is none which beats this one about 'heart-burning' in sheer sophistry. In fact the Hindu society has always operated a very rigorous scheme of reservations, which was internalised through caste system. Eklavya lost his thumb and Shambhk his neck for their breach of caste rules of reservations.

The present furore against reservations for OBCs is not aimed at the principle itself, but against the new class of beneficiaries, as they are now clamouring for a share of the opportunities which were all along monopolised by the higher castes.

Quantum and Scheme of Reservations

Scheduled Castes and Scheduled Tribes constitute 22.5% of the country's population. A pro-rata reservation of 22.5% has been made for them in all services and public sector undertakings under the Central Government. In the States also, reservation for SCs and STs is directly proportional to their population in each State.

The population of OBCs, both Hindu and non-Hindu, is around 52% of the total population of India. Accordingly 52% of all post under the Central Government should be reserved for them, but this provision may go against the law laid down in a number of Supreme Court judgements wherein it has been held that the total quantum of reservations under Articles 15(4) and 16(4) of the Constitution should be below 50%.

In view of this the proposed reservation for OBCs would have to be pegged at a figure which, when added to 22.5% of SCs and STs, remain below 50%. In view of this legal constrain, the commission is obliged to recommend a reservation of 27% only, even though their population us almost twice this figure.

States which have already introduced reservation for OBCs exceeding 27%, will remain unaffected by this recommendation. With the general recommendation regarding the quantum of reservation, the Commission proposes the following overall scheme of reservation for OBCs:

- Candidates belonging to OBCs recruited on the basis of merit in an open competition should not be adjusted against their reservation quota of 27%.
- The reservation should also be made available to promotion quota at all levels nitika goyal (3) Reserved quota remaining unfilled should be carried forward for a period of three years and deserved thereafter.
- Relaxation in the upper age limit for direct recruitment should be extended in the same manner as done in case of SCs and STs.
- A roster system for each category of posts should be adopted by the concerned authorities in the same manner as presently done in respect of SC and ST candidates.

The scheme of reservations in its toto should be made applicable to all recruitment to public sector undertakings both under the Central and State Governments, as also to nationalised banks.

All private sector undertakings which have received financial assistance from the Government in one form or the other should also be obliged to recruit personnel on the aforesaid basis.

All universities and affiliated colleges should also be covered by the scheme of reservation. To give proper effect to these recommendations, it is imperative that adequate statutory provisions are made by the Government to amend the existing enactments, rules, procedure, etc., to the extent they are not in consonance with the same.

Educational Concessions

Our educational system is elitist in character, results in a high degree of wastage and is least suited to the requirements of an over-populated and developing country. It is a legacy of the British rule which was severely criticised during the independence struggle, and yet, it has not undergone any structural changes. Though it is least suited to the needs of backward classes, yet, they are forced to run the rat-race with others as no options are available to them.

As 'educational reform' was not within the terms of reference of the Commission, we are also forced to trend the beaten track and suggest only the palliative measure within existing framework. Various State Governments are giving a number of educational concessions to other backward class students like exemption of tuition fees, free supply of books and clothes, mid-day meals, special hostel facilities, stipends, etc. These concessions are all right as far as they go.

But they do not go far enough. What is required is, perhaps, not so much the provision of additional funds as the framing of integrated schemes for creating the proper environment and incentives for serious and purposeful studies. It is well known that most backward class children are irregular and indifferent students and their drop-out rate is very high.

There are two main reasons for this. First, these children are brought up in a climate of extreme social and cultural deprivation and consequently, a proper motivation for schooling is generally lacking. Secondly, most of these children come from very poor homes and their parents are forced to press them into doing small chores from a very young age. Upgrading the cultural environment is a very slow process.

Transferring these children to an artificially upgraded environment is beyond the present resources of the country. In view of this it is recommended that this problem may be tackled on a limited and selective basis on two fronts. First, an intensive and time bound programme for adult education should be launched in selected pockets with high concentration of OBC population. This is a basic motivational approach, as only proper motivated parents will take serious interest in educating their children. Secondly, residential schools should be set up in these areas for backward class students to provide a climate specially conducive to serious studies. All facilities in these schools including board and lodging, will have to be provided free of cost to attract students from poor and backward homes, separate Government Hostels for OBC students with the facilities will be another step in the right direction.

A beginning on both these fronts will have to be made on a limited scale and selective basis. But the scope of these activities should be expanded as fast as the resources permit. Adult education programme and residential schools started on a selective basis will operate as growing-points of consciousness for the entire community and their multiplier effect is bound to be substantial. Whereas several States are extended a number of ad hoc concessions to backward class students, few serious attempts have been made to integrate these facilities into a comprehensive scheme for a qualitative upgradation of educational environment available to OBC students.

After all, education is the best catalyst of change and educating the backward classes is the surest way to improve their self image and raise their social status. As OBCs cannot afford the high wastage rates of our educational system, it is very important that their education is highly biased in favour of vocational training. After all reservation in services will absorb only a very small percentage of the educated backward classes and the rest should be suitably equipped with vocational skills to enable them to get a return on having invested several years in education.

It is also obvious that even if all the facilities are given to OBC students, they will not be able to compete on an equal footing with others in securing admission to technical and professional institutions. In view of this it is recommended that seats should be reserved for OBC students in all scientific, technical and professional institutions run by the Central Government as well as State Governments. This reservation will fall under Article 15(4) of the Constitution and the quantum of reservation should be the same as in the

Government services, *i.e*, 27%. Those States which have already reserved more that 27% seats for OBC students will remain unaffected by this recommendation. While implementing the provisions for reservation it should also be ensured that the candidates who are admitted against the reserved quota are enable to derive full benefits of higher studies.

It has been generally noticed that these OBC students coming from an impoverished cultural background, are not able to keep abreast with other students. It is, therefore, very essential that special coaching facilities are arranged for all such students in our technical and professional institutions. The concerned authorities should clearly appreciate that their jobs is not finished once candidates against reserved quota have been admitted to various institutions. In fact the real task starts only after that special coaching assistance to these students, not only these young people will feel frustrated and humiliated but the country will also be landed with ill-equipped and sub-standard engineers, doctors and other professionals.

Financial Assistance

Vocational communities following hereditary occupations have suffered heavily as a result of industrialisation. Mechanical production and introductions of synthetic materials has robbed the village potter, oil crusher, blacksmith, carpenter, barber, etc. of their traditional means of livelihood and the popularization of these classes is a well-known phenomenon in the countryside. It has, therefore become very necessary that suitable institutional finance and technical assistance is made available to such members of village vocational communities who want to set up small-scale industries on their own. Similar assistance should also be provided to those promising OBC candidates who have obtained special vocational training.

Of course, most State Governments have created various financial and technical agencies for the promotions of small and medium scale industries. But it is well known that only the more influential members of the community are able to derive benefits fro these agencies. In view of this, it is essential that separate financial institutions for providing financial and technical assistance are established for the backward classes. Some State Governments like Karnataka and Andhra Pradesh have already set up separate financial corporations etc, for OBCs. Cooperative Societies of occupational groups will also help a lot.

But due care should be taken that all office-bearers and members of such societies belong to the concerned hereditary occupational groups and outsiders are not allowed to exploit them by infiltrating into such cooperatives. The share of OBCs in the industrial and business life of the country is negligible and this partly explains their extremely low income levels. As a part of its overall strategy to uplift the backward classes, it is imperative that all State Governments are suitably advised and encouraged to create a separate network of financial and technical institutions to foster business and industrial enterprise among OBCs.

Structural Changes

Reservations in Government employment and educational institutions, as also as possible financial assistance will remain mere palliatives unless the problems of backwardness is tackled at its root. Bulk of the small land-holders, tenants, agricultural labour, impoverished village artisans, unskilled workers, etc. belong to Scheduled Castes, Scheduled Tribes and Other Backward Clàsses.

"Apart from social traditions, the dominances by the top peasantry is exercised through recourse to informal bondage which arises mainly thorough money-lending, leasing out of small bits of land and providing house-sites and dwelling space to poor peasants. As most of the functionaries of the Government are drawn from the top peasantry, the class and caste linkage between the functionaries of Government and the top peasantry remain firm.

This also tills the socio-political balance in favour of the top peasantry and helps it in having its dominance over others." The net outcome of the situation is that not with standing their numerical preponderance, backward class continues to remain in mental and material bondage of the higher castes and rich peasantry. Consequently, despite constituting nearly 3/4th of the countries population, Scheduled Castes, Scheduled Tribes and Other Backward Classes have been able to acquire a very limited political clout, even though adult franchise was introduced more than three decades back.

Through their literal monopoly of means of production of higher castes are able to manipulate and coerce the backward classes into acting against their own interests. In view of this, until the stranglehold of the existing production relations is broken through radical land reforms, the abject dependence of under privileged classes on the dominant higher castes will continue indefinitely. In fact there is already a sizeable volume of legislation on the statue books to abolish zamindari, place ceilings on land holdings and distribute land to the landless. But in actual practice its implementation has been halting, half-hearted and superficial. The States like Karnataka, Kerala and West Bengal which have gone about the job more earnestly have not only succeeded in materially helping the Backward Classes, but also reaped rich political dividends into the bargains.

It is the Commission's firm Conviction that a radical transformation of the existing production relations is the most important single step that can be taken for the welfare and upliftment of all backward classes. Even if this is not possible in the industrial sector for various reasons, in the agricultural sector a change in this nature is both feasible and overdue. The Commission, therefore, strongly recommends that all the State Governments should be directed to enact and implement progressive land legislations so as to effect basic structural changes in the existing production relations in the countryside.

At present surplus land in being allotted to SCs and STs. A part of the surplus land becoming available in future as a result of the operation of land ceiling laws etc. should also be allotted to the OBC landless labour.

Miscellaneous

- Certain parts of some occupational communities like Fishermen, Banjaras, Bansoforas, Khatwes etc. still suffer from the stigma of untouchability in some part of the country. They have been listed as O.B.Cs. by the Commission, but their inclusion in the lists of Scheduled Castes / Scheduled Tribes may be considered by the Government.
- Backward Classes Development Corporations should be set up both at the Central and State levels to implement various socio-educational and economic measures for their advancement.
- A separate Ministry / Department for O.B.Cs. at the Centre and States should be created to safeguard their interests.
- With a view to giving better representation to certain very backward parts of O.B.Cs like the Gaddis of Himachal Pradesh, Neo-Buddhists in Maharashtra, Fishermen in the Coastal areas, Gujjars in Jand, it is recommended that areas of their concentration may be carved out into separate constituencies at the time of delimitation.

Central Assistance

At present no Central Assistance is available to any State Government for implementing any welfare measures for Other Backward Classes. The 18 States and Union Territories which have undertaken such measures have to provide funds from their own resources.

During the Commission's tours practically every State Government pointed out that unless the Centre is prepared to liberally finance all special schemes for the upliftment of OBCs, it will be beyond the available resources of the States to undertake any worthwhile programme for the benefit of Other Backward Classes.

The Commission fully shares the views of the State Governments in this matter and strongly recommends that all development programmes specially designed for Other

Backward Classes should be financed by the Central Government in the same manner and to the same extent as done in the case of Scheduled Castes and Scheduled Tribes. Regarding the period of operation of the Commission's recommendations entire scheme should be reviewed after twenty years.

We have advisedly suggested this span of one generation, as the raising of social consciousness is a generational progress. Any review at a shorter interval would be rather arbitrary and would not give a fair indication of the impact of our recommendations on the prevailing status and life-styles of O.B.Cs.

IMPLEMENTATION

All the recommendations of the report are not yet implemented. The recommendation of reservations for OBC's in government services was implemented in 1993. As on 27 June 2008 there is still a backlog of 28, 670 OBC vacancies in government jobs. The recommendation of reservations in Higher educational institutes is implemented in 2008.

CRITICISM

The National Sample Survey puts the figure at 32%. There is substantial debate over the exact number of OBC's in India, with census data compromised by partisan politics. It is generally estimated to be sizable, but lower than the figures quoted by either the Mandal Commission or and National Sample Survey.

There is also an ongoing controversy about the estimation logic used by Mandal commission for calculating OBC population. Famous Indian Statistician, Mr.Yogendra Yadav who supports Reservations agrees that there is no empirical basis to the Mandal figure. According to him "It is a mythical construct based on reducing the number of SC/ST, Muslims and others and then arriving at a number."

National Sample Survey's 1999-2000 round estimated around 36 per cent of the country's population is defined as belonging to the Other Backward Classes (OBC). The proportion falls to 32 per cent on excluding Muslim OBCs. A survey conducted in 1998 by National Family Health Statistics (NFHS) puts the proportion of non-Muslim OBCs as 29.8 per cent L R Naik, the only Dalit member in the Mandal Commission refused to sign the Mandal recommendations. He said that there are two social blocks among the OBCs: upper caste (Jat and Gujjar) and upper OBCs (Yadavs, Kurmis, etc.) and Most Backward Classes (MBCs). He feared that upper OBCs would corner all the benefits of reservation.

Here we shall present the study of the Mandal Commissions's list of the OBC for the state of West Bengal only for the sake of brevity. In this list, Urao (along with its synonyms Bandot, Haro, Karkata, Luidu, Shitheo, Tigga and Tirki) has been listed as an OBC (OBC No.176). On the other hand, it is already in the list of Scheduled Tribes for the state with a slight difference of spelling "Oraon" (ST 33).

Similarly, Scheduled Tribes Kharia (OBC 105; synonym of Lodha, ST 23 in the ST List), Kherwar (OBC 107; ST 17, with a spelling Kharwar), Koda (OBC 113; ST 20, spelled Kora), Bhotia (OBC 33; ST 5, spelled Bhutia), Brijia (OBC 39, ST 7, with a spelling Birjia), Gonda (OBC 68; ST 12, spelled Gond) and Lakra (OBC 123, and Lakar OBC 122, which is actually a surname adopted by many members of the Scheduled Tribe Munda), which are already declared STs for the state. Tharu (OBC 171) is a widely studied scheduled tribe.

Thapa (OBC 170) is a synonym of ST Sherpa (ST 5, same as Bhutia, Tota, Dukpa, Kagatay, Tibetan, Yolmo). Many famous ST surnames have been listed as OBC Mahato (OBC 129), etc. Other anthropologically famous scheduled tribes listed as OBC are Kuki (OBC 118), Lushei (actually Lushai; OBC 124), Koli (OBC 116) and Rohangia.

Similar manipulation has been done with many Scheduled Castes also. For example in the state of West Bengal, Bhangi has been listed as OBC (No. 26), with a rider "excluding those in the Scheduled Caste". On the other hand the SC list for West Bengal shows that Bhangi (at place no. 22 in the SC list) is an unconditional SC for the whole of the territory of the state. Halalkhor has also been listed as an

OBC (No. 73) with a similar condition but this caste is also an unconditional SC (No. 21, spelled Halelkhor). A sub-caste of Dom (Maghaiya-Dom) has been listed as OBC at place No. 126. Dom as a whole has been a Scheduled Caste (No.17 in West Bengal SC list) for ages.

Bahelia (SC No. 2) has been listed by its synonym Chirimar (OBC 45). Bagal (OBC 11) is already there in the SC list at place number 1, with a spelling Bagll. Although Nat is an SC (No. 47), its sub-caste Karwal-Nat has been made an OBC (OBC 97). Jaliya Kaivartta (SC 23) is just the Sanskritized name of Machua listed as OBC (OBC 125). All the Nav-Buddhists (Neo-Buddhist) have been include in the OBC list, which is again an anomaly, because the Nav-Buddhists enjoy their SC status.

Not only synonyms or alternative spellings of the SCs and STs have been recorded as OBC, but also there are other types of manipulations like same OBC caste has been listed twice or sometimes thrice in the list of the same state. An example of this type of manipulation is Kahar in Bihar list (No. 23 as well as No. 70), Kewat (at no. 115 as well as 84.) At any rate the list is vitiated by such inclusions.

The Kuki tribes (ST) actually live in Nagaland, Meghalaya, Mizoram and Tripura, none of which are neighboring to West Bengal. Even if any member of the tribe migrates to West Bengal or anywhere else in India, either it retains its ST status of the mother state or becomes General population. It is difficult to believe that some Kuki tribes live in West Bengal as OBC. Lushai tribe (ST) live mainly in Mizoram and are the principal Mizo tribe.

They are also found in Manipur as ST. Koli (ST) are found in a widespread area ranging from Orissa to Rajasthan up to Karnatak. Rohangia ((OBC 158) are actually a distant tribe which mainly live in Myanmar but are also found in Bangla Desh-Myanmar-Tripura border areas). Introduction of such castes to the West Bengal OBC list seems to be an act of fertile brain and raises doubt whether any actual survey was done at all. At any rate a small number of these tribes could be present in the former East Bengal (now Bangla Desh) in areas adjoining former state of Assam and Myanmar before partition. Some OBC caste names given in the list are obsolete of forward castes. Tyagi is an upper caste, which lives in UP, Haryana and Delhi. This caste was earlier called Taga. But with a general trend of all the North Indian castes to Sanskritize their names, Taga people adopted a new name Tyagi which was similar to Taga.

But still in the remote village especially by the illiterate people Tyagis are often called Taga. We find the name of Taga in Haryana Mandal list (OBC 74), Delhi (OBC 81) and Uttar Pradesh (OBC 109, as Taga-Bhat). The principles and norms set in the very beginning regarding the criterion for the Non-Hindu communities have been violated flagrantly, hence now the Roman Catholic is not a religion but a caste in the eyes of the Mandal Commission (Latin Catholic, OBC 106, Kerala). Anglo-Indians, who are the off-springs of the British rulers, have also been made an Other Backward Caste (OBC 6, Kerala). Although it has been decided at the outset that only occupational castes among the Muslims and Christians and the castes bearing the same name as a Hindu OBC or SC will be included as a Muslim or Christian OBC caste, the set rule was violated wherever political expediency dictated.

For example Kayastha (Muslim) has been made an OBC (OBC 93, Uttar Pradesh) which does not fulfill the criteria set for inclusion of non-Hindu castes. A last word about credibility of the Mandal survey.

Presence of obsolete and archaic caste names like Taga (for Tyagi in Haryana, Delhi and UP), Bhuihar (for Bhumihar in Bihar), Domb (for Dom in all the southern states), listing of Kuki, Lushai, Rohangia tribes in West Bengal which are not found in West Bengal today but actually some of each of them lived in East Bengal in undivided India neighbouring Tripura, Meghalaya etc, and many such factors cannot be explained unless it is assumed that the Mandal list is not result of a recent survey, but it has been compiled by editing the caste list of 1931 census. But the editing was most inefficient. These names could not have crept in unless the old united Bengla caste list of 1931 was just copied and some named SC and ST, as well as well known forward caste names were just deleted, to arrive at the current OBC list of Mandal. Every state's OBC list has the same story. The entire list seems to be manipulated, but most carelessly and inefficiently manipulated.

Most famous scheduled castes like Dusadh (Dhari), Mochi, Domb (Dom) and Bhangi have been put as OBCs in many states. If the Government does not reject this whole Mandal list, all the SCs and STs listed as OBC will have to be deleted from the respective SC and ST lists. Because the Mandal Commission was a constitutional body which had done a survey and this survey was done at a later date than the surveys for the SC and ST, which were done during the British period without the authority of our present Indian Constitution.

Indeed any act (or survey) done under the authority of Indian Constitution automatically supersedes any act (or survey) of the British administration if there is an overlap or confusion.

PROTEST

A decade after the commission gave its report, V.P. Singh, the Prime Minister at the time, tried to implement its recommendations in 1989.

The criticism was sharp and colleges across the country held massive protests against it. Soon after, Rajiv Goswami, student of Delhi University, committed self-immolation in protest of the government's actions.

His act further sparked a series of self-immolations by other college students and led to a formidable movement against job reservations for Backward Castes in India. First student to die due to self immolation was Surinder Singh Chauhan on Sep 24, 1990.

ARGUMENTS AGAINST RESERVATIONS

The opponents of the issue argue:

- Allocating quotas on the basis of caste is a form of racial discrimination, and contrary to the right to equality. Although the exact relation between caste and race is far from well established

- As a consequence of legislating to provide reservations for Christians and Muslim, religious minorities in all government education institutions will be introduced which is contrary to the ideas of secularism, and is a form of anti-discrimination on the basis of religion.
- Most often, only economically sound people (and rather rich) from the so-called lower castes will make use of most of the reserved seats, thus counteracting the spirit of reservations. Political parties know reservations are no way to improve the lot of the poor and the backward. They support them because of self-interest of the "creamy layer", who use the reservations to further their own family interests, and as a political flag of 'achievement' during election campaigns. In fact, several studies show that the OBC class is quite comparable with the general caste in terms of annual per capita consumption expenditure, and the top strata of OBC is ahead in a host of consumption areas.
- The quality of these elite institutes may go down, because merit is severely being compromised by reserving seats for certain caste-based communities.
- There are no efforts made to give proper primary education to truly deprived classes, so there is no need to reserve seats for higher studies. The government schools in India have absolutely no comparison to the public schools in the developed countries, and only about 65% of the Indian population is literate,. The critics argue that "reservation" only in higher institutions and jobs, without improving primary and secondary education, cannot solve this problem.
- The government is dividing people on the basis of castes for political advantages.
- The caste system is kept alive through these measures. Instead of coming up with alternative innovative

ideas which make sure equal representation at the same time making the caste system irrelevant, the decision is only fortifying the caste system.

- The autonomy of the educational institutes are lost.
- Not everyone from the so-called upper classes are rich, and not all from so called lower classes are poor.
- The reservation policy of the Indian Congress will create a huge unrest in the Indian society. Providing quotas on the basis of caste and not on the basis of merit will deter the determination of many educated and deserving students of India.
- Multinational companies will be deterred by this action of the government, and foreign investment in India may dry down, hurting the growth of the Indian economy. Doubtless, urgent actions to improve the lot of the majority, which has not benefited from development — not achieved after 55 years of reservations for scheduled castes — are essential. But this must not hazard improving the economy's competitiveness in a very competitive world.
- There are already talks of reservations in the private sector. If even after providing so many facilities to reserved categories during education, if there is no adequate representation of those people in the work force, there must be some problems with the education system.

Critics of the Mandal Commission argue that it is unfair to accord people special privileges on the basis of caste, even in order to redress traditional caste discrimination. They argue that those that deserve the seat through merit will be at a disadvantage.

They reflect on the repercussions of unqualified candidates assuming critical positions in society (doctors, engineers, etc.). As the debate on OBC reservations spreads, a few interesting facts which raise pertinent question are already apparent. To begin with, do we have a clear idea what proportion of our population is OBC? The Mandal Commission (1980) it is 52 per cent. In 2001 Indian Census, out of India's population of 1,028,737,436 the Scheduled Castes comprise 166,635,700 and Scheduled Tribes 84,326,240, that is 16.2% and 8.2% respectively.

There is no data on OBCs in the census. However, just as to National Sample Survey's 1999-2000 round around 36 per cent of the country's population is defined as belonging to the Other Backward Classes (OBC). The proportion falls to 32 per cent on excluding Muslim OBCs.

A survey conducted in 1998 by National Family Health Statistics (NFHS) puts the proportion of non-Muslim OBCs as 29.8 per cent. The NSSO data also shows that already 23.5 per cent of college seats are occupied by OBCs. That's just 8.6 per cent short of their share of population just as to the same survey.

Other arguments include that entrenching the separate legal status of OBCs and SC/STs will perpetuate caste differentiation and encourage competition among communities at the expense of national unity. They believe that only a small new elite of educated Dalits, Adivasis, and OBCs benefit from reservations, and that such measures do nothing to lift the mass of people out of backwardness and poverty.

ARGUMENTS IN SUPPORT OF RESERVATIONS

- Affirmative Action has helped many - if not everyone from underprivileged and/or under-represented communities to grow and occupy top positions in the world's leading industries. Reservation in education is not the final solution, it is just one of the many solutions. Reservations is a means to increase representation of hitherto under-represented caste groups and thereby improve diversity on campus.
- Although Reservation schemes do undermine the quality of education but still affirmative Action schemes are in place in many countries including USA, South Africa, Malaysia, Brazil etc. It was

researched in Harvard University that Affirmative Action programmes are beneficial to the underprivileged. The studies said that Blacks who enter elite institutions with lower test scores and grades than those of whites achieve notable success after graduation. They earn advanced degrees at rates identical to those of their white classmates. They are even slightly more likely than whites from the same institutions to obtain professional degrees in law, business and medicine. They become more active than their white classmates in civic and community activities.

- Although Reservation schemes do undermine the quality of education but still they are needed to provide social justice to the most marginalized and underprivileged is our duty and their human right. Reservation will really help these marginalized people to lead successful lives, thus eliminating caste-based discrimination which is still widely prevalent in India especially in the rural areas. (over 60% of Indian population stays in Villages).
- But meritrocracy is meaningless without equality. First all people must be brought to the same level, whether it elevates a part or delevels another, regardless of merit. Only after that merit becomes meaningful. Privileged people have never known to go backward due to reservations or lack of "meritrocracy". Reservations have only slowed down the process of the 'forward' becoming richer and backward becoming poorer.
- In a perfectly functioning society the institutions and various walks of life must represent the many parts roughly in proportion to their share in population. In India it is clearly not the case and hence the need for reservations.
- India does not have the economic or institutional capacity for undertaking a grassroots based solution to the problem, so reservations remain the only practical solution for social anti-discrimination

- People who support reservations keenly invite all the anti-reservationists to lead the life of a backward class citizen and live within the means that they have for themselves. It is their contention that in a experimental set-up like this the differences in achievement/performance would disappear or reduce down to experimental errors/random error. Underlying idea being that everyone is born equal but into an unequal circumstances. And when the circumstances have been a result of a social system then the system either needs to be abandoned or reformed.
- Reservations are a political necessity in India because vast influential parts of voting population. All governments have supported maintaining and/or increasing reservations. Reservations are legal and binding. As shown by Gujjar agitations (Rajasthan, 2007–2008), increasing reservations is also essential for peacekeeping in India.
- Reservations will go a long way in capacity building with regard to the human resource of the country. In the long run, it has tremendous economic benefits as it will raise the productivity of the majority of the potential workforce of the country
- The government of India, is bound and empowered by the constitution of the country to secure for all citizens equality in social, economic and political sphere.

NAMANTAR ANDOLAN

Namantar Andolan was started by Dalit Panthers. Namanter Andolan is a movement to change Marathwada University's name to Dr. B.R. Ambedkar University.

Marathwada is made up of five districts — Aurangabad, Parbhani, Beed, Nanded and Usmanabad — out of 28 districts that were part of the earlier Hyderabad state ruled by the Nizam of Hyderabad. The Marathwada part of the state was merged with Maharashtra after its trifurcation in 1956. As per the 1971 census, the population of this region was 8,058,347. This consisted of 80% Hindus; 9.52% belonged to Scheduled Castes; 11.8% Muslims, 7.2% Buddhists, and the rest were of other communities. Marathwada is an economically backward region of the state. 82% of the people are occupied in farming, as against the figure of 65% for the whole state. At that time (1971 census), industrial activity was almost nil, with only two persons out of 1,000 engaged in industry compared to 100 industrial workers out of every 1,000 in Mumbai.

Further, Dalits comprised about 17% (9.5% of Scheduled Castes and 7.2% of the population compared to about 12% for the whole of Maharashtra. About 75% of the Dalit population consisted of farm labourers, and 90% of the Dalit lived below the poverty line. The literacy rate among the Dalits in Marathwada was about 19% as compared to the general literacy rate of 35%. Among the Dalits, the Mahar community was supposed to be relatively better off and socially more conscious and with a higher rate of literacy. Unemployment was a severe problem in Marathwada. For example, on 23 March 1974, 2,000 youths who came to Parbhani town looking for jobs were told that only 40 posts were to be filled up. There was no scope for the youths in farming or in industry.

Thus education was the only field where there was a concentration of Dalit youths. After one united march with Panthers there was a split in the students' advisory committee, allegedly provoked by Panthers. The differences of opinion among the leaders of the committee were also caused by the meeting they had with Vasantrao Patil. Those opposing the renaming move organized themselves under the banner of 'Marathwada Vidyarthi Kriti Samiti'. This Samiti gave a call of colleges in Marathwada remained closed from 12 to 26 September 1977. The Samiti also organized a total Marathwada bandh on 19 September.

DALIT BUDDHIST MOVEMENT

The Dalit Buddhist movement (dubbed as Navayana by certain Ambedkerites) is arguably the most influential of a series of 19th and 20th century Buddhist revival movements in India. It received its most substantial impetus from B. R. Ambedkar's call for the conversion of Dalits to Buddhism in the context of a caste based society that considered them to be at the lowest end of the hierarchy.

ORIGINS

Buddhism was once dominant through much of India, it had however begun to decline by the 12th century. The Buddhist revival began in India in 1891, when the Sri Lankan Buddhist leader Anagarika Dharmapala founded the Maha Bodhi Society The Maha Bodhi Society mainly attracted upper-caste people, most of whom did not identify themselves specifically as Buddhists, seeing no significant difference between Buddhism and Hinduism.

South India

In 1890, Pandit C. Ayodhya Dasa (1845-1914), better known as Iyothee Thass, founded the Sakya Buddhist Society (also known as the Indian Buddhist Association). The first president of the Indian Buddhist Association was the German born American Paul Carus, the author of The Gospel of Buddha (1894).

Thass, a Tamil Siddha physician, was the pioneer of the Tamil Dalit movement. He argued that Tamil Dalits were originally Buddhists. He led a delegation of prominent Dalits to Henry Steel Olcott and asked for his help in the reestablishment of "Tamil Buddhism." Olcott helped Thass to visit Sri Lanka, where he received diksha from Bhikkhu Sumangala Nayake.

After returning to India, Thass established the Sakya Buddhist Society in Madras with branches in many places including Karnataka. Thass established a weekly magazine called Oru Paisa Tamizhan ("One Paisa Tamilian") in Chennai in 1907, which served as a newsletter linking all the new branches of the Sakya Buddhist Society. The magazine discussed traditions and practices of Tamil Buddhism, new developments in the Buddhist world, and the Indian subcontinent's history from the Buddhist point of view. Brahmananda Reddy, a Dalit leader of Andhra Pradesh, was also fascinated by Buddhism.

Uttar Pradesh

In the early 20th century, the Barua Buddhists of Bengal under the leadership of Kripasaran Mahasthavir (1865-1926), founder of the Bengal Buddhist Association in Calcutta (1892), established viharas in cities such as Lucknow, Hyderabad, Shillong and Jamshedpur. In Lucknow, Bodhanand Mahastavir (1874-1952) advocated Buddhism for Dalits. Born Mukund Prakash in a Bengali Brahmin family, he was orphaned at a young age, and was then raised in Benaras by an aunt. He was initially attracted to Christianity, but became a Buddhist after a meeting with Buddhists monks from Ceylon at a Theosophical Conference in Benares.

He later lived in Lucknow where he came in contact with Barua Buddhists, many of whom were employed as cooks by the British. In 1914, Prakash was ordained Bodhanand Mahastavir in Calcutta in the presence of Kripasaran Mahasthvir. He began preaching Buddhism in Lucknow. He founded the Bharatiye Buddh Samiti in 1916, and set up a vihara in 1928.

In his book Mula Bharatavasi Aur Arya ("Original Inhabitants and Aryans"), Mahastavir stated that the shudras were the original inhabitants of India, who were enslaved by the Aryans. Bodhanand Mahastavir wrote another book on Buddhist rituals called Baudha Dvicharya. His associate, Chandrika Prasad Jigyasu, founded the Bahujan Kalyan Prakashan.

The two co-authored a book on the life and teaching of the Buddha. Acharya Ishvardatt Medharthi (1900-1971) of Kanpur also supported the cause of the Dalits. He had studied Pali at Gurukul Kangri and Buddhist scripture was well known to him. He was initiated into Buddhism by Gyan Keto and the Lokanatha in 1937. Gyan Keto (1906-1984), born Peter Schoenfeldt was a German who arrived to Ceylon in 1936 and became a Buddhist. Although Medharthi heavily criticized the Indian caste system, he didn't criticize Hinduism. He claimed that the Dalits ("Adi Hindus") were the ancient rulers of India and had been trapped into slavery by the Aryan invaders. He also claimed that the sanatana dharma was the religion of "Adi Hindus", and tried to reconcile Buddhism with the Sant Mat. Another Bhikkhu of Kanpur, Bhikshu Uttam, was a strong supporter of the Arya Samaj and the Jat Pat Todak Mandal, the anti-caste wing of the Arya Samaj.

B. R. AMBEDKAR

At the Yeola conference in 1935, prominent Dalit leader B. R. Ambedkar declared that he would not die a Hindu, saying that it perpetuates caste injustices. Ambedkar was approached by various leaders of different denominations and faiths.

Meetings were held to discuss the question of Dalit religion and the pros and cons of conversion. On May 22, 1936, an "All Religious Conference" was held at Lucknow. It was attended by prominent Dalit leaders including Jagjivan Ram, though Ambedkar could not attend it. At the conference, Muslim, Christian, Sikh, and Buddhist representatives presented the tenets of their respective religions in an effort to win over Dalits.

Buddhist monk Lokanatha visited Ambedkar's residence at Dadar on June 10, 1936 and tried to persuade him to embrace Buddhism. Later in an interview to the Press, Lokanatha said that Ambedkar was impressed with Buddhism and that his own ambition was to convert all Dalits to Buddhism. In 1937, Lokanatha published a pamphlet Buddhism Will Make You Free, dedicated to the Depressed Classes of India from his press in Ceylon.

In early 1940s, Ambedkar visited Acharya Ishvardatt Medharthi's Buddhpuri school in Kanpur. Medharthi had earlier been initiated into Buddhism by Lokanatha, and by the mid-1940s, he had close contacts with Ambedkar. For a short while, Ambedkar also took Pali classes from Medharthi in Delhi. Bodhananda Mahastvir and B. R. Ambedkar first met in 1926, at the "Indian Non-Brahmin Conference" convened by Shahu IV of Kolhapur. They met on two more occasions and for a short while in the 1940s, where they discussed dhamma. Mahastavir objected to Dr Ambedkar's second marriage because his bride was a Brahmin. Later, his followers actively participated in Ambedkar's Republican Party of India.

Ambedkar's Conversion

After publishing a series of books and articles arguing that Buddhism was the only way for the Untouchables to gain equality, Ambedkar publicly converted on October 14, 1956 at Deekshabhoomi, Nagpur.

He took the three refuges and the Five Precepts from a Buddhist monk, Bhadant U Chandramani, in the traditional manner and then in his turn administered them to the 380,000 of his followers that were present.

The conversion ceremony was attended by Medharthi, his main disciple Bhoj Dev Mudit, and Mahastvir Bodhanand's Sri Lankan successor, Bhante Pragyanand. Ambedkar would die less than two months later, just after finishing his definitive work on Buddhism. Many Dalits employ the term "Ambedkar(ite) Buddhism" to designate the Buddhist movement, which started with Ambedkar's conversion and many converted people called themselves as "Nava-Bauddha" *i.e.* New Buddhists.

22 Vows of Ambedkar

After receiving ordination, Ambedkar gave dhamma diksha to his followers. The ceremony included 22 vows given to all new converts after Three Jewels and Five Precepts. On 16 October 1956, Ambedkar performed another mass religious conversion ceremony at Chanda.

He prescribed 22 vows to his followers:

1. I shall have no faith in Brahma, Vishnu and Maheshwara nor shall I worship them.
2. I shall have no faith in Rama and Krishna who are believed to be incarnation of God nor shall I worship them.

3. I shall have no faith in Gauri, Ganapati and other gods and goddesses of Hindus nor shall I worship them.
4. I do not believe in the incarnation of God.
5. I do not and shall not believe that Lord Buddha was the incarnation of Vishnu. I believe this to be sheer madness and false propaganda.
6. I shall not perform Shraddha nor shall I give pinddan.
7. I shall not act in a manner violating the principles and teachings of the Buddha.
8. I shall not allow any ceremonies to be performed by Brahmins.
9. I shall believe in the equality of man.
10. I shall endeavor to establish equality.
11. I shall follow the noble eightfold path of the Buddha.
12. I shall follow the ten paramitas prescribed by the Buddha.
13. I shall have compassion and loving kindness for all living beings and protect them.
14. I shall not steal.
15. I shall not tell lies.
16. I shall not commit carnal sins.
17. I shall not take intoxicants like liquor, drugs etc.
18. I shall endeavor to follow the noble eightfold path and practice compassion and loving kindness in every day life.
19. I renounce Hinduism, which is harmful for humanity and impedes the advancement and development of humanity because it is based on inequality, and adopt Buddhism as my religion.
20. I firmly believe the Dhamma of the Buddha is the only true religion.
21. I believe that I am having a rebirth.
22. I solemnly declare and affirm that I shall hereafter lead my life just as to the principles and teachings of the Buddha and his Dhamma.

Nowadays many Ambedkarite Organisations are working for these 22 vows (*i.e.* 22 Pratigya). They believe that these vows only are responsible for the existence and rapid growth of present Buddhism in India. The umbrella organization known as the 22 Pledges Practice and Propagation Movement (*i.e.* in Hindi- 22 Pratigya Aacharan aur Prachaar Abhiyan) is fully devoted for this purpose. This totally non-political movement is the brain-child of Arvind Sontakke, and comprises around 5,000,000 volunteers (Pracharaks) including many regional and local groups throughout India.

DALIT BUDDHISM MOVEMENT AFTER AMBEDKAR'S DEATH

The Buddhist movement was somewhat hindered by Dr. Ambedkar's death so shortly after his conversion. It did not receive the immediate mass support from the Untouchable population that Ambedkar had hoped for.

Division and lack of direction among the leaders of the Ambedkarite movement have been an additional impediment. The 2001 census, there are currently 7.95 million Buddhists in India, at least 5.83 million of whom are Buddhists in Maharashtra.

This makes Buddhism the fifth-largest religion in India and 6% of the population of Maharashtra, but less than 1% of the overall population of India. The Buddhist revival remains concentrated in two states: Ambedkar's native Maharashtra, and Uttar Pradesh — the land of Bodhanand Mahastavir, Acharya Medharthi and their associates.

Developments in Uttar Pradesh

Acharya Medharthi retired from his Buddhapuri school in 1960, and shifted to an ashram in Haridwar. He turned to the Arya Samaj and conducted vedic yajnas all over India. After his death, he was cremated just as to Arya Samaj rites. His Buddhpuri school became embroiled in property disputes. His follower, Bhoj Dev Mudit, converted to Buddhism in 1968 and set up a school of his own.

Rajendranath Aherwar appeared as an important Dalit leader in Kanpur. He joined the Republican Party of India and converted to Buddhism along with his whole family in 1961. In 1967, he founded the Kanpur branch of "Bharatiya

Buddh Mahasabha". He held regular meetings where he preached Buddhism, officiated at Buddhist weddings and life cycle ceremonies, and organized festivals on Dr. Ambedkar's Jayanti (birth day), Buddha Jayanti, Diksha Divas (the day Ambedkar converted), and Dr Ambedkar Paranirvan Divas (the day Ambedkar died).

The Dalit Buddhist movement in Kanpur gained impetus with the arrival of Dipankar, a Chamar bhikkhu, in 1980. Dipankar had come to Kanpur on a Buddhist mission and his first public appearance was scheduled at a mass conversion drive in 1981. The event was organized by Rahulan Ambawadekar, an RPI Dalit leader. In April 1981, Ambawadekar founded the Dalit Panthers (U.P. Branch) inspired by the Maharashtrian Dalit Panthers. The event met with severe criticism and opposition from Vishwa Hindu Parishad and was banned.

In 2002, Kanshi Ram, a popular out-caste political leader from a Sikh religious background, announced his intention to convert to Buddhism on October 14, 2006, the fiftieth anniversary of Ambedkar's conversion. He intended for 20,000,000 of his supporters to convert at the same time. Part of the significance of this plan was that Ram's followers include not only Untouchables, but persons from a variety of castes, who could significantly broaden Buddhism's support. However, he died October 9, 2006 after a lengthy illness; he was cremated as per Buddhist rituals. Another popular Dalit leader, Bahujan Samaj Party chief Mayawati, has said that she and her followers will embrace Buddhism after the BSP gains control of the government.

Maharashtra

Japanese-born Bhadant Nagarjun Surai Sasai is an important Buddhist leader in India. Sasai came to India in 1966 and met Nichidatsu Fuji, whom he helped with the Peace Pagoda at Rajgir.

He fell out with Fuji, however, and started home, but, by his own account, was stopped by a dream in which a figure resembling Nagarjuna appeared and said, "Go to Nagpur".

In Nagpur, he met Wamanrao Godbole, the person who had organized the conversion ceremony for Dr. Ambedkar in 1956. Sasai claims that when he saw a photograph of Dr. Ambedkar at Godbole's home, he realised that it was Ambedkar who had appeared in his dream.

At first, Nagpur folk considered Surai Sasai very strange. Then he began to greet them with "Jai Bhim" (victory to Ambedkar) and to build viharas. In 1987 a court case to deport him on the grounds that he had overstayed his visa was dismissed, and he was granted Indian citizenship. Sasai is one of the main leaders of the campaign to free the Mahabodhi Temple at Bodh Gaya from Hindu control.

Organized Mass Conversions

Since Ambedkar's conversion, several thousand people from different castes have converted to Buddhism in ceremonies including the twenty-two vows. The Tamil Nadu and Gujarat governments passed new laws in 2003 to ban "forced" religious conversions.

These laws were later withdrawn due to heavy opposition:

- 1957: In 1957, Mahastvir Bodhanand's Sri Lankan successor, Bhante Pragyanand, held a mass conversion drive for 15,000 people in Lucknow.
- 2001: A prominent Indian Dalit Buddhist leader and political activist, Udit Raj, organized a large mass conversion on November 4, 2001 where he gave the 22 vows, but the event met with active opposition from the government.
- 2006, Hyderabad: A report from the UK daily The Guardian said that some Hindus have converted to Buddhism. Buddhist monks from the UK and the U.S. attended the conversion ceremonies in India. In response, Hindu nationalists asserted that Dalits should concentrate on illiteracy and poverty rather than looking for new religions.
- 2006, Gulbarga: On October 14, 2006 hundreds of people converted from Hinduism to Buddhism in Gulburga (Karnataka).

- 2006: A Buddhist source claimed that "300,000 Dalits are estimated" to have converted to Buddhism as part of 50th year celebrations of Ambedkar's deeksha in 2006. Non-Partisan sources put the number of attendees (not converts) at 30,000. The move was criticized by Hindu groups as "unhelpful" and has been criticized as a "political stunt."
- 2007, Mumbai: On May 27, 2007 tens of thousands of Dalits from Maharashtra gathered at the Mahalakshmi racecourse in Mumbai to mark the 50th anniversary of the conversion of Ambedkar. The number of people who actually converted, however, versus the number of people in attendance was not clear. The event was organized by the Republican Party of India leader Ramdas Athvale.

Criticism of Conversions

Hindu critics have argued that efforts to convert Hindus to Ambedkarite Buddhism are political stunts rather than sincere commitments to social reform. In addition, several Dalit leaders have stated that they are not against the upper castes *per se*.

Leaders of the Dalit Bahujan Samaj Party have said that they are being branded as "anti-Hindu" because of the publicity associated with the conversions is largely the work of "manuvadi vested interests, including political parties and parts of the media" and that they are only interested in peaceful dialogue with the Brahmins.

DISTINCTIVE INTERPRETATION

Dr. Gail Omvedt, an American-born and naturalized Indian sociologist and human rights activist:

- Ambedkar's Buddhism seemingly differs from that of those who accepted by faith, who 'go for refuge' and accept the canon. This much is clear from its basis: it does not accept in totality the scriptures of the Theravada, the Mahayana, or the Vajrayana. The question that is then clearly put forth: is a fourth yana, a Navayana, a kind of modernistic enlightenment version of the Dhamma really possible within the framework of Buddhism?

Most Dalit Indian Buddhists espouse an eclectic version of Buddhism, primarily based on Theravada, but with additional influences from Mahayana and Vajrayana. On many subjects, they give Buddhism a distinctive interpretation. Of particular note is their emphasis on Shakyamuni Buddha as a political and social reformer, rather than merely as a spiritual leader.

They point out that the Buddha required his monastic followers to ignore caste distinctions, and that he was critical of the social inequality that existed in his own time. Ambedkar's followers do not believe that a person's unfortunate conditions at birth are the result of previous karma.

9

Globalisation Status of Dalits

INTRODUCTION

The plethora of literature on globalisation paradoxically seems to induce more confusion than clearing out the true nature of its dynamics. For many, it is not at all a new phenomenon; it has been there in essence in the cross border trade that went on centuries ago and in an identifiable form in the nineteenth century capitalism insofar as it lent both labour and capital substantially mobile, gave fillip to international trade and when national economies were kept in kilter by the operation of the gold standard.

This attempt at universalising the theory as well as praxis of globalisation tends to imply futility of resistance to globalisation. Many proffer a TINA (There Is No Alternative) argument as per which despite adverse impact of globalisation on masses of people, there is no alternative for the world than adopting the globalisation model. This argument, while reflecting the admission of the adverse impact of globalisation and therefore sounding more credible, tends to indicate accrual of more benefits than costs.

It tends to neutralise the theoretical arguments against globalisation and therefore cripples the resistance movement much before its articulation. Then there are sponsored authorships that ceaselessly contribute multi-dimensional arguments in support of these policies. They could range from out right theoretical distortions to empirical amplification. The sheer number of such studies claiming all kinds of success stories as attributes of these policies and all kinds of failures as due to absence of them overwhelms and enfeebles the truth to the contrary. The main theme of globalisation is pivoted on the promise of development and its "trickle down" to the subaltern parts of the society. Notwithstanding the total contrary evidence, the glitter created by the free markets misleads one into believing that the benefits of globalisation reached the weak and poor of the society.

After nearly a decade of adoption of these policies in our country and on the eve of the launch of so called second phase of Reforms, it is time that we examined the magnitude and direction of the impact of these policies on the dalits representing the oppressed people in India. This document seeks to attempt this task with the help of available statistics.

GLOBALISATION IN A HISTORICAL PERSPECTIVE

The doctrinal basis of today's globalisation is provided by the "neo-liberalism" that represented revival of economic liberalism propounded by Adam Smith in 1776 in his famous book titled, "Wealth of Nations". Economic liberalism advocated the abolition of the government intervention in economic matters; it considered fee trade was the best way for a nation's economy to develop.

These ideas were "liberal" in the sense of no controls. Underneath their democratic facade, promotion of individualism and encouragement of free enterprise, they came to mean free hand for the capitalists for exploitation of labour and to make huge profits at any cost. These ideas ruled the world through the 1800s and early 1900s till the great depression of the 1930s eclipsed them with the theory of a British economist named John Maynard Keynes.

This theory propounded that full employment is necessary for capitalism to grow and it can be achieved only if governments and central banks intervened to increase employment. It worked well through the post World War II reconstruction period and thereafter through the mid sixties. The USA which had emerged as the major economy of the world long before the World War II, immensely benefited from the state-coordinated wartime economy so as to assume the reigns of global capitalist order. It zealously guarded the capitalist system against the radical nationalism sprouting at many places, invariably with the use of force under the peculiar terminology of falsehood like "protection against the threat to stability" (a case of overthrow of the first democratic government of Guatemala in 1954 or a blatant military intervention planned in Italy in 1948 in the wake of election results sensing the undesired outcome). With over half of the world's wealth, the USA performed the role of world's banker in the post-World War II system.

However, with the increasing financial crisis of the debt-ridden countries, the Nixon administration decided to dismantle this system, giving rise to huge explosion of unregulated capital flows that totally marginalized the real economy. The composition of the international financial transaction shifted from real economy to speculation. Within just two decades form 1971 to 1990, the percentage of transactions related to real economy came down from 90% to paltry 10% and further declined to 5% over next five years. The capitalist crisis over the last 25 years, with its shrinking profit rates, inspired the corporate elite to revive economic liberalism into neo-liberalism.

This neo-liberalism is opeartionalised through "the Washington Consensus". This phrase significantly refers to the structural adjustment programmes designed by the government of the United States and the international financial institutions that it largely dominates. These institutions are the core of "*de facto* world government" representing the interests of transnational Corporations, banks and investment firms in a new Imperial age. With regard to the operational features of the neo-liberalism, none other than its patron saint Adam smith had exposed its inherent class bias.

Writing about the society of his times he pointed out that the "principal architects" of policy in England were "merchants and manufacturers", who used state power to serve their own interests, however "grievous" the effect on others, including the people of England. The "principle architects" of the neo-liberal "Washington Consensus" are the masters of the private economy, mainly huge Corporations that control much of the international economy and have the means to dominate policy formation as well as the structuring of thought and opinion. The institutional structure through which the globalisation is being promoted is basically subservient to the interests of big capital, particularly that of US who seeks to leverage its dominant role in global economy through essentially a short-term, profit-maximization model.

Its anti-labour, anti-people characteristics are deeply embedded in its architecture that is incapable of anything but perpetuation of poverty, inequality and environmental degradation.

CRISIS DRIVEN' REFORMS: INDIA INTO GLOBAL ORDER

The Brettonwood institutions have been the main instrument to spread the wings of globalisation. However, it came be adopted by every nation state in the form of some kind of local initiative, euphemistically called as Reforms. The conditionalities accepted as a rescue package were declared here as economic reforms by the government. These Economic Reforms launched in July 1991 in India were in nature of a crisis management response to the economic and political crises that erupted in early 1991.

The economic crisis comprised a steep fall in the foreign exchange reserve, galloping inflation, large public and current account deficits and mounting of domestic and foreign debt. In politics, the fall of two governments in a short span of four months, from November 1990 to March 1991; deferment of presentation of the union budget, fairly long political interregnum till the elections, the assassination of a former prime minister Rajiv Gandhi in their midst and the emergence of a minority government with a leader sans charisma, reflected an unprecedented crisis.

These events led to a sharp erosion of confidence in India among lenders, down gradation of India's credit rating and consequently snapping of international credit lines from private or commercial sources. Indian Reforms thus, were essentially of a 'crisis driven' variety. They did not represent strategic choice with a vision of long-term development of Indian people. The blue print for the Reforms was provided by the combination of macro-economic stabilisation and structural adjustment programme of International Monetary Fund (IMF) and World Bank respectively, which had been adopted by many countries before in similar situations.

The typical measures under these programmes are:

Macro-economic Stabilisation:

- Complete autonomy of the central bank to pursue independent monetary policy,
- Devaluation of currency for making exchange rate more realistic,
- Elimination/ reduction of all subsidies,
- Introduction of financial structure reforms and free entry of foreign financial institutions,
- Reduction/ elimination of fiscal and balance of payments deficits,
- Removal of all controls on prices, exchange and interest rate, and
- Withdrawal of restrictions on imports.

Structural Adjustment:

- Decontrol of industries,
- Privatisation of government-owned entities,
- Structural changes in the economy aimed at export-led growth,
- Free entry of foreign capital and technology without any let, hindrance or conditions,
- Free entry and exit of foreign firms including financial and services industries,
- Free cross border movement of capital and other funds,
- Legislative safeguards for protection of intellectual property rights,
- Creation of legal climate for enforcement of legal contracts, private property rights, and free entry and exit of business, industrial and financial firms.

The underlying economic philosophy of these programmes stems from the theories of neoliberalism that propounds the rule of market, reduction in the role of State, cutting public expenditure on social services and eliminating the concept of public good; deregulation, and general replacement of public with private. It is based on the premise that the public sector leads to inefficient allocation and utilisation of economic resources and that the enterprise of private sector overcomes it through the dynamics of free market.

Dalits in India

Dalits, as the ex-untouchables prefer to be called, are a very distinct social group. While belonging to a broad class of have-nots they suffer an additional disability of social oppression. Economically, most of them are still the poorest of poor. The balance minuscule minority has managed to escape poverty limits and to locate itself on to a continuum ranging up to a reasonable level of prosperity. The main factor that has catalysed this transition is the reservation policy, which has provided them a basic opportunity to enter the modern sectors of economy. In social terms however, all dalits, irrespective of their economic standing, still suffer oppression. This social oppression varies from the crudest variety of untouchability, still being practised in rural areas, to the sophisticated forms of discrimination encountered even in modern sectors of urban areas. Although the statistics indicate that dalits have made a significant progress on almost all parametres during the five post-independence decades, the relative distance between them and non-dalits seems to have remained the same or increased.

More than 75 per cent of the dalit workers are still connected with land; 25 per cent being the marginal and small farmers and balance over 50 per cent are the landless labourers. In urban areas, they work mainly in unorganised sector. Out of the total dalit population of 138 million, the number of dalits in services falling in the domain of reservations does not exceed 1.1 million; a mere 0.8 per cent.

Organisation of Study

Corresponding to dual disabilities of the dalits, the main body of the document is divided in two parts:

1. The impact on dalits as a part of the class of have-nots
2. The impact on dalits as a disadvantaged social group.

In the first part, impact of the Reforms in relation to the three most critical factors affecting the poor people is studied.

They are:

- Food security,
- Inflation
- Employment.

Poverty, which represents the combined influence of all deprivations, is also reviewed separately. In light of the vast data available on the impact of similar reforms in other countries, this part is sub-divided so as to outline 'Indian experience' and 'international experience' separately. The second part focuses on the influence of the Reforms on the specific three disabilities suffered by the dalits in addition to their poverty.

They are:

- Educational backwardness,
- Discrimination in employment,
- Atrocities
- Socio-cultural suppression.

The last concluding part sums up the study with the observations regarding certain prerequisites for the Reforms to be more responsive to the problems of people, particularly the dalits.

IMPACT OF THE REFORMS ON THE POOR

Impact of the Reforms on poor people can be assessed along several dimensions but here the study confines itself to the three most predominant ones, *viz*, food security, inflation and employment. Implementation of the Reforms over the last five years in India has generated huge data so as to enable meaningful and autonomous assessment of our native experience. This is covered in the first part. The Reforms however were implemented many years before and in many countries. This vast treasure of information that is available can be used to validate or correct the inferences from the study. This is covered in the second part.

INDIAN EXPERIENCE

Food Security

Food security mainly relates with the production, distribution and pricing of food grains and thus brings agriculture, Public Distribution System (PDS) and the subsidy structure in to focus. The Reform measures that predominantly affect them are reduction in fiscal deficit, reduction in subsidies, devaluation of Rupee, export orientation and reduction in agricultural credit. Considering the pattern of the budgetary outlays of the government, the fiscal contraction inevitably resulted in a disproportionate cut in capital expenditure.

The capital expenditure slid from 5.10 per cent of GDP in 1990-91 down to 2.74 per cent in 1995-96. In terms of percentage of total expenditure, it fell from an average of 32.8 per cent during the preceding five years of the Reforms, to average of 22.05 per cent during the succeeding five years of the Reforms. In 1995-96 (BE), it was as low as 17.82 per cent. Agriculture sector also bore the share of this cut. The average annual increase in public sector outlay on agriculture and irrigation during 1985-90 fell from ₹ 1.3 billion to an average of ₹ 0.68 billion during 1990-92. This cut is bound to have a depressing effect on the agricultural production in coming years.

The subsidy on fertilizer had played a crucial role in quadrupling food grain production from 46 million tonnes for a population of 363 million in 1951 to 170 million tonnes in 1991 for a population of 832 million. But, after the launch of the Reforms, the subsidy was reduced. It slid from 0.82 per cent of GDP in 1990-91 to 0.75 per cent of GDP in 1995-96. The prices of the phosphatic and potassium based fertilizers were decontrolled and that of nitrogen based fertilizers were reduced by 10 per cent. The prices of phosphatic and potassium based fertilizers soared to international level resulting into sharp fall in their consumption. Consumption of phosphatic one fell from 3.3 million tonnes of nutrients in 1991-92 to 2.7 million tonnes in 1993- 94 and that of potassic fell from 1.4 to 0.9 million tonnes in the same period. Some amount of substitution effect raised the consumption of nitrogen-based fertilizer from 8 million tonnes in 1991-92 to 10.8 million tonnes in 1995-96 resulting in skewing of the nutrient balance.

As against the consumption ratio of a mix of nitrogenic, phosphatic and potassic fertilizer of 5.9:2.4:1 in 1991-92, closer to the deemed ideal of 4:2:1, it deteriorated to 9:3:1 in 1994-95. This imbalance is said to have an adverse effect on soil quality and in turn on its productivity. The nutrient imbalance apart, a study of Andhra Pradesh, Maharashtra and Karnataka by Gaiha (1994) has noted a significant reduction in per hectare fertilizer consumption during the Reform period, which expectedly showed up in the decline in food grain production. This inherent threat to food security is further magnified by the devaluation of rupee by about 25 per cent effected in July 1991. It resulted in making our food grains cheaper in the international market. As a result, even the ordinary (non-aromatic) rice (besides the usually exported superfine aromatic (basmati) rice was exported in huge volumes.

The policy impetus to export of rice and wheat is reflected in the actual exports overshooting the targets. For example, in 1995- 96 (October- September) actual rice export had reached 5.51 million tonnes as against the target of 2.5 million tonnes. Increasing exports and free market sales of foodgrains have contributed to a drastic reduction in the stocks of foodgrains with the public procurement agencies. For example, by September 1996, there was a whooping reduction of 10 million tonnes in the stock of foodgrains. In case of wheat, it dipped down to 10.36 million tonnes, even lower than the prescribed minimum norm of 13.1 million tonnes. The policy thrust on agricultural exports has moreover resulted in diversion of land to the export production of non-food primary products. There has been a spurt in corporate farming for export horticulture and floriculture products, etc. As per one FAO report, this trend of shifting land for exportable non-food grain crops had already set in even in the decade ending 1991. The prospects for this trend lies in the fact that there is a huge demand in the developed countries for some 9000 varieties of edible non-food grain primary products which grow in sub-tropical and tropical regions of the developing countries.

Likewise, there is an exportable surplus of foodgrains and dairy products in the developed countries that craves for markets. Surely, as some economists apprehend, India may turn to be a net importer of foodgrains in not so a distant future. The international market for agri-products being a oligopsony of three to six giant companies whose control over the market extends to 80 to 90 per cent, export thrust in this area may not moreover be cost effective. As the experience of some African countries shows, the increasing export of foodgrains for same level of foreign exchange earning certainly impairs the food security of people.

The reforms in banking led to a severe squeeze on agriculture lending. The share of agriculture in net bank credit consistently declined and fell from 17.4 per cent to 12.4 per cent during March 1990 to March 1995. Expressed in constant (1980-81) rupees, it fell from ₹ 81,470 million in 1989-90 to ₹ 70,500 million in 1994-95. Considering, the hike in input costs, the impact of this squeeze could have only been deleterious on food grains production. As a measure of ensuring food security to the large mass of Indian population, public distribution system was instituted in India in the wake of the calamity of the Great Bengal Famine of 1942-43 and the World War-II.

The system comprises over 4,24,000 fair price shops spread all over the country in rough proportion of the population. The food distributed through PDS is subsidised by the Government to the extent of the difference between the issue price of foodgrains and their economic cost to Food Corporation of India (FCI) - the agency that incurs the cost of transportation, storage and administration in respect of the stock of food grain. It devours a significant part of the government subsidy. For example, in 1990-91 out of total food subsidy of ₹ 26,000 million, FCI -costs amounted to ₹ 10,000 million, which works out to a whooping 38.5 per cent. With the FCI-costs ever increasing, the impact of any reduction in subsidy has to hit the poor directly.

For ensuring supply of foodgrains to the PDS system in face of export attraction due to the devaluation of rupee, for maintaining their level of production in spite of sharp rise in input prices and for political consideration of assuaging the rich farmers' lobby, the government had to increase the procurement prices of rice and wheat. The procurement prices of rice and wheat were raised by 67.56 per cent and 62.8 per cent respectively between 1989-90 and 1993-94.

This rise was passed on to the consumers by increasing the issue prices of these commodities by 85.81 per cent and 75.14 per cent respectively between June 1990 and February 1994, apparently for reducing the food subsidy. The impact of this rise was reflected in a significant fall in the off-take of food grains. After the Reforms, off-take of wheat and rice as a percentage of the allocation has shown considerable decline. In the years from 1990- 91 to 1992-93 this percentage was generally over 80 but in the next three years from 1993-94 to 1995-96, it came down to below 50 per cent in case of wheat and to little over 60 per cent in case of rice.

The export - attraction of wheat has already led to shortages from situation of surplus, which had to be met with expensive imports. The promising income from wheat crop has resulted in wheat extensively substituting coarse cereals - the main food of poor people in many parts of the country, as can be seen from the dwindling output of the latter. The latest data show that it fell from 36.6 million tonnes out of a total foodgrains output of 179.5 million tonnes in 1992-93 to 30 million tonnes out of a total output of 185 million tonnes in 1995-96.

Since, the difference between the consumer-end PDS retail prices and market prices became marginal, the not-so-poor left the PDS and owing to unaffordable prices the poor cut their consumption. The resultant effect on nutrition and hunger had to be borne by the people in direct proportion to their poverty. One study revealed that the families of landless labourers and marginal and small farmers reduced their off-take by over 50 per cent. Considering their extremely low level of food consumption, below or around the subsistence minimum calories defined by the poverty line, the impact of further reduction of intake by over 50 per cent may have led many people to starvation deaths. Recently, on the advice from the World Bank, the government has decided to make the PDS targeted at the real poor.

The real intention however appears to be the reduction in food subsidy. With the narrowing spread between the market and the PDS retail prices, the so-called non-poor are already out of its net. Even the back-of-envelope kind calculation will show that the people below the poverty line (at the 1991 level) require 46.5 million tonnes of foodgrains as against the actual distribution of only 16.6 million tonnes, a mere 36 per cent of the requirement.

The new scheme based on the executive reluctance to acknowledge poverty is bound to push many more people to starvation. The cumulative effect of the above could be clearly seen in a trend of falling per capita net availability of cereals per day for the Indian population. During two years of the Reforms, there was 8.43 per cent fall in per capita availability of cereals and 12.02 per cent fall in that of pulses. Considering the acute inequality of Indian population, the impact of this declining trend on the poorer and particularly the disadvantaged parts like the dalits would be far more severe than revealed by the averages.

Pulses being the only source of vegetable protein for poor people, a sharp decline in their availability certainly indicates malnutrition. The incidence of malnutrition further would be disproportionately injurious to women and children because of the male preference in Indian tradition. The evidence of this disaster has already come in the form of malnutrition deaths of over 350 children in the Amaravati district of Maharashtra - the most industrialised and relatively progressive state in India.

Inflation

Inflation hits poor people the hardest. Being employed mainly in the unorganised sector, they do not have even the partial protection that their counterparts in the organised sector have by way of dearness allowance. Most of their earning is spent on the basic needs like food, clothing and shelter, and hence any price rise directly dampens their level of consumption.

The policy measures unleashed under the Reforms that directly contributed to inflation are:

- Reduction in the budget and fiscal deficit,
- Devaluation,
- Privatisation,
- Elimination or reduction in subsidies
- Export promotion.

The reduction in the budget and fiscal deficits predominantly resulted in curtailment of capital expenditure and consequently in the decline in capital formation. Between 1990-91 and 1993-94 the real fall in capital expenditure was 31 per cent. The real gross fixed capital formation as percentage of GDP reflects a consistent decline from 21.3 in 1990-91 to 19.8 in 1993-94. Its fall for the public component is far more precipitous, from 8.6 to 7.8 for the same period. This could lead to fall in future output and with inelastic wages, would cause an inflationary pressure in the economy. Reduction in budgetary support to the public sector effected under the Reforms serves dual objective.

One, it contributes to containment of the budgetary deficit and two; it constitutes a step in the direction of privatisation. The budgetary support to the PSUs was reduced by 6.1 per cent over the balance budgetary period of nine months in the very first post- Reforms budget of 1991-92 and consistently thereafter. The budget prescribes the supplementary resources and their sources to the PSUs. For example, in 1992-93 it showed a marginal increase in the amount to be mobilised through sale of bonds but a growth of 320 per cent in the costlier funds obtained through commercial debts and suppliers' credit. These methods are not always feasible and hence the PSUs had to resort to increasing prices of their products to make the two ends meet. For example, in the same budget, the impossible target given to Sail Authority of India to raise its internal generation from ₹ 4,910 million to 9,720 million was met by the 15 per cent increase in steel prices, giving significant fillip to the inflationary spiral in the economy. Devaluation of currency directly contributes to inflation by raising the cost of imports that enter into domestic production or consumption.

Large part of our import comprises petroleum crude and its products; chemicals, machinery, iron and steel, etc. which enter as raw or intermediate materials in our production processes. Most of these products are of common use in the economy. Any escalation in their cost therefore directly contributes to the rise of general price level. The last administrative price rise of petroleum products could be a case in point. The devaluation of rupee made it dearer domestically, causing deficit in the oil pool account to mount. Eventually, it entailed hefty price rise of petroleum products. Insofar as petroleum products are consumed directly or indirectly by all, their price rise impelled the general price level to go up with a multiplier effect.

All the studies on the Economic Reforms are unanimous in their conclusion that the Reforms have significantly contributed to inflation. A recent study by the EPW Research Foundation revealed significant price rise all across. Based on the wholesale Price Index (WPI), the price rise of the primary substances of consumption ranged from 42 per cent to 93 per cent. The WPI for all substances increased by 44.4 per cent registering an annual compound growth of 10.3 per cent. In the decade preceding the Reforms (1980-81 to 1990-91) this increase was only 7 per cent, despite the 17 per cent growth in money supply. Prof. Kurien's study isolates four periods of significant price rise from 1950; *viz,*

- 1964-65 to 1968-69,
- 1972-73 to 1976-77,
- 1979- 80 to 1983-84
- 1991-92 to 1995-96.

He clearly finds extraneous force majure situations being responsible for the price rise in the three periods before the Reforms but no such tangible reason for it in the fourth period. There were severe famines in the first and the third periods and huge increase in the international prices in the third period that caused the prices to rise. On the contrary, during the post-Reforms fourth period, there was an unprecedented long spell of good monsoons for continuous seven years, and relative stability in international petroleum prices. Therefore, the only inescapable inference Prof. Kurien reached was to attribute the price rise to the steps taken under the Reforms. For example, it is the Reforms that caused the price of chemical fertilizer to rise by 100.6 per cent, electricity by 65.9 per cent and coal by 58.1 per cent.

Devaluation of rupee and emphasis on the export-led growth caused pressure on the prices of products depending on their import content. The exact effect of simultaneous reduction of customs duty and excise duty is not easy to assess but as some micro studies indicate, they also added to the rise of general price level. For example, there being no significant customs duty on the imported medicines before the Reforms, the reduction therein did no difference to their prices. However, the devaluation of rupee pushed them sky rocketing. The aggressive export promotion of many primary substances also resulted in their price-rise in the domestic market. The increase in money supply resorted to thwart the revaluation of rupee in the face of huge inflow of foreign exchange during 1992-93 to 1994-95 also contributed to elevating the general price level. The price rise of food grains owing to the cuts in food and fertilizer subsidies and consequent adjustments have particularly been harsh.

In the preceding decade of the Reform the per annum price of rice had risen by 7 per cent and that of wheat by 3.3 per cent. But in the next four years of the Reform period, they registered the rise of 13.5 per cent and 18.1 per cent respectively. Other foodgrains also behaved approximately in similar fashion. The price-rise for pulses has been 97.2 per cent; that for vegetables 163.4 per cent, for fruits 74 per cent; and for eggs, meat and fish group 102.5 per cent. The free market unleashed by the Reforms also indirectly but significantly has contributed to the price rise.

Employment

The rate of growth of employment in the organised sector dropped from more than 1.7 per cent per annum in the late 1980s to 1.2 per cent in 1991-92 and to 0.6 per cent in 1992-93. Creation of jobs in the public sector fell from 11.0 million in the preceding four years to the 6.2 million in the succeeding four years of the Reforms. For the Private Sector, the corresponding figures showed a slight rise from 2.08 million to 2.49 million on account of free market euphoria. In the Central Government establishment there were 4.03 million jobs on 1st March 1991, which went up next year to 4.14 million. But for the next two years, they came down to 3.97 million and 3.84 million respectively. Similar picture of declining employment opportunity is held out in the statistics of Employment Exchanges.

The notified vacancies had come down from 0.59 million in 1989-90 to 0.4 million in 1992-93 and to 0.38 million in the subsequent year. Similar decline is seen in the statistics of appointments. The appointments issued during the three years were 0.29 million, 0.23 million and 0.22 million respectively. The ratios of appointments to the notified vacancies for these years also shows a striking decline, *viz,* 8.5 per cent, 7.9 per cent and 6.7 per cent respectively.

The contraction in public expenditure and the consequent reduction in aggregate demand could not but adversely affect employment in the unorganised sector, whether non-agricultural rural employment or urban informal sector employment, given the casual nature of such employment. The policy reforms made benefits of the small sector available to the big industrial houses.

National Council of Applied Economic Research had cautioned that the Reforms relating to deregulation of the big industries, withdrawal of the licence system and global reduction of custom duties would exert adverse impact on the small industries. The statistics of the industrial sickness show a marked deterioration during the Reform period. For example, in 1990, there were 2,21,097 sick industries, which represented a 8.86 per cent decline from the previous year. But after the Reforms were launched, this figure went up to 2,23,809 in 1991 and further to 2,47,724 in 1992 indicating the 1.23 per cent and 10.69 per cent growth respectively, over previous years.

Entrepreneurship Development Institute of India, Ahmedabad had surveyed the impact of the Reforms on small scale industries in 1993, and saw clear deterioration in their situation.

It attributed this deterioration to three factors:

1. General recession in 1991-92,
2. Reduction in the budgetary support to the public sector
3. Liberalisation of imports of the capital goods.

The cumulative impact of these factors has been in the total collapse of demand for their products. Small-scale industries based on imports had a tough time due to devaluation of rupee. Increasing competition, increasing costs and pressure on prices has made the very survival difficult for many. Today more than 4,00,000 small-scale industries are either sick or closed. The reforms in financial sector permitted the banks to charge interest as per the credit rating of debtors and manage their profitability. This also added to the difficulty of small-scale industries.

For, getting loans from banks at affordable interest rates now became a formidable task for them. One study clearly concluded that the Reforms had an adverse impact on the new job opportunities in the small-scale industries. In rural areas there has been a significant cut in the bank credit to the agriculture and nonagriculture industries. The bank credit to these sectors was 40 per cent till the launch of the Reforms. It came down to 38.7 per cent in 1992 and 35 per cent in July 1994. The bank credit to agriculture as a percentage of net bank credit fell consistently to 12.4 per cent in March 1995 from 17.4 per cent in March 1990. It has had an adverse impact on these industries and in turn on rural employment. A study on the unemployment in 1993 estimated that out of 25 million unemployed, approximately 10 million came from the unorganised sector of urban areas and the non-agricultural sectors of the rural areas and were identified as the victims of the Economic Reforms.

The Economic Reforms lay excessive reliance on foreign investment not only for industrial development but also to solve the unemployment problem faced by the country. In this context, the observation of United Nations, in the Human Development Report of 1993 is quite revealing. It says that the TNCs and their associate companies had made significant investments in developing countries but it could not generate significant employment.

The amount of jobs created by the foreign investment in the entire third world during 1990 to 1993 is not even equal to the number of people entering the job market in India in a single year! The companies in the Fortune 500 list of 1992 together said to have had 5,472 billion dollars sales and 25 million jobs in 1992. Although this sales figure is 27 times India's GDP, the employment figure does not reach even its one third.

The impetus to export agriculture in the Reforms is bringing in corporate and contract system in the agriculture sector. The government has already declared that the Land Ceiling Act identified as the main obstacle in the process, would be suitably changed. Directionally, the emergent corporate farms will gobble up small holdings of the marginal to middle farmers and push them into the herd of job seeking millions.

Corporatisation of agriculture always leads to depeasantisation and simultaneously reduction in labour absorption. The cropping pattern of these capitalist farms makes unskilled agricultural workers redundant. This emergent scenario is certainly going to aggravate the unemployment problem further rather than solving it. The theme of export-led growth emphasised by the Reforms will expose the Indian industry to the vagaries of international markets, which can have very negative effect on employment in the long run. Export thrust, unmindful of the demands of the domestic requirements can be quite harmful as has been experienced in the case of cotton thread case. In this case, large scale export of the coarse cotton thread had catapulted 110 weavers in Andhra Pradesh to starvation deaths. There are many such case studies in the international repertoire of experience with such Reforms.

The import of modern technology and investment constitutes an important rationale for the economic Reforms. Many facilitating provisions have been adopted for attracting the same. It is a different matter that the flow of both technology as well as investment follows the capitalist logic of maximisation of long-term profits. This logic is evident when Pepsi brings in its great technology to convert our potatoes and sell them in chip form at a price 80 times over. There is a virtual boom in strategic alliances, joint ventures, technological collaborations etc. that act as vehicles for bringing in foreign technology and capital.

They invariably depend upon the marketing muscle of the foreign partner represented in their powerful brands. The influx of foreign brands is bound to displace Indian brands, not by virtue of their intrinsic superiority but because of their sheer financial and organisational muscle. The process will virtually spell deindustrialisation of the domestic industry. The modern factories replacing them cannot generate even a fraction of the employment lost in displaced manpower. The imperatives of global competitiveness moreover, will increasingly impel companies to re-engineer their business processes that necessarily results in 'down sizing' of the company rendering the millions jobless.

The relative mobility of capital vis-à-vis labour also holds an ominous prospect for future jobs. The buzzword of competition has suddenly awakened one and all in the business world to the necessity to restructure their companies. Since, this exercise is envisaged to prepare the companies to face global competitions, every one engaged a foreign consultancy firm that claimed the requisite experience and know how for millions of dollars. Already this phenomenon has threatened the well-meaning native consulting firms into seeking some kind of alliance with these foreign firms for sheer survival. These exercises overtly aimed at creating sharper customer focus essentially end up in cutting jobs. Strangely, more than the private companies the State owned units operating as monopoly or oligopoly seem to feel greater pressure to so reorganise.

Nationalised banks have already threatened to declare 4,00,000 persons surplus, Railways have stopped recruitment, Department of Post and Telecommunication intend to retrench 2,00,000 workers. The examples indeed are legion. A study conducted by EPW Research Foundation in early 1994 found that the total employment which showed an increase in first two years of the Reforms, had slumped thereafter; that the bulk of employment had occurred in contract and other forms of non-regular employment, the share of which in total employment had gradually risen to one-third by March 1993, and that regular employment fell by 3.3 per cent in 1992-93 even as the value of fixed assets of the sample companies rose by some 27 per cent.

The competitive pressure of the free market scenario has impelled managements to adopt labour flexibilisation strategies as noticed by the International Labour Organisation as early as 1989. The spurt in restructuring exercises in corporate India already reflects the trend towards 're-engineering' by concentrating on core or flagship businesses and spinning off non-core businesses through subcontracting or outsourcing. It is reinforced with an HRD strategy that envisages workers to develop new skills and get exposed to various aspects of work so that they can become multi-skilled and can do varied tasks in a flexible work environment.

This is leading to 'individual contact', thereby eliminating the vary basis of the trade unionism. The directional thrust of the Reforms is already evident in the tremendous growth of the informal sector, which is characterised by the rampant use of casual labour, hiring and firing practices, and all kinds of exploitation of labour.

Poverty

Poverty is a sum total of all the deprivations. In India governmental definition of poverty is based on the sole criterion of minimum food requirement for survival. Thus the poverty line is decided by the income sufficient to buy food equivalent of 2400 calories in rural and 2100 calories in urban areas. The database for poverty estimates is provided by the quinquenial surveys of NSS. NSS also collects the consumer expenditure data by decile group on an annual basis. The Reforms have reversed the two decades long declining trend of poverty.

The rural poverty went up from the pre-reform low of 33.7 per cent to 41.7 per cent in 1992 and slightly declined to 40.2 per cent in 1993-94. The urban poverty also showed the same trend shooting up from the pre-Reform low of 36 per cent to 37.8 per cent and then coming down to 36.2 per cent. The ratio of ultra poverty (*i.e,* extreme poverty) to total poverty showed a marked increase after the Reforms.

In 1990-91, this ratio was 68.95%, it went up to 71.04% in 1991 and to 74.64% in 1992. The corresponding figures for urban area were 72.99, 73.14 and 74.20 per cent. In 1992, the rural workers in secondary and tertiary sectors showed a decline of 6.3% and 1.3% respectively from the pre-Reform level in 1989-90.

Curiously, the primary sector showed a hefty increase of 10.1% in the same period. In rural area nearly 50% farming households have less than one acre land. They need supplementary work in nonagricultural sector for meeting the two ends. In absence of this work however, they land up engaging themselves with the sundry work related to their tiny farms and declare themselves as the agriculture workers. This increase in the primary sector jobs thus indicates partial unemployment of workforce.

The decline in non-agricultural jobs and the overall employment are attributed to the cut in the government expenditure on various poverty alleviation programmes, during the Reform period. Notwithstanding their extremely low transfer efficiency and ineffectiveness in targeting the poor, these programmes played a role in poverty reduction during the eighties. They are operated on the 80:20 basis by the Centre and the State. In the first flush of enthusiasm the government effected drastic reductions in all of these programmes till it was alarmed by the havoc it created and its political implication in the ensuing general election.

It attempted to reverse this trend in 1994-95 and 1995-96 budgets under the much-propagandised 'human face to reforms'. Even after taking all these increased outlays into account its resultant effect barely equals provision of less than 20 days work at ₹21 for a person, in a year. The central transfers constitute a major resource for the states to conduct the programmes under the Social sector. These transfers show consistent decline during the Reform period on all the heads except for the payment of interest, over a period 1990-91 to 1993-94.

This decline amounts to whooping 18.52 per cent. The central assistance to states for some specific schemes likewise has been on consistent decline from much before the start of the Reforms but the states seem to have managed the expenditure profile. However, the Reform-ethos has eroded this expenditure after 1990-91.

The maximum cut was effected in the expenditure on disease-prevention and control programme which relate with the poverty prone diseases like T.B, Malaria, Fileria, Leprosy etc. Its direct manifestation has been aplenty, in form of reemergence of the epidemics of Plague, T.B, Malaria, Jaundice, Influenza, Pneumonia and very recently, Dengue. Inequality is a corollary of growing poverty for the upper layers seldom suffer degradation.

Based on the available data on consumption expenditure, the share of the bottom 30% people, which was growing consistently from 1987-88 up to 1990-91, both in rural as well as in urban areas, had a sudden reversal soon after the Reforms were launched. In rural area, it was 15.57% in 1987-88, which rose up to 15.96% in 1990-91, but thereafter slid down to 15.79% in 1991 (July - December) and further to 15.60% in 1992 (July-December). For the urban area, the corresponding figures are 13.33%, 13.74%, 12.74% and 13.17%, indicating a slight upturn in the terminal year. The share of the middle 40% population also dwindled in the same manner in both rural and urban area. The loss of these 70% population appears to have benefited the top 30% population. Their share for the pre-Reform period was on consistent decline, which has suddenly jumped up in the Reform period.

EXPERIENCE OF OTHER COUNTRIES

Many protagonists of the economic Reforms tend to discount the Indian experience as premature. Fortunately, there are many countries in which similar Reforms are being worked for many years. There are numerous studies assessing their efficacy and impact on various parts of population. Most of them are unanimous in noting the precipitous fall in standard of living of the majority population of the subject country that has led to widespread riots and socio-political unrest.

The thrust of the Reforms is on economic growth, which as per their apologists would 'trickle down' to the people. Notwithstanding the metaphorical argument that trickle can never be equal to that may be required in terms of distributive justice to the poor, the growth generating capacity of these Reforms itself appears to be in question. In Latin America, after adoption of the Reforms economic growth rates had actually fallen.

In the pre-Reform period, Latin America's economic growth rates had exceeded the average growth rate of the industrial countries and that of USA for over a decade. But, it suffered a historical reversal soon after the Reforms were launched. From 1980 to 1985, the average real growth rates of per capita income in Argentina, Brazil, Chile, Mexico and Peru were negative and per capita income levels had gone back by a decade to those prevailing in the 1970s. For Peru and Chile, they had slipped back even to pre-1970 levels. Although, the growth rates of GDP in cases of Argentina and Chile appear to have risen in 1992, the reasons therefor do not quite belong to the standard Reform-package. In Chile, the government's huge investments in copper mines projects, forestry, and document projects; extension of cheap credit to the new export industries and other such interventions during 1973 to 1990 came to fruition, in form of the spurt in economic growth rates. In Argentina, a totally different phenomenon seems to have caused the economy to look up in 1992.

The fall in the American interest rates had caused the dollars stacked in the American banks by the Argentinean capitalists, to flow back to Argentina into its emerging financial markets. Besides these examples, there are many countries where the GDP-growth rate seems to have deteriorated in 1992. In Brazil, it fell down from 9.1% in 1980 to 7.9% in 1985 and further to - 0.9% in 1992.

For the same years, the GDP- growth rates for Columbia were 4.1%, 3.3% and 2.7%; those for Peru were 3.1%, 2.1% and -2.8% and for Mexico they were 8.4%, 7.9% and 2.6% respectively. In some other countries like Ghana, Indonesia, Ivory Coast etc, notwithstanding their individual economic characteristics, the growth rates appear to be simply erratic. Contrary to the assertions of the IMF and the World Bank, there is thus no concrete evidence that these type of Reforms really lead to incremental economic growth in the subject countries. There is enough evidence however, that these Reforms have heaped many kinds of miseries on the majority of population of these countries. In Latin America between 1980 and 1984, open unemployment went up from 7 to 11 per cent. In Chile, Columbia, Peru and Venezuela, the unemployment rates jumped by 50 and 100%.

A sizeable decline has taken place in industrial wages in the same period in African and Latin American countries. It fell by 40% in Tanzania, 33% in Zambia and Mexico and 24% in Peru. This decline ranged from 30 to 60%, between 1980 - 87 in Argentina, Bolivia, Chile, Costa Rica, Egypt and Kenya. The real wages of the government employees have fallen almost everywhere. The decline is of the order of 30 - 40% in the African countries during 1975 to 1985 and between 10 - 120% in Latin America between 1980 to 1987. Most of the countries (*e.g*, Argentina, Brazil, Chile, Columbia, Ivory

Coast, Mexico, Peru, Philippines etc.) that adopted these IMF/ World bank sponsored Reforms showed a clear decline in Gross Domestic Investment during the period from 1980 to 1992. There was a sharp decline in the share of social expenditure in the Latin American countries and West Asia. In the former, it fell from 36% to 24.3% and in the latter, from 20.3% to 17.2% between 1980 and 1987. In terms of share of capital expenditure, investment in social infrastructure has suffered in Sri Lanka; the spending on health, education and food subsidy having declined from 38% of current expenditure in 1977 to 22% during 1980 - 82.

There was a relatively sharper decline in similar expenditure in Turkey, Guyana and Sudan. In Somalia and Tanzania the share of primary education in such expenditure further declined. Per capita expenditure on education and health was reduced by 11% and 5% respectively in Morocco, by 29% and 35% in Ecuador and by 20% in Chile. The former Soviet Russian countries and the east European countries have been implementing these Reforms since 1989.

Whatever may be the pitfalls of the socialist regimes in these countries, it had provided its entire people with basic necessities of living. What has become of these countries after the Reforms were launched is very well documented in a report published by UNICEF. In Bulgaria 53.6% families were living in poverty in 1992. In 1989, Hungary had 10.1% poverty, which within next two years of Reforms had more than doubled to 21.3% in 1991.

In Czech Republic it went up from 5.7% in 1989 to 18.2% in 1992. It jumped from 21.8% to 41.4% in Poland during the same period. It went up from 27.3% to 51.1% in Rumania; from 5% to 43.8% in Russia and from 8.9% to 30.2% in Slovakia. In Poland 57.6%, in Rumania 70.1% and in Slovakia 41.3%, children live in poverty. In Mongolia the Reforms catapulted 25% population below the monthly 10 dollars - poverty line. The mortality rate between 1989 and 1993 also increased significantly in these countries due to drastic decline in living standard. Unemployment rates have soared in most of the east European countries. About 6.5 million people were registered as unemployed in December 1992 - a rise from 5 million a year ago. Inflation is still a major problem. In Poland, which was the pet success story of the Reforms for free market advocates, more than 50% people say that the Communist system was better. More than 16% are unemployed in industrial cities and more than that in the rural areas; almost 14% of the people in the country are on doles and about one third of the total families now live below the official poverty line.

The notable exception is the experience of East Asian countries. The proportion below the poverty line in this region, comprising People's Republic of China, Indonesia, Korea, Malaysia, Philippines, Thailand and Indochina declined from 35% to 10% over this period. The key social indicators, *viz*, life expectancy, infant mortality, adult literacy and population growth for these countries also improved very impressively. However, it is not the Reforms that have caused this miracle. The real reasons have been analysed as their specific historical setting, their creation of pre-conditions for success and the strategies they employed.

For instance, almost all of them had undertaken effective land reforms, achieved high levels of literacy, particularly female literacy; and substantially better health standards. Better female participation in the labour force led to rapid increase in household and overall domestic saving rates. The higher level of social consumption with relatively better distribution of incomes and wealth vastly widened the demand of those economies and facilitated more broad based development.

Higher literacy and health standards were the most crucial factors in enhancing labour productivity, which in turn went to facilitate significant import substitution and export promotion. Under the influence of these Bretton Wood institution sponsored reforms, inequality in the world has been consistently growing. Between 1988 and 1993, the per capita income of the lowincome countries of the world fell by 35% from ₹ 584 to ₹ 380. As against this the same for the rich countries went from ₹ 17,080 to 23,090. The share of the lowincome countries in total income also fell from 5.44% to 4.83% in the same period. For the block of Latin American countries famous as the test bench for these reforms, the picture is strikingly dismal in terms of inequality. In Brazil, the ratio of income or consumption of the top and the lowest 20% people increased from 26.1% to 32.1% between 1983 and 1989. In Columbia, between 1988 and 1991, the same had gone up from 13.3 to 15.5%.

In all these countries the consumption of the bottom 20% population as a share of total consumption ranged from paltry 2.1 to 8.7%. The gap between poor and rich of the world has increased by 30% over the last decade along with the spread of these kinds of Reforms.

During 1987 to 1994, the number of billionaires in the world showed a remarkable increase. In USA, it went up from 49 to 120; in the Asia Pacific region, from 40 to 86; in Europe, from 36 to 91 and in west Asia and Africa, it went up from 8 to 14. The brief life sketches of these billionaires given in the Forbes magazine of July 18, 1994 show how these Reforms have been instrumental in enriching them.

IMPACT OF THE REFORMS ON DALITS AS A DISADVANTAGED SOCIAL GROUP

The social disadvantage suffered by the dalits in India was taken note of in the Constitution of India, which was drafted under the chairmanship of Dr. Ambedkar - a person who had spearheaded the most momentous anti-caste movement of the depressed classes. It provided the dalits with many safeguards, *viz,*

- Social, educational, cultural and religious safeguards,
- Economic safeguards,
- Political safeguards,
- Safeguards for employment.

The free market ethos unleashed by the Reforms, conceptually can neither confirm to the democratic spirit of the Indian Constitution of 'one vote, one value', nor can it coexist with the system of positive discrimination embodied in these safeguards. For, the market grants moneyed person more value, and overtly believes in the jungle law of 'might is right'. To a large extent, the primary motivation behind these Constitutional provisions was liberal democratic aspirations that characterised the freedom movement. However, these aspirations and the initial ideological zeal of the founding fathers withered away in no time and what survived was its utilitarian dimension for the electoral politics. The sorry state of the executive compliance with these Constitutional provisions amply bears out the fangs of the intrinsically iniquitous Indian society.

The Reforms will bring a kind of legitimacy to this attitudinal resistance of the upper castes and classes to the movements for change by the downtrodden. These safeguards will stand eroded as the Reforms gain in momentum. Influence of the Reforms is bound to be all pervasive. However, only a few issues of importance to the dalit masses have been picked up for discussion here.

RESERVATION AND FINANCIAL ASSISTANCE IN EDUCATION INSTITUTIONS

Reservation in the educational institutions and the financial assistance in the form of scholarships and freeships constitute perhaps the most important factor in the development scheme for dalits. For, it is primarily responsible to make the basic input of education available and affordable to them.

Without education, all the constitutional safeguards including the reservation in services would be infructuous. Under this scheme the dalit students whose parental income is below a specified level, get freeship, reservation in admissions to all the colleges getting grants-in-aid from the government, and scholarships.

Without this assistance, even today, it would be difficult even for the second-generation educated dalits to send their children to school. The Reforms have already resulted in freezing the grants to many institutions and in stagnating, if not lowering, the expenditure on education. The free market has entered the educational sphere in a big way.

Commercialisation of education is no more a mere rhetoric; it is now the established fact. Commercial institutions offering specialised education that signify essential input from utilitarian viewpoint, have come up in a big way from cities to small towns.

Their product-prices are not only based on the demand-supply consideration in their market segment but also are manipulated by their promotional strategies. In a true spirit of globalisation, many foreign universities are invading the educational spheres through hitherto unfamiliar strategic alliances with non-descript commercial agencies, of course at hefty dollar equivalent prices.

Many elite institutions like IIMs and IITs, suddenly facing fund crunch had to resort to raising their fee structure and other prices many fold. They were already beyond the reach of the dalits. When they eventually turn self-financing, their prices would be benchmarked against their international counterparts, which any way would be affordable to the same top market segment that constitutes the focus of all the Reform-talk. As the job markets become acutely competitive, owing to a sharp decline in job opportunities, the polarisation between the elite and commoner would also sharpen.

Various kinds of price barriers would be erected to thwart the entry of downtrodden to the portals of development. Even the sphere of primary education the coverage of which has been so miserably inadequate as to leave out multitude of children in villages as illiterate, could not remain unaffected, notwithstanding its already existing divide between the vernacular and English schools.

Corporatisation has entered this arena, transforming the education into an enterprise for profits. The quality of input these expensive schools will provide will benchmark the products in the contracting job markets. Even today, because of preponderance of the English language in business circles, the divide between village and towns is almost complete in the field of education. It is so difficult for a village student, educated in vernacular medium to compete with his convent educated (now an understatement!) counterpart in cities and towns. If this is the situation of general village population, the plight of the dalits who besides being the poorest of the village population carry additional burden of social discrimination, is indeed a worrisome matter. Despite several kinds of State assistance, the dalits are plagued with alarming rate of school dropouts.

This may be explained out as much by the need for dalit children tc supplement their meagre family incomes for making the two ends meet as also by the erosion of their faith that education could be the instrument to change the pathetic course of their lives. This sense of alienation is going to grow with the progress of the Reforms, giving rise to increasing lumpenisation and criminalisation of the dalit youth.

RESERVATIONS IN SERVICES

Whatever may be the other costs, the government policy of reservations in employment sphere has undoubtedly played an important role in the process of advancement of the dalits. The policy broadly envisages representation of the dalits in proportion to their population in all the public services, which includes the government, the public sector, autonomous bodies and other institutions that receive grant-in-aid from the government.

A cursory glance at the figures of this representation is enough to get a pathetic state of implementation of this policy. Howsoever, unsatisfactory the results of implementation may be, the importance of reservations from the dalit viewpoint cannot be over emphasised. As could be evidenced by the organised private sector, where it would be difficult to find a dalit employee (save of course in scavenging and lowliest of the similar jobs), without reservations the dalits would have been totally doomed.

The importance of reservations thus could only be assessed in relation to situations where they do not exist. Whatever be their defects and deficiencies, they have given certain economic means of livelihood and some social prestige to the sons and daughters of over 1.5 million landless labourers. Whether they get real power or not, over 50,000 dalits could enter the sphere of bureaucratic authority with the help of reservations. More importantly these tangible benefits to few have instilled a hope in entire dalit people to strive for their betterment. This hope predominantly manifests in the form of spread of education among them. Their emotional bond with the nation and its Constitution despite heaps of injustice and ignominy they bear every moment of their life may also be significantly attributable to the Reservation Policy. The winds of privatisation under the Economic Reforms have already shaken the very foundations of Reservations.

Wherever the Reforms patterned on the Structural Adjustment Programme of the World Bank were carried out, denationalisation and privatisation of the public sector have come in a big way. Being a late starter, India has not reached the scales achieved by others, say, the Latin American countries. However, the start has not been any less impressive. Within a short time, almost all the sectors of economy stand opened up for private investment. The disinvestment in existing public sector companies has already been allowed up to 49 per cent by the policy.

The public stake being more than 50 per cent, the 'public sector' as such is not yet dismantled in the policy. It continues to be the State as before, and hence attracts application of the reservation policy. However, the Reform package has already endangered, if not abolished, the reservations through numerous back doors.

In the name of preparing the Public Sector Undertakings (PSUs) for global free market regime, the PSUs are being allowed/ encouraged to have strategic alliances with private companies from India and abroad. As such, over the last five years, many profit making PSUs have formed the joint venture companies (JVC).

Most of the PSU investments continue to be channelled through the JV route despite repeated failures of the joint ventures. These JVCs are strategically structured so as not to fall in the PSU-framework. The typical equity stake for the PSU and private could be 49:51. There appears to be a great deal of receptivity for this scheme in the government circles. There are no policy barriers on the business to be pursued by these JVCs. Theoretically, an existing PSU can hive off its business divisions into private JVCs and transform itself into a financial holding company with a Board of Directors and skeleton staff.

Even if such an entity technically remains a PSU and follows the reservation policy sincerely, it would still have little or no scope to absorb the dalits in its staff. Whatever may be the strategic considerations, the fall out of this process practically amounted to shutting the doors of these new age companies to the dalits and to potential neutralisation of the reservation policy.

The policy of limited disinvestment of the PSUs not being in conformity with the spirit of the Reforms, is bound to be relaxed in favour of privatisation any time. But still, all the PSUs may not get privatised at once. The better ones would be gobbled up by the bigger sharks. The worst ones may be closed down or distress-sold. And the middle ones may for quite some time, continue to be the relic of their past. Whatever the scenario, the residual structures of the 'reformed' PSUs are never going to be the same, as far as the dalits are concerned.

The privatisation and the excuse of global competition, superimposed on the traditional caste prejudice, will never allow reservations to happen, any more. Other public services are also bound to slip out of the reservation policy. Most of the sectors, which were the traditional domain of the government investment, have already been released for the private investment.

ATROCITIES

The caste atrocities are an integral feature of the dalit life. The government machinery keeps on collecting their statistics year after year and issues it in a report of its Commissioner for the SCs and the STs (now the National Commission for the SCs and the STs). There are at least three Articles (15,17 and 23) in the Constitution of India, which seek to mitigate the evil.

To give effect to these Constitutional provisions the following acts also have been in operation:

- The Untouchability (Offences) Act, 1955, later amended anc retitled as the Protection of Civil Rights Act, 1955
- The Scheduled Castes and Scheduled Tribes (Prevention of Atrocities Act) 1989 and The Bonded Labour System (Abolition) Act, 1976

Despite this, the statistics of the registered atrocities read like a balance sheet of a blue chip company with consistent rise every successive year. It is pertinent to remember that owing to the dependency relationship of the dalits with the perpetrators of atrocities, not every occurrence of the atrocity gets registered.

Rather, it can be safely assumed that behind each registered atrocity over ten atrocity cases go unreported. As per the latest statistics, every day nearly 50 cases of atrocities are registered all over the country. Over three dalit women are raped and six are disabled on each day round the year. The National Commission analysed the causes of each of the atrocities in a sample of 45 cases.

The analysis shows that out of 45 cases 13 are clearly attributable to the economic reasons. The balance can also be explained out by some kind of weakness of the dalits. Coupled with the weakness of the dalits, their growing assertiveness and the refusal to submit to the casteist dictates of the village lords, rebellion assimilated through the Ambedkarian struggle and the process of general awareness, also cause atrocities to increase. Atrocities are basically a rude reassertion of power over the powerless by the powerful in the wake of threat.

It is thus an expression of insecurity by the powerful who perceive power slipping their hand. In the pre-colonial closed loop production system of a typical village since everyone followed his or her calling under the divine authority of religion, there were no atrocities of the kind we experience in the saner age of globalisation today. If any one questioned or defied this system, the religious code provided for the punishment. In this scheme, it was more important to fortify the religious control on populace than physically taming them to comply. Although the emphasis was on enslavement of mind, physical punishment did exist as a contingency measure. Atrocities on the dalits today are in essence a physical punishment for their act of forsaking the bondage. The physical punishments or atrocities presuppose material power in the hands of perpetrators of atrocities.

Not only that the dalits lit the fire of anger in materially powerful upper castes by defying their notion of caste authority but also they added fuel to it by coming in competition for partaking scarce resources. The emergence of the land owning middle castes during the post-independence development process who at the one end replaced the traditional upper castes and wore their mantle of superiority but who at the other end found itself in competition with the dalits for resources like education and employment moreover led to accentuation of atrocities.

These middle castes lacked the cunning and sophistication of the upper castes and enraged themselves into physical response on slightest provocation. They could not stomach the dalits who were utterly dependent on them in the village setting asserting their human rights or competing with them on equal platform for scarce resources and eventually winning them away in some cases with the help of reservations. This commonplace experience is amplified by the vested interests of the ruling classes to make out all the dalits as robbers of the share of these middle castes.

Thus, the essential ingredients for atrocities on the dalits can be identified as the existence of material power in the hands of perpetrators of atrocities, enduring sense of social superiority, increasing scarcity of resources, and growing popularization of the masses.

The directional impact of the Reforms on the atrocities on the dalits therefore can be inferred from the effect it would have on the existing dependency relationship in the villages that the dalits are engaged in with the powerful middle castes; on the caste system itself; on the availability of certain critical resources like jobs; health care, education etc.; and on the income distribution to the people. Atrocities are seen to occur where the dependency relationships are more pronounced. Villages, where the dalits as landless labourers depend upon landlords or rich farmers for their livelihood and where the traditional caste equations have a potential to yield economic surplus to the latter, provide ideal setting for atrocities. What impact would the new regime have on the socio-economic setting of Indian villages?

In face of it, this relationship cannot be altered till the dalits get land. Can the new regime afford this economic empowerment of the dalits? Can it, for instance, grant them land? The answer to all these questions will be in negative. Instead of talking about land reforms, the new regime will promote depeasantisation of Indian agriculture and consolidation of their holdings to start corporate farming. The capital influx in the rural areas will have natural ally in the rich farmers who have hegemonic hold over their areas. These parts will be the main beneficiaries of the improved terms of trade and capitalist development in the rural areas. The form that the new system may take will have the corporate structure of management and beneath the local vendors to provide various inputs and services.

While the rich farmers may assume the roles in this organisation as big or petty capitalist, the erstwhile landless labourers, marginal and small farmers shall together constitute the vast army of jobseekers. Although in notional terms the dalits might get rid of the old relationships, in reality they will still be dependent on their upper caste employers and certainly far more vulnerable than before.

With regards to impact of the economic Reforms on the caste system, the optimists and protagonists rely upon an old rhetoric of contradiction between feudalism and capitalism. The problem of annihilation of castes subsumes the change in the economic structure of the society in favour of the dalits and simultaneously a massive cultural movement to cleanse the minds of people of the caste notions and implant in its place the attitude of scientificism and virtue of liberty, equality and fraternity. Having seen that far from striving for economic equality, the Reforms are going to accentuate the existing inequalities, we can just examine its attitude towards the caste system. Will the Reforms promote the cultural movement for social equality? Does it have the wherewithal or motivation to catalyse struggles against the caste system?

The answers to these questions will also have to be in negative. The old rhetoric that capitalism will completely displace feudalism evokes positive expectations in some people about the prowess of the Reforms to annihilate castes. They would argue that the unbridled capitalism inherent in the Reforms is not compatible with any feudal structure and hence implementation of the latter should remove these last blots of the caste system.

This simplistic thumb rule does not seem to be entirely validated by the developmental experience in India. The capitalism in India did not have to sprout through the bedrock of contradictions of feudalism as in Western Europe. It was planted in the fertile soil of the Indian feudalism. It has grown here on its nutrients. The caste institution has defied the classical mould of feudalism by possessing many unique features, the most important being its resilience and adaptability.

What we experience in the mysterious growth of casteist politics today in India is precisely this ability of caste to adapt to changing times. The vast army of unemployed created by the developmental dynamics of the economic Reforms will need appropriate instruments for being controlled. The history bears ample testimony to the fact that whenever the people tended to come together with a common identity, the ruling classes have deftly used the time-tested weapon of castes to divide them.

Caste with its divisive potential will never be abandoned by any iniquitous regime. Its resilience may diffuse its contours but in its essence the caste would coexist with the Reforms. Privatisation and free market components of the Reforms are certainly impacting very adversely on the job situation. Many resources for public consumption shall also be scarce, as they would be produced in private enterprises for profits. They would be beyond the reach of common people. The impact of the Reforms in terms of increasing inequality has been established beyond doubt. Therefore, it can be inferred that the Reforms are potentially incapable to alleviate the pain of dalit masses. In sum, the atrocities on the dalits not only shall continue but may also be increased on account of the Reforms.

SOCIO-CULTURAL SUPPRESSION

Privatisation, which is the pivotal component of the Economic Reforms, will eliminate the very basis of the reservation policy in its present form. Since the Reforms envisage minimalist role for the State, the space for the public domain and therefore for the reservations shall be greatly constricted. Reservation policy that represented the strategic response of liberal bourgeoisie to the aspirations of the dalit movement not quite unlike that of the colonial State at the time of its inception, was never swallowed by the civil society as rightful share of the dalits.

Its response initially reflected feudal magnanimity but once the first generation of the dalits started pouring out of the university portals into the job markets and claimed their share of pie, the reaction reflected feudal ferocity. The cunning of upper caste dominated State apparatus was evident in full measure in the manner the circulars proclaiming this policy were issued.

Their convoluted language facilitated the unwilling bureaucracy to thwart it to the possible extent and judiciary to be labour over several years on what should have been so evident. The broad statistic on the implementation of this policy is enough to reveal the extent of prejudice of the State machinery as well as the civil society.

One of the provisions of the policy states that a dalit candidate qualifying without any concession should not be placed in the reserved seat, implying thereby that the percentage representation of the dalits in services or the educational institutions would be more than its prescribed value. But, over the five decades of implementation of the reservation policy it refuses to reach even the prescribed levels confirming the casteist notion still prevalent in society that the dalits are intrinsically an inferior specie. Despite this vile attitude of the establishment the reservations by far has been the sole contributor to advancement of the dalits. Privatisation is meant to directly hit it.

The benefits of the reservation policy to the dalit community have been more indirect than direct. Directly it benefited a few but indirectly it has created hope for advancement in the entire dalit population. This hope is already faded even when not much of privatisation has happened so far.

Their ideological amount is proving insufficient to resist it. There is a visible alienation, hopelessness and dejection setting in among them, which is getting manifested in increasing lumpenisation and criminalisation of dalit youth. This trend portends doom not only for the dalits but also for the entire oppressed people thirsting for some radical change. For, no radical change is possible in this country without dalit participation. The dalit consciousness formed over centuries of struggle is getting obliterated by the contemporary compulsions created by the Reforms.

This phenomenon will catapult dalit masses back onto the vicious spiral of backwardness and fortify reactionary regimes in the similar proportion. This irrevocable loss would prove dearest to the dalits. While privatisation might set in slowly, the free market that it engenders much before could hit the dalits really harder through the legitimacy it grants to the base instincts against any emancipation project. For, the likely victims of the privatisation is still a miniscule part of the dalit population but the impact of these social would engulf entire dalit population.

Howsoever base the individual conviction might have been, the yesteryears had nearly forbidden them from surfacing openly. But, now the emergent free market is not only permitting but also promoting the vilest and venomous discourse against the dalits and the minorities. The vehemence with which the reservations or any kind of subsidy or any positive discrimination are derided today has a qualitatively distinctive edge. It is interesting to note that there is not yet a dalit voice raised against this fascist hegemony. It would indeed be difficult for the dalits to resist this onslaught. The emergence of right wing politics to national prominence is merely a corollary or consequence of this transformation. Social consequences of the economic miseries associated with these Reforms are indeed ominous for the dalits.

On one side they shall be subject to increasing popularization and on the other stand in competition with the multitude of masses in the job market. Increasing tendency of businesses to downsize, virtual abolition of the reservation system through privatisation, the strategies of flexibilisation and informalisation of labour; corporatisation and depeasantisation of farming etc. will release vast numbers of people to the job market. The resident caste prejudices in such situations will certainly get activated to the detriment of the dalits.

CONCLUSION

The economic reforms in the mould of macro-economic stabilisation and structural adjustment programme of IMF and World Bank have essentially a pro-rich bias. Wherever they were implemented, they have worsened the situation of the masses of poor people in absolute as well as relative terms. Some contrary data to this general observation are rather attributed to the departures from the standard blueprint given by the Bretton Wood institutions.

The dalits in India, being the poorest of the poor have been hit the hardest. Their social disabilities, largely reinforced by and sustained on the economic deprivations, are bound to get accentuated with these policies. The Indian reforms were essentially 'crisis driven' and not 'strategy driven' when they were adopted. There have since been changes in the formation and key persona.

The new government for instance has imparted them a form of 'strategy' through their Common Minimum Programme. However, there has not yet been any evidence of this strategy being any different from the course followed by the previous government. The complete discourse of the Reforms appears to be either grossly off the mark of Indian reality or to assume out its momentous features. The broad Indian reality is that India has too many poor. As per the Human Development Report, 1996, there are 229 million income poor but more than twice as many, 554 million are capability poor.

In terms of capability poverty, its 61.5% population is poor. Its rank just as to descending poverty among the 174 countries of the world is 135. Even today India is predominantly an agrarian economy, with over 70 per cent of its population living in villages. No statistics moreover can adequately capture the heinous socio-cultural inequality that is an abiding part of the Indian reality. It has acute inequalities not only in economic terms but also in the socio-cultural terms. The free market oriented reforms ought to take this grave Indian reality into consideration.

Unless there is a wide spread purchasing power in the economy the market can never be free and sustainable. The reform strategy thus should embody sustainable economic empowerment of the rural masses; investments to enhance their capability and effective measures for accelerated development of the disadvantaged parts like the dalits. The pre-requisite to reforms therefore could be the radical land reforms, massive investments in rural areas into agriculture-related infrastructural projects, universalisation of primary education, primary health care system and reinforcement of positive discrimination in favour of the dalits.

The devil of casteism could be tamed only by freeing general masses of the people from the anxieties and uncertainties about basic survival. The general condition of deprivation has rendered them vulnerable to be the preys to the frequent machinations of the vested interests that make them see the enemy within their own class. The relative equality thus can be the bedrock for launching the socio-cultural offensive in the form of mass-education programmes. But this all may still not be enough. The policy of positive discrimination in favour of the dalits will have to be reinforced much more vigourously in all the sectors of economy, than ever before. They need to be reframed and simplified for the effective implementation. Unlike the current provisions, this may be stopped once their representation in services comes on par with the general population. The specific reform package can be formulated in terms of the conditions existing then. There arises a question of capital.

Where will the capital for the investment in basic reforms come from? Not an easy question to answer, indeed. But some pointers may not be impertinent. It is acknowledged since number of years that India has a parallel economy in black money. The recent spate of scams is a mere corroboration of this hypothesis. The Reforms appear to have given them a boost. Whatever little has surfaced can be likened to a tip of iceberg.

Some five years ago, an unofficial estimate by the World Bank had put the unaccounted money of Indians kept in various tax havens at ₹ 100 billion. As per Finance India, the range of capital outflows was from ₹ 1065 million to ₹ 370 million just in one single year - 1993. Much of the ₹ 10 billion money in the non-resident account is said to be belonging to the resident Indians.

The evidence of this kind abounds. As against this vast sum of our own money, what the government aims at out of the Reforms is the paltry sum of some four to five billion dollars of foreign direct investment a year to come in the country! The size of the money that rightfully belongs to the people of the country may be good enough for the task. But to unearth this treasure certainly requires a political will. India does not need capital as much as it does the political will to better its destiny.

Bibliography

Ahuja, R.: *Violence against Women*, Maharashtra: Pune Publication, 2000.

Balagopal, K.: *Subdivision of SC Reservation in Andhra Pradesh*, Andhra Pradesh: Economic and Political Weekly, 2001.

Bandhu, P.: *Dalit Women's Cry for Liberation: My Rights are Rising Like the Sun, Will you Deny this sunrise?* New Delhi: Long Life Publication, 2003.

Bapat, Gururao V.: *Yakshagaana Performance and Meaning—A Semiotic Study*, Karnataka: Regional Resources Centre for Folk Performing Arts, 2002.

Bhargav, G.: *Human Rights of Dalits: Societal Violation*, Hyderabad: Self Publication, 2005.

Bhat, Chandrashekhar: *Emerging Ethnic Identity and Social Mobility Among the Waddars of South India*, New Delhi: Concept Publishing Company, 2003.

Charsley, Simon R.: *Dalits and State Action: The 'SCs'. In Challenging Untouchability*, New Delhi: Sage Publications, 2006.

Charsley, Simon: *Evaluating Dalit Leadership: P.R. Venkatswamy and the Hyderabad Example*, Hyderabad: Economic and Political Weekly Press, 2005.

Chitnis, V.: *Human Rights of the Vulnerable Groups*, Pune: Futuristic Digital, 2005.

Clough, John E.: *The Story of a Man, A Mission and a Movement*, New York: The Macmillan Company, 2001.

Coburn, Thomas B.: *The Crystallization of the Goddess Tradition*: Delhi, Motilal Banarsidas Press, 2000.

Deliege, Robert: *Replication and Consensus: Untouchability, Caste and Ideology in India, Man,* London: Cambridge University, 2003.

Jogdand Mahipal, *Indian Social Reality and Inequality in to the Human Right Violence of Dalit,* Mumbai: College of Social Work, 2001.

Jogdand, P.: *Dalit Women, Issues and Perspectives,* New York: Cambridge University Press, 2000.

Kale, R.: *Kolhatyachre Por,* London: Cambridge MA: Perseus Publishing, 2006.

Kumar, N.: *Dalit Policies, Politics and Parliament,* Shipra Publication, Banglore, 2004.

Michael, S.: *Dalits in Modern India, Vision and Values,* Toronto: Thomson Nelson, 2008.

Omvedt, G.: *Dalit Women and Communalism,* Hyderabad: Self Publication, 2007.

Pal, R.: *Human Rights of Dalits: Societal Violation,* Hyderabad: Self Publication, 2000.

Pandit, V.: *Handbook on Prevention of Atrocities (SC/ST), Maharashtra: Vidnayak Sansod Prakashan, Ujgaon,* Maharashtra: Pune University, 2002.

Paswan, S.: *Encyclopedia of Dalits in India,* Kolkotta: Kolkotta University, 2002.

Punalekar, S.: *On Dalitism and Gender, Dalit Women's Issues and Perspectives,* New Delhi: Gyan Prakashan, 2001.

Raj, M.: *Dalit Leadership in Panchayats,* New York: Institute of Modern Studies. 2006.

Tirmare, P.: *Violation of Human Rights of Dalit Women: Issues and Facts,* Maharashtra: Pune University, 2000.

Webstar, J.: *Dalit's in Modern India, Vision and Values,* New Delhi: Vistar Publication, 2001.

Zelliot, E.: *Dr. Ambedkar and the Empowerment of Women: Caste and Gender Kali for Women,* New Delhi: Jain Publication, 2003.

Index